Narrowed Lives

Meaning, Moral Value, and Profound Intellectual Disability

Simo Vehmas & Reetta Mietola

STOCKHOLM
UNIVERSITY PRESS

Published by
Stockholm University Press
Stockholm University
SE-106 91 Stockholm, Sweden
www.stockholmuniversitypress.se

Supporting Agency (funding): Department of Special Education,
Stockholm University

First published 2021
Cover Illustration: "Kristo"
Cover illustration credit: Jyri Pitkänen
Cover designed by Stockholm University Press

ISBN (Paperback): 978-91-7635-151-2
ISBN (PDF): 978-91-7635-148-2
ISBN (EPUB): 978-91-7635-149-9
ISBN (Mobi): 978-91-7635-150-5

DOI: https://doi.org/10.16993/bbl

Suggested citation:
Vehmas, S. and Mietola, R. 2021. *Narrowed Lives: Meaning, Moral Value,
and Profound Intellectual Disability*. Stockholm: Stockholm University Press.
DOI: https://doi.org/10.16993/bbl. License: CC-BY 4.0.

To read the free, open access version of this book online,
visit https://doi.org/10.16993/bbl or scan this QR code with
your mobile device.

Endorsements from Readers

For people with profound intellectual and multiple impairments, what is a good life? Who is responsible for trying to ensure that such a life is possible? This sobering, no-nonsense book about individual people who live in Finnish care homes is a timely and vital contribution to thinking about both the possibilities and the limitations of care, empathy and moral engagement.
— Don Kulick, Distinguished University Professor of Anthropology, Uppsala University

This important book boldly challenges many pervasive and harmful assumptions about people with profound disabilities. Through powerful illustrations of how the external world can constrain, limit, and deny the worth of disabled persons, the authors confront difficult but essential questions that must be asked in order to combat ableism and enable flourishing.

By combining philosophical analysis with in-depth research into lived experience and relationships, this book is a call to critically reconsider how meaning is assigned, and how moral values are embodied in everyday practices. *Narrowed Lives* boldly asserts that the varied and complex lives of people with profound disabilities need not be narrow at all.
— Licia Carlson, Professor of Philosophy, Providence College

Provocative... this book provides answers to questions of the human that unconsciously abound in any conception of intellectual disability and, crucially, urges all researchers to consider the lives of people with intellectual disabilities.
— Dan Goodley, Professor of Disability Studies and Education, University of Sheffield

Editorial Board

Peer Review Policies

Stockholm University Press ensures that all book publications are peer-reviewed. Each book proposal submitted to the Press will be sent to a dedicated Editorial Board of experts in the subject area. The full manuscript will be reviewed by chapter or as a whole by two external and independent experts.

A full description of Stockholm University Press' peer-review policies can be found on the website: http://www.stockholm universitypress.se/site/peer-review-policies/

The Editorial Board for Narrowed Lives applied a single-blind review while assessing the manuscript. Meaning that the author's name was revealed to the reviewers, while the reviewer names were only disclosed to the author at the end of the editing process.

Recognition for reviewers

Stockholm University Press and the Editorial Board would hereby like to express their sincere gratitude to the reviewers of this book:

Reviewers of the Book Proposal

- Christopher Goodey, Professor Emeritus, UK.
- Phillippa Wiseman, PhD, Lecturer in Research Methods, Institute of Health and Wellbeing, University of Glasgow, UK

Reviewers of the Book Manuscript

- Iva Strnadova, Professor in Special Education and Disability Studies, University of New South Wales, Sydney, Australia
- Philippa Wiseman, PhD, Lecturer in Research Methods, Institute of Health and Wellbeing, University of Glasgow, UK

For
Eva Feder Kittay

Contents

Acknowledgements

This book is based upon a research project entitled *Profound Intellectual and Multiple Disabilities and a Good Life*, funded by the Academy of Finland (SA 275988), which we acknowledge with gratitude. We thank our colleague Sonja Miettinen for her contributions in the data collection and initial analysis of it. We also thank our research assistant Johanna Snellman for her invaluable help in transcribing and coding the data.

We would like to thank two of our colleagues who were pivotal in the making of this research project. Eva Feder Kittay's work inspired Simo to engage with the philosophical issues related to moral status. Discussions with Eva, and visiting the Center for Discovery (https://thecenterfordiscovery.org), where her daughter Sesha lives, were crucial motivators for Simo to understand better the everyday lives of persons with profound intellectual and multiple disabilities. We perhaps do not agree with Eva on everything – and she probably does not agree with everything said in this book. But her passion for what is right and fair has truly been an inspiration without which this project and this book would not have materialised.

Nick Watson initially posed Simo the idea of forming an empirical research project building upon the philosophical debates on moral status and profound intellectual disability. Nick helped Simo to focus the research agenda, and has been a tremendous support throughout the project. And, considering that Nick is a sociologist, he is actually a lot of fun.

Especially in the beginning of the project, the members of our advisory group provided us with invaluable insights and advice in relation to the ethnographic fieldwork in particular. Thank you, Chris Hatton, Bill Hughes, Lucy Pickering, Sara Ryan, Ben Simmons, Kerstin Stalker, John Vorhaus and Nick Watson.

In June 2017, we organised a multidisciplinary workshop by the Baltic Sea just outside Helsinki, where scholars from the fields of anthropology, disability studies, law and philosophy presented and discussed work in progress in relation to profound intellectual disability. Thank you, Ben Curtis, Marion Godman, Matti Häyry, Don Kulick, Eva Feder Kittay, Erik Olsman, Chrissie Rogers, Lucy Series, Tom Shakespeare, Ben Simmons, Stacy Clifford Simplican, John Vorhaus, Jan Walmsley, Nick Watson and Jonathan Wolff. Three days with this group of people was an unforgettable celebration of intellectual rigour, ethical engagement and academic fellowship.

We are indebted to the following friends and colleagues who contributed to this book by discussing with us, providing us with information or reading and commenting different parts of the manuscript: Liz Adams Lyngbäck, Jan Grue, Matti Häyry, Heli Leppälä, Markku Mattila, Mina Sedem, Tom Shakespeare, Magnus Tideman, Hannu Vesala and Nick Watson. Presenting work in progress in conferences and research seminars has also been crucial for the development of this book's analyses and arguments. We would especially like to thank participants in research seminars at the University of Amsterdam, the University of Glasgow, Lund University and the University of Southampton.

Don Kulick read the whole book manuscript. With great patience, as well as uncompromising frankness and professionalism, he provided us with detailed, critical comments that helped us to make this book a lot better than it would otherwise have been. We are privileged to have a colleague like him. Thank you.

We also thank two anonymous reviewers and members of the Editorial Board for their constructive comments for the first draft of the manuscript.

We are indebted to the Department of Special Education at Stockholm University, and its head, Diana Berthén, for providing financial support that enabled this book to be published in open access format. Reetta would also like to thank ALL-YOUTH project (SA 312689) for the chance to finalise this book while working in the project.

Finally, we offer our deepest gratitude and debt to those who cannot be named: the care workers that allowed us to follow and take part in their work, and the family members who gave us the permission to take part in the lives of our research participants, and who agreed to talk to us about their experiences. Most importantly, we thank our research participants Anna, Ella, Frida, Hugo, Leo and Sebastian, who allowed us to be parts of their lives for a short period of time. Our aim was to understand their lives better, and possibly somehow contribute to making things better for them.

Authors and Their Contributions

Simo Vehmas is professor of special education at Stockholm University, Sweden, and a visiting professor at Høgskolen i Innlandet, in Lillehammer, Norway. He recently co-edited, with Nick Watson, the *Routledge Handbook of Disability Studies* (2nd edition).

Reetta Mietola works as a research fellow at the University of Helsinki, Finland, where she directs a four-year research project on Finnish disability activism in past and present.

Benjamin L. Curtis is a senior lecturer of philosophy at Nottingham Trent University, United Kingdom, with research interests in ethics and metaphysics, and the intersection between the two.

The research project which this book is based upon was conceived by Simo. The empirical data was collected by Reetta, and Sonja Miettinen (Sonja took no part in writing this book). The empirical findings were discussed by the three of us throughout the project. The analysis of the data was discussed by Simo and Reetta during the writing process of the book. Simo wrote Chapters 1, 6, 7 and 8. Reetta wrote Chapters 2, 3 and 4, which were revised and edited by Simo. Reetta and Simo wrote Chapter 5 together. Benjamin and Simo wrote the appendix.

A Note on Language

We have chosen the term 'intellectual disability' instead of terms like 'learning disability' or 'learning difficulty' simply because it is the generic term used in the international scientific community. While one may disagree the appropriateness of a given term, at least one knows roughly what the term 'intellectual disability' means and to what kinds of people it is usually applied to. As for the expression *persons/people with PIMD*, we use it to refer to a group of people that has been categorised under the diagnostic category of *profound intellectual and multiple disabilities*. The reason we mostly refer to them specifically as *persons* is that this project was founded upon the ethical notion that they are persons in the moral sense of the term, meaning that they are as valuable and worthy of respect as any other human being. When we write about our individual research participants with PIMD, however, we use their names (all pseudonyms). We hope that the reader can tell when we talk about a class property, a social construct called PIMD, rather than of the individuals to whom this label is applied to because we are very much aware that the term PIMD tells very little about them as individual human beings.

However, we acknowledge that the PIMD abbreviation is annoying, perhaps even disrespectful for some readers – despite the fact that many disabled people refer to themselves with abbreviations (e.g. 'people with MS', 'MND', 'ALS' or 'SCI'). Having said that, using *profound intellectual and multiple disabilities* throughout the book would make the text too burdensome. Also, we do not want to use exclusively the term *profound intellectual disability* because in our view it is important that the reader is reminded throughout the book that this group of people do not merely have an intellectual disability but multiple disabilities as well. Therefore, we mostly use expression *persons* or *people with PIMD*. As for 'person-first' language ('person with disability') and 'disability-first' language ('disabled person'), we follow the example of scholars such as Kulick and Rydström (2015), Linton (1998) and Wendell (1996), and alternate between the two.

Chapter 1: Introduction

'But she can walk! People with PIMD don't walk, do they?'

It was either Reetta or Simo who expressed this doubt during a discussion we had during the process of recruiting research participants for our fieldwork. The discussion was about walking – the ability to be able to walk, or not – and it arose in relation to a middle-aged woman, Ella. We thought Ella was especially interesting regarding our research because she challenged the conventional understanding of profound intellectual and multiple disabilities (PIMD) as people who lack all competence. It is usually assumed that persons with PIMD are not able to be physically active, let alone walk.

Most studies on motor activity do not include people with PIMD, which means that the extent to which individuals who have been given that diagnosis are in fact physically active is still largely unknown (van der Putten, Bossink, Frans, Houwen, & Vlaskamp, 2017). However, Simo ended up having a discussion with a medical professional who had long experience in working with people with intellectual disability about the definition of PIMD. For her, it was important to distinguish PIMD as a category in which individuals simply do not walk. Simo told her about Ella with the goal of opening a discussion on the medicalised narrative of PIMD. The doctor smiled politely and replied, 'Well, if she walks, she is not an individual with PIMD.' End of discussion.

The question of walking illuminates epistemic power struggles surrounding PIMD. Who gets to represent the voice of those who

How to cite this book chapter:
Vehmas, S. and Mietola, R. 2021. *Narrowed Lives: Meaning, Moral Value, and Profound Intellectual Disability*. Pp. 1–27. Stockholm: Stockholm University Press. DOI: https://doi.org/10.16993/bbl.a. License: CC-BY 4.0.

have very limited means to express it themselves? How to reliably separate persons with PIMD from others within the category of intellectual disability? Most of all, the question of whether people with profound intellectual and multiple disabilities possess the ability to walk demonstrates what defining PIMD is often all about; it is about ticking boxes of deficiency, of what one is not able to do (see Chapter 3). In Ella's case, all the boxes regarding intellectual and adaptive functioning (e.g. American Psychiatric Association, 2013, p. 33) seem to get ticked. Except that she could walk. So, is she a person who can justifiably be put under the ambiguous category of PIMD, and what difference does that make anyway?

Conceptions presented in major diagnostic manuals about persons with PIMD direct the focus and content of their care (see Chapter 3). They are conceptualised as a group of people who need constant help in just about everything: they have extremely limited capacities to understand instructions, they are incapable of expressing themselves verbally, they are incapable of taking care of their basic needs, and so on (e.g. American Psychiatric Association, 2013; WHO, 1992). Philosophical theories of well-being tell us that what makes one's life go well may depend on its experiential quality, whether it satisfies one's desires, or whether it is in line with some objective criteria for a good quality of life (e.g. Wasserman & Asch, 2014). If one is seen to lack understanding, communication, and the ability to do much at all, it would be only logical to think that people with PIMD have extremely limited possibilities regarding well-being and a good life.

Conceptions about the nature of PIMD and its significance regarding quality of life set the foundations and limits for the services that ultimately make up the lives of people with PIMD – lives that are very much embedded in institutional practices of disability service systems. The expression 'narrow lives' was used by one of the care workers in our data when he was explaining the lack of engagement and effort in the service system to make the lives of persons with PIMD more active, more meaningful. The impairment effects related to PIMD have undeniable consequences and set boundaries for persons in this group. But it was not the impairments of people with PIMD that implied a 'narrow life' in the care worker's account. Rather, it was limited resources, combined with a mechanical, unimaginative care culture and slight ambition or means to find out what a good life might mean for a particular individual with very limited means to express his or her dreams, wishes, hopes and desires.

What this book aims to do is to shed light on what 'narrow lives' means in the case of persons with PIMD, why their lives are narrow(ed), and what the ethical implications of all this are. In order to do this, in the following chapters we will provide theoretically informed empirical descriptions about the lives of our research participants on issues such as the way conceptions of their competence manifest in care work practices, or what explains the lack of social relations in their lives. Also, we will explore related theoretical issues such as the significance and meaning of chronological age in the lives of persons with PIMD, and the ethical complexities related to enabling their sexuality, as well as one of the main motivation for our study: the issue of the moral status, namely why people with PIMD merit the same moral consideration as the rest of us.

The devaluing of persons with PIMD in philosophy

Whether or not Ella is a person with PIMD, she *is* referred to as being someone with 'profound intellectual disability'. That was crucial regarding our research interest. The research project, and this book, were initially motivated by philosophical debates about the personhood and moral worth of people with profound intellectual disability. In those debates (which will be analysed in the appendix),[1] physical impairments have a marginal role but limited cognitive and emotional capacities are at the centre of the debate. They are seen crucial in determining who is worth of full moral consideration and who is not. To lack these capacities also implies a lower level of well-being than is attainable to so-called

---

[1] This philosophical analysis included in the book as an appendix was a parallel, collaborative project between Benjamin and Simo, adding to our ethnography. It differs from the rest of the book in in that it concentrates on unpacking the strengths and weaknesses of different philosophical arguments without discussing the issue in the light of our data.

normal people. These kinds of views motivated Simo to develop a research project that would examine, in the light of empirical data, what makes a good life for this group of people. The lived experiences of persons with PIMD would be observed in various contexts. We would also talk to their families and carers, and this way construct a detailed account of their everyday lives. The aim was to rectify the lack of empirical data that makes philosophical discussions often so sterile.

Simo had been struggling with ethical issues related to intellectual disability on and off since the late 1990s, and he got drawn back to discussions on moral status when he first familiarised himself with the debate between the prominent philosophers Eva Feder Kittay, Jeff McMahan and Peter Singer (e.g. Kittay, 2005, 2010; McMahan, 2002, 2009; Singer, 1993, 2009). There are several puzzling features in these debates. The first is the way McMahan and Singer portray humans with PIMD as psychologically comparable to pigs and dogs, the kinds of beings who are able to attain only the level of well-being that of 'a contented dog' (McMahan, 2002, p. 153), and whose moral worth is consequently lower than that of so-called 'normal' people. To many people, such comparison means that one would need to see a person with PIMD as a dog or pig. And that is 'the moment of revulsion', as Eva Kittay (2010, p. 399) argues. But, even if one did not find the comparison offensive as such, the way it is presented in McMahan's and Singer's texts is, at least in our reading, dismissive, even contemptuous of people with PIMD and the meaningfulness of their lives. The second perplexing feature in these kinds of casual remarks in McMahan's and Singer's texts is that they are made without any appeal to (or real knowledge of) empirical evidence.

Eva Kittay (2005, 2010) has criticised McMahan and Singer for their lack of engagement with the lived realities of persons with PIMD. She has a daughter, Sesha, who is now a middle-aged woman with profound intellectual and multiple disabilities. Kittay has used her personal experience and knowledge about her daughter to refute the claims made by McMahan and others. However, she engages only very little with empirical research literature on PIMD. Thus, philosophical debates on the moral significance of PIMD are mostly informed by personal experience or anecdotal evidence about intellectual disability. This is partly because there is so little actual research on the lives of people with PIMD. There *is* a significant body of research literature on the quality of life of persons with intellectual disability (in relation specifically to persons with PIMD, see Nieuwenhuijse, Willems, van Goudoever, Echteld, & Olsman, 2019), but, as Lyons (2011) has demonstrated in his extensive literature review, most of the pertinent research on quality of life has focused on persons with mild and moderate intellectual disability, has been quantitative, and has not engaged in depth with ethics and politics.

A basic question prompted by people with PIMD is how society might engage with them in ways that ensure their dignity as individuals, and facilitate their flourishing. People with PIMD challenge liberal understandings of citizenship because their rights are often not balanced by the duties usually associated with citizenship (such as the duty to enter into gainful employment) (e.g. Kittay, 1999; Nussbaum, 2006). They complicate the ethics of reciprocity in that they do not necessarily offer gratitude or reciprocity for the services and goods they receive from others.

A striking feature of the philosophical discussions about people with PIMD is that they often proceed in a largely theoretical modality, as though there is little difference between the people under this category, who, in fact, are as diverse as any other group of people. In order to nuance understanding of the lives lived by people with PIMD, we need material that focuses on them as individuals. This book contributes to that goal. It will focus on documenting the meanings of a good life for people with PIMD, and the practices that enable (or not) such a life in the institutional settings that ultimately dictate what kinds of lives they live. What kind of moral, social, interactional and affective value is accorded to individuals with PIMD by the people who work and live with them most closely? How do practices of care contribute (or not) to people with PIMD being recognised as fellow human beings worthy of dignity?

People with PIMD cannot reach levels of well-being that require highly developed intellectual capacities. In many philosophical accounts this implies that they cannot live *the* good life: a life that is line with some objective moral criteria (e.g. in Aristotle's

eudaimonian ethics, living in accordance with virtue and reason). We decided to put aside objective criteria for the good life,
and try to see what *a* good life could mean to people with PIMD
(see Kittay, 2019, pp. 49–54). What kinds of things and activities
seemed to be important or enjoyable to our research participants?
Did the service system provide persons with PIMD a genuine opportunity to pursue them?

We were not convinced that any particular theory of well-being
or good life would be expedient in unpacking the lived realities
of people with PIMD, or engaging with the ethical issues PIMD
gives rise to. The theory that was most discussed at the beginning
of the project as a potential analytical tool was the capabilities
approach, a theory of social justice developed by the economist
Amartya Sen (1992) and the philosopher Martha Nussbaum
(2006). The capabilities approach argues that justice should be
evaluated in terms of what valuable doings or beings people are
capable of achieving. Also, a society has a duty to ensure that all
citizens have a minimum level of a number of central capabilities that are necessary for human dignity and well-being. Such
capabilities include, for example, bodily health, bodily integrity,
affiliation and control over one's environment (Nussbaum, 2006,
pp. 69–81).

The capabilities approach worked in our project as a framework
that informed our discussions regarding what things generally are
considered important for a good life and social justice. Rather
than setting in advance particular theories that would be applied
in data analysis, we thought it would be more expedient to proceed
inductively, to see which activities, arrangements, surroundings
and people are present in the lives of persons with PIMD and only
after that ponder what theory would be suitable to the analysis of
the issue (such as age-appropriateness or sexuality) in question.

The exclusion of PIMD in disability studies

One of our aims with this book is to counteract the erasure of
persons with PIMD in the disability studies literature. Disability
studies as a discipline has grown out of a need for alternative
forms of knowledge concerning disability and disabled people. The

discipline is characterised by its close relationship to the disability rights movement, sharing a political commitment to illuminating and eradicating social discrimination faced by disabled people. In order to implement this political commitment, new approaches to research practice have been sought after the realisation that *research on disability* has historically in its part marginalised disabled people by producing knowledge *about* them, not *for* and *with* them. Disability studies has aimed at developing an alternative research paradigm that is inclusive of and empowering to disabled people. In order to change the social relations of research production (Oliver, 1992), disability scholars turned to critical social research traditions to develop an 'emancipatory research paradigm' for disability studies. This paradigm entails, for example, a political commitment to the struggles of disabled people for self-emancipation and willingness only to undertake research that will be of practical benefit to the self-empowerment of disabled people (Barnes, 2003; Barton, 2005; Stone & Priestley, 1996). While not all research in the field of disability studies can be characterised as emancipatory, there is a strong consensus among the discipline concerning its political aim of promoting social justice by listening to and representing the voices of disabled people.

Considering the drive towards the empowerment of disabled people within disability studies, it is astonishing that people with PIMD are virtually missing from key theoretical and methodological discussions, as well as from empirical studies in the field (e.g. Barnes, 1990; Davis, 2013a; Oliver, 1990). It is thus reasonable to argue that people with PIMD are probably the most marginal group of disabled people both in society and in research (Boxall & Ralph, 2010). This group is the last to benefit from the changes in the policy and service system that have followed from the political recognition of disability rights. In Finland this has manifested, for example, in living arrangements: group homes were for long considered to be insufficiently functional for individuals with PIMD, with the result that they were forced to live in institutions longer than people with 'milder' forms of intellectual disability. And, still, people with PIMD often continue to live heavily institutionalised lives (Mietola, Teittinen, & Vesala, 2013, pp. 86–90).

At the same time as the social positioning of persons with PIMD calls for academic attention, they have been mostly neglected by disability studies. It seems that the emancipatory research paradigm, with its emphasis on self-empowerment, has made some disabled voices heard, but it has not been able to offer alternative approaches to include those who may not be able express themselves clearly. As Barton (2005, p. 325) notes, there is a need to pay more attention to 'the extent to which we are aware of and able to engage with some voices', particularly voices of 'those individuals who do not communicate through speech'.

Disability studies has traditionally concentrated on examining various social, structural and cultural practices and mechanisms that exclude disabled people from social participation. In the materialist Marxist tradition, the focus has been on the material, mainly economic factors that have placed disabled people at the fringes of society (e.g. Oliver, 1990). Various social constructionist and poststructuralist accounts, on the other hand, have produced genealogies and cultural analyses exploring the origins of ableist, discriminatory and oppressive ideas and values (e.g. Goodley, 2014; Hughes, 2020). Since the focus in virtually all theoretical traditions in disability studies has been on societal and cultural factors, individual experiences and properties, such as impairments and their role in people's disablement, have often been ignored (Vehmas & Watson, 2014). Unsurprisingly, intellectual disability (especially PIMD) has been at the margins of disability studies because it involves the kinds of serious, all-inclusive impairment effects that cannot be explained merely by social arrangements (Chappell, 1998; Shakespeare, 2006; Vehmas, 2010).

Thus, apart from a few exceptions (Björnsdottir, Stefansdottir, & Stefansdottir, 2017; Brigg, Schuitema, & Vorhaus, 2016; Jones, 2004), PIMD has been researched mainly outside disability studies, in an impairment-specific research tradition that does not shy away from alliance with medical research (in journals such as the *American Journal on Intellectual and Developmental Disabilities*). However, there is body of work that recognises the social and cultural elements related to disablement but that does not necessarily identify with disability studies or any of its theoretical narratives as such (e.g. Bigby, Clement, Mansell, & Beadle-Brown, 2009; Clement & Bigby, 2009; Goodwin, 2020;

Granlund, Wilder, & Almqvist, 2013; McCormack, 2020; Nind, 2007; Pawlyn & Carnaby, 2009; Samuel, Nind, Volans, & Scriven, 2008: Simmons & Watson, 2014; Talman, Wilder, Stier, & Gustafsson, 2019; Tilley, Ledger, & Haas, 2020; Vorhaus, 2013, 2014). Alongside these kinds of contributions, our work can be seen to be in the same league as the work of Clement and Bigby (2013) on living arrangements, Goode's (1994) ethnographic research on children with congenital deaf-blindness and intellectual disability, Johnson and Walmsley's (2010) contribution on the meaning of a good life with reference to current policies and ideologies, and Vorhaus's (2016) empirically informed philosophical work on children with PIMD.[2]

Notwithstanding some similarities, this book is different from the ones mentioned above. This is because of the way our work is based on the fusion of the research method, the focus of the research, and the ways the findings have been theorised: this book is based upon ethnographic fieldwork with adults with PIMD, and many of the empirical findings are analysed philosophically. There is very little ethnographic research on adults with PIMD and, as a result, there is only very little engagement with some aspects of their lives, like the significance of age and related issues such as sexuality.

In what follows, we will present an overview of the history of intellectual disability, and concentrate on issues that relate to our research interests such as the conceptualisation and moral significance of intellectual disability. The second subchapter unpacks the history of the Finnish intellectual disability service system and its underpinning values and ideologies.

---

[2] To some extent, our work resembles McKearney's (2018a, 2018b, 2019) anthropological research, which aims to re-evaluate the agency of those with significant intellectual disability. His work is highly interesting but we have difficulties relating to it mainly because of its reliance on theology. The care work that McKearney observed, provided by the Christian charity called L'Arche, was motivated by religious, at times sentimental ideas that to us would merit a more critical appraisal than McKearney's sympathetic reading. Also, it is a somewhat unclear whether his research participants were, in fact, people with PIMD.

The meaning of intellectual disability – historical overview

Naming people with limited intellectual capacities has a long and colourful history. Within the last century alone, persons with intellectual disability have been seen to suffer from backwardness, cretinism, developmental disability, dullness, feeble-mindedness, idiotism, imbecility, intellectual handicap, intellectual impairment, learning difficulties, mental deficiency, mental handicap, mental retardation, moronism and oligophreny, just to name a few classificatory terms (Goodey, 2011, p. 4). It would be simplistic to assume that these terms are merely different names of the same, objectively existing phenomenon. Each of them portrays slightly different kinds of individual depending who says the term in question, who hears it, and where and when he or she hears it.

It is impossible to evaluate the number of people with intellectual disability in different eras on the basis of archaeological data (human remains, grave goods, art objects, ancient written descriptions) or legal and medical records (Berkson, 2004; Goodey, 2011; Scheerenberger, 1983). This is because of the problems related to defining intellectual disability; it is based on the evaluation of behaviour, and thus inevitably context-bound. Undoubtedly there have always been people who have had difficulties in understanding and executing basic everyday activities. However, the content and the significance of those activities to human lives has always depended more or less upon the social context.

So, one may well analyse what 'simple-mindedness' meant in Plato's texts (Goodey, 1992), or 'idiocy' in medieval English law (Neugebauer, 1996) but ultimately these historical concepts did not have all that much in common with current notions of human intelligence or intellectual disability. Goodey (2001) argues that intellectual disability as a diagnostic category is very much a modern product that started to slowly take shape in the 17th century, when for the first time humans were seen as persons, phenomenological continuums that started from birth and ended in death. For the first time, many human characteristics were seen as congenital, incurable individual properties that constituted a person's identity. Also, the growing tendency to separate mind from the body as distinct entities, as well as classifying intelligence and rationality as species-specific, laid the foundation for the category of intellectual disability; while the Greeks and their medieval successors defined rationality loosely as a metaphysical entity that could belong to gods, humans and sometimes even animals, now rationality was deduced from each species' natural endowments (Berrios, 1995, p. 226; Goodey, 2001, pp. 7–9; 2011, p. 17). The new, modern understanding thus consisted of three ingredients, which conceptualised intellectual or mental deficiencies as '(a) congenital and incurable, (b) purely mental and (c) classifiable by strict laws of nature' (Goodey, 2001, p. 9).

Understanding and defining intellectual disability did not rise at that time from psychology (which was not a discipline separate from others) but, rather, it was discussed under the heading of philosophy (Goodey, 2001). A philosopher who had a considerable effect on the understanding on intellectual disability and mental illness was John Locke. He argued, for example, that 'the mad' have the capacity to form and have ideas but they join them together wrongly and so make wrong propositions, whereas 'the idiot' scarcely puts ideas together or has the capacity to reason at all (Locke, 1998, book II, ch. XI, 13). Locke's thought, and the weight he put on the ability to reason and think abstractly, had a great effect on modern, medicalised classifications and definitions of intellectual disability (Goodey, 1995; Goodey & Stainton, 2001). For Locke, these faculties differentiated humans from animals, which in its part gave room for the growing notion that idiots were not essentially human. Locke argued that all human beings were born as blank slates but gradually developed psychological capacities to be autonomous reasoners. Some humans, however, stayed in the state of idiocy without developing the capacity to form abstract ideas (Goodey, 2001, pp. 12–13).

Altogether, the meaning of idiocy was in flux due to various changes in legal, religious and medical thinking, which all were interwoven. Medicine made tremendous advances in the 19th century and part of that progress was the increasing medico-scientific explanations of intellectual disability. The rate of one's developmental disability was determined mainly on the basis of one's speech and language (Scheerenberger, 1983, p. 63). For example, Jean Etienne Dominique Esquirol (1772–1840), an early

French pioneer in psychiatry, divided individuals with intellectual disability into imbeciles and idiots: imbeciles use limited intellectual, affective and verbal facilities but would 'never reach the degree of reason, nor the extent and solidity of knowledge, to which their age, education, and social relations, would otherwise enable them to attain', whereas idiots represented 'the utmost limit of human degradation': 'They hear, but do not understand; they see but do not regard. Having no ideas, and thinking not, they have nothing to desire; therefore have no need of signs, or of speech' (Scheerenberger, 1983, p. 54).

In the late 19th century, attention turned to intelligence testing and to the heredity of intelligence and intellectual disorders. One of the most important pioneers of intelligence testing was Francis Galton, the father of eugenics, alongside the French physicians Alfred Binet and Theodore Simon, whose psychometric tests were largely used in the pursuit of finding children who were uneducable (Harris & Greenspan, 2016, p. 14). Intelligence was assumed to be hereditary and stable, a universal, objective and a measurable phenomenon that consisted of things such as information-processing, logical reasoning and abstraction (Goodey, 2011, pp. 5–9, 39–46). Intelligence tests were believed to be scientific and objective, and, in part, they legitimised the category of intellectual disability and especially the institutional responses to individuals categorised as such (e.g. segregation to special schools and institutions). But, at the same time, the various limitations of such tests were acknowledged that resulted in frequent revisions to enhance each test's reliability and validity. Intelligence tests became increasingly suspect, especially regarding their discriminatory effects to, for example, ethnic minorities (Scheerenberger, 1987, pp. 27–33). Although intelligence tests still play a role in the diagnostics of intellectual disability, IQ test scores are now seen as approximations of conceptual functioning that 'may be insufficient to assess reasoning in real-life situations and mastery of practical tasks' (American Psychiatric Association, 2013, p. 37).

The early diagnostic terms such as idiocy and imbecility continued to exist in diagnostic manuals until the mid-1900s, when the American Association on Mental Deficiency (later the American Association on Mental Retardation, AAMR, and since 2007 the American Association on Intellectual and Developmental Disabilities, AAIDD) introduced the term 'mental retardation' in 1961: 'Mental retardation refers to subaverage general intellectual functioning which originates in the developmental period and is associated with impairment in adaptive behavior' (Scheerenberger, 1987, p. 11). This definition was the first to introduce the dual criteria and levels for intelligence and adaptive behaviour (mild, moderate, severe, profound), and it was nearly universally adopted and remained virtually the same for the next 30 years. The new definitions in 1992 and especially in 2002 and 2010 marked significant changes, especially in the sense that the new definitions acknowledged the socially constructed nature of intellectual disability; it is neither a mental disorder nor a medical disorder, not an absolute trait of an individual but, rather, a state of functioning expressed in the interaction of an individual and the environment (Harris & Greenspan, 2016, p. 16; Scheerenberger, 1987, pp. 11–17).

Thus, according to the influential definitions by the AAIDD, the World Health Organization (WHO, ICD/ICF), and the American Psychiatric Association (DSM-5), intellectual disability is characterised by significant limitations in both intellectual functioning (learning, reasoning, problem solving etc.) and adaptive behaviour, which is a collection of conceptual (language, money, time etc.), social (interpersonal skills, the ability to follow rules etc.) and practical skills (personal care, schedules and routines etc.). As for profound intellectual disability, the WHO defines it in the following way:

> The IQ [of those] in this category is estimated to be under 20, which means in practice that affected individuals are severely limited in their ability to understand or comply with requests or instructions. Most such individuals are immobile or severely restricted in mobility, incontinent, and capable at most of only very rudimentary forms of non-verbal communication. They possess little or no ability to care for their own basic needs, and require constant help and supervision. (WHO, 1992, p. 230)

According to DSM-5, individuals with profound intellectual disability may understand only some simple instructions due to their limited conceptual skills, can express themselves only through non-verbal, non-symbolic communication, and are dependent on others for all aspects of daily physical care, health, and safety (American Psychiatric Association, 2013, p. 36). Since profound intellectual disability typically includes other impairments (most typically visual and physical, the latter causing immobility or severely restricted mobility), or other health conditions like epilepsy or impaired sense of touch, temperature and pain, the term applied to them is usually profound intellectual and multiple disabilities (PIMD) (Pawlyn & Carnaby, 2009, p. 7).

It is difficult to estimate the exact number of individuals who meet the diagnostic criteria of PIMD simply because of the ambiguity of such criteria. However, it is generally estimated that the prevalence of intellectual disability varies between 1% and 3% globally, and that severe and profound disability affects approximately 4% and 2% of that population, respectively (Maulik, Mascarenhas, Mathers, Dua, & Saxena, 2011). In Finland, the average prevalence of intellectual disability among the population of 16–64 years of age is estimated to be 0.81% (Westerinen, 2018).

Development of the Finnish intellectual disability services

State care for people with intellectual disability in Finland began at the turn of the 20th century. At the time, conceptions and terms signifying intellectual disability varied greatly in different contexts. In medicine, intellectual disability was seen as a subtype of mental illness that typically emerged during childhood. In everyday usage, the division between 'congenital idiots' ('*synnynnäinen idiootti*'/'*tylsämielinen*') and 'mentally ill' ('*mielisairas*'/'*mielenvikainen*') was not common, and such terms were often used interchangeably. In special education, intellectual disability began to be seen in the late 1800s as a developmental backwardness instead of a mental illness, which meant that it was something that could be worked upon through education. This new approach took place when students with intellectual disability were placed at schools for deaf children. Teachers soon noticed the difference between learning difficulties caused by a lack of hearing and those caused by limited intellectual capacities. Students with intellectual disability were seen as burdens in deaf schools, and therefore special classes and institutions specifically for such students were established, at first usually in connection to deaf schools (Harjula, 1996, pp. 61–62).

When the first statistics were compiled on mental illness and idiocy, in 1883, the latter was defined as a defect of the brain that could damage one's intellectual capacities, emotional and moral characteristics, or all of them. Local parishes were in charge of collecting data for the early disability statistics. Criteria and terminology in their lists were vague, confused and inconsistent with the definitions used by policymakers. Terms like '*halfidiot*' (half idiot), '*helidiot*' (total idiot), '*stollig*' (kooky, crazy), '*slö*' (dull), '*pehmeäpäinen*' (soft headed), '*puupää*' (blockhead) or '*pöljä*' (thickheaded)[3] were used by teachers, priests and the common people interchangeably. As a result, there were no reliable statistics on the number of people who could have been classified as idiots, or that could provide information about the level of their capacities. The main motivation for developing a clear definition and classification system for idiocy was to establish criteria for the developmental potential of intellectually disabled children, and especially whether they were educable ('*koulutuskelpoinen*'/'*bildbar*'). Educability became the main criterion for distinguishing feeble-minded from idiots:[4] the feeble-minded ('*tylsämielinen*'/'*andesvag*') were those with limited intellectual capacities, but who had the potential to develop and learn – they were thus educable and should be placed in special education classes or schools. Idiots, on the other hand, were vegetative 'creatures at the lowest level' with a complete lack of intelligence or mental qualities such as emotions, will or comprehension. They were uneducable and belonged to institutions. These classifications and descriptions were presented in late 1890s by Edvin Hedman (1863–1915), the leading figure of the early Finnish care and education system for people with intellectual disability, and they

---

[3] Some of the original terms were Finnish, some Swedish, due to the fact that both were (and still are) official languages in Finland.

[4] We use original terms such as 'feeble-minded' and 'idiot' in this subchapter without quotation marks, according to the conventions at the time.

guided the Finnish care system for the next 20–30 years (Harjula, 1996, pp. 62–64).

The first institutions for people with intellectual disability, like most societal responses to disability in late 1800s, were built upon traditional Christian philanthropic principles; charity was extended to feeble-minded individuals, who were seen as persons that needed to be protected from society, from its neglect and abuse. The largest and the leading institution in Finland was the Perttulan Tylsämielisten Kasvatuslaitos (Perttula Institution and Training School for the Feeble-Minded), where Christian philanthropy was very soon replaced by eugenics. It was no longer the feeble-minded who needed protection from society but the other way round. Society needed to be protected from the threat the feeble-minded posed as they were heritably degenerated individuals who could pass on their deficiencies to the next generations (Mattila, 1999a, p. 51). Societal interests became the basis for disability services and the criterion for the value of an individual human being.[5] The founder of the Perttula Institution, Edvin Hedman, was a devout eugenicist who in 1887 had already described feeble-mindedness as a degeneration and a decline of human nature (Harjula, 1996, p. 131). It was Hedman who set the foundation for the institutional responses to intellectual disability in Finland, and his work (including his values) was continued by his wife, Emma, as the director of Perttula 1915–1927, and later his son Reidar, who was the director of Perttula from 1927 until 1944 (Mattila, 1999b, pp. 226–229). Accordingly, in 1912 the Perttula Institution started to sterilise their residents *alegally*[6] until 1922, when the Finnish National Board of Health pointed out that such operations could be seen as *illegal* (similar alegal practices were prevalent at the

---

[5] Edvin Hedman's son Reidar argued in 1927 that classifying people either as normal, useful or abnormal, or as entitled (or not) to full human rights was not only justified but necessary. The nation's success were to be placed first. Should an individual fail to meet its requirements, he or she needed 'to be labelled as below the standard without pity' (Harjula, 1996, p. 135).

[6] This means that sterilizations were neither legal nor illegal as the law at the time included no provision that could have been applied directly to sterilization – it was thus a matter lying outside the sphere of law.

time in many other countries, such as Sweden) (Mattila, 1999b, pp. 66–70, 229–230).

Realism was the guiding principle in the education of fe-eble-minded students; education cannot overcome laws of nature so the aim of school could not be to make idiots into human be-ings, as Edvin Hedman put the matter. Rather, the aim, for tho-se who actually had the potential to develop, was to teach them practical and social skills, and possibly even rudimentary literacy and mathematical skills. If the child did not learn to communicate with other people, he or she was to be removed from school.[7] One of the Perttula Institution's teachers argued in 1924 that the minimum aim of their work was to make a feeble-minded indi-vidual 'tolerable to the environment by habituating him to hu-man manners'. Controlling sexuality and teaching virtues such as chastity, decency and self-discipline were also central in the institutional order guiding the lives of the feeble-minded (Harjula, 1996, pp. 78–82, 87).

Discussions about the moral worth of certain human lives and whether some humans were suitable for death were part of the eugenic discourse (Harjula, 1996, pp. 131–132). Such discussions continued even after World War II. Erkki Saari[8] (1957, pp. 25–28, 50–51) in his book *Sielullisesti poikkeavat lapset* (*Mentally Deficient Children*)[9] (which was used in teacher education in Finnish universities) pondered whether the lives of idiots – those who are unable to learn to read or even speak, to dress them-selves, or in general to take care of themselves – were useless. He concluded that individuals who are nothing but a burden to society actually suffer from sickness, and therefore ought to be treated and taken care of rather than be exterminated. It would be absurd to kill those with smallpox, alcoholism or syphilis

---

[7] At the Perttula Institution, during 1890–1927 some 33–37% of the students were expelled because they were considered to be incapable of development (Harjula, 1996, p. 98).

[8] Erkki Saari was head of a reformatory (Järvilinnan vastaanottokoti) in 1945–1970 and an influential scholar in child welfare issues.

[9] The first edition of the book was published in 1949. The third edition, from 1957, includes a statement on the second cover page: 'Kouluhallituksen hyväksymä opettajainvalmistuslaitosten oppikirjaksi' ('Approved by the National School Board as a textbook for teacher training institutions').

and so it would be to do so in the case of idiots. Saari argued that killing such individuals would fail to eliminate the cause of deficiency – general 'social hygienic measures', such as sterilisation, were needed instead (Saari, 1957, p. 51).

Until the 1950s there were only few institutions for people with intellectual disability and no legislation to guide their services.[10] The need for such legislation arose as part of a preventive welfare agenda where feeble-minded people were seen as a societal risk; the main motivation for the organised care of the feeble-minded was to protect society from social problems caused by this group of people. In particular, the care of uneducable idiots was seen to be a pressing issue by medical and education professionals as it was estimated in the 1940s that the need for institutional places for idiots was three times more than the actual number of places at the time. Therefore, Vajaakykyisten lasten huoltokomitea (the Committee for the Welfare of Handicapped Children) was set up to make a general plan for the care of disabled children and especially children with intellectual disability. The committee concluded that the only way to solve the issue of feeble-mindedness efficiently was to develop their institutional care, which in practice meant enlarging the existing institutions and building new ones[11] (Leppälä, 2014, pp. 44–52).

The institutional care of the feeble-minded was arranged according to the 'Danish model', which meant organising large central institutions that had separate wards for each group of the feeble-minded according to their level of development and need of support. The Committee for the Welfare of Handicapped Children argued that this model was better than the decentralised system used, for instance, in Sweden, with small, regional institutions. The decentralised model was seen problematic because small institutions could not guarantee appropriate

---

[10] In 1927 there were 152 places in Finnish intellectual disability institutions, in 1933 228 and in 1945 735 places. In addition, some people with intellectual disability were placed in mental hospitals but there is no knowledge about the number of such individuals (Vesala, 2003).

[11] In 1947–1958 the number of the feeble-minded placed in institutions increased from 735 to 1,620. At the beginning of the 1960s, Finland had 12 institutions for the feeble-minded, with 2,018 residents (Leppälä, 2014, pp. 52, 95).

grouping of residents according to their characteristics (especially according to their additional special features such as epilepsy, physical or sensory impairments) and because it would allegedly include the risk of great disparity between different regions, where some institutions would be overcrowded while others would be half empty. Also, large institutions with several hundred residents were seen as more cost-effective and efficient than smaller units regarding care work (Leppälä, 2014, pp. 95–96).

The only places for people with intellectual disability to live outside their childhood homes in the 1960s were intellectual disability institutions (in 1969 ca. 4,300 residents with ID), mental hospitals (in 1969 ca. 1,960 residents with ID) and old people's homes (in 1969 ca. 2,500 residents with ID). But alongside the building of new residential institutions, a new form of organised care started to develop: community care. Instead of providing all care and services within institutions, the needed support and services were to be arranged within one's community, and one's home. The first day activity centres ('*päivähuoltola*' or '*eksternaatti*'), which took care of people with intellectual disability during the daytime, were established in the late 1950s. Their main function was to ease the burden of the families taking care of their disabled children and to enable them to continue to live at home. Day centres provided activities and teaching of practical skills (e.g. hygiene, table manners), and for the more advanced students even schools subjects, mostly for children under the age of 16. In 1961 there were only nine day centres, with 476 customers, and, by 1969, 1,189 customers (Leppälä, 2014, pp. 110–112; Vesala, 2003).

Parents of children with intellectual disability, who started to get organised in the late 1950s, were one of the driving forces of the development of community care. Many parents did not wish to place their children in institutions,[12] which caused bafflement among experts (e.g. medical doctors, child welfare and public health officials), who were virtually unanimous that institutions

---

[12] One finding of doctoral research published in 1966, which the candidate found surprising, was that only some 25% of parents wanted to place their children with intellectual disability into institutions (Leppälä, 2014, p. 115).

were the best solution not only for the disabled children but for their families as well. The relationships between parents and experts were often strained as experts tended to see parents as impediments to the implementation of appropriate care for their children. Many parents were seen to be unfit to care for their children and experts accused them of denying the reality of their child's disability in cases where parents attempted to keep their children in regular schools. However, institutions did not have sufficient places for all persons with intellectual disability, so the development of community care was a practical necessity (Leppälä, 2014, pp. 112–117).

The general ethos guiding disability policy in Finland started to change in the 1960s, when society's interests were replaced by the interests and social rights of individuals. For the first time, (re)habilitation was seen (especially by academics and professionals in social policy and intellectual disability care) as profitable and possible for people with intellectual disability, something they might actually benefit from – even in the case of those with the most profound disability. It was emphasised that, regardless of possible utilitarian considerations, all individuals had the right to pursue and realise their potential, and live lives that were as meaningful as possible. Also, persons with intellectual disability not only needed their basic care needs to be met but impulses and activities to fulfil their emotional and social needs as well. Admittedly, habilitation would never make these individuals productive citizens who could support themselves. But, even though the development gained through habilitation may have seemed modest to other people, they were pivotal to the individuals with intellectual disability themselves, and to their quality of life. It was not utility but, rather, humanity that should motivate habilitation; society was seen to have a duty to secure the dignity and human rights of people with (profound) intellectual disability. The focus of habilitation (instead of *re*habilitation, because it was about developing each person's individual potential rather than restoring lost capacities) was on primary adaptive functions (hygiene, dressing, eating, communication etc.) and strengthening each person's potential capacities in order to attain as high a level of proficiency as possible (Leppälä, 2014, pp. 125–129).

The sexuality of persons with intellectual disability was virtually unthinkable until the 1960s. They were considered either too infantile, too dangerous or too perverted to have legitimate sexual needs. One function of institutions had been from early on to control the sexuality of their residents. One example of this policy in Finland was to place residents into rooms of either one or three, in order to prevent homosexual relationships. But, from the 1960s onwards, things like homosexual relations and masturbation began to be seen, slowly but surely, to be harmless and normal, and, importantly, as human rights issues. An individual's sexuality belonged now to herself; it was not primarily something that society ought to control. One manifestation of sexual liberation was new legislation. The new Marriage Act (1969) and Sterilization Act (1970) no longer categorically denied people with intellectual disability the chance to get married or to have children. However, in practice the new laws and more liberal attitudes regarding sexuality within the disability service system did not make a dramatic difference in the lives of people with intellectual disability. Their sexual relationships, marriages and procreation continued to be seen as problematic even by the professionals in charge of their care: people with intellectual disability were not seen to have the necessary understanding about the emotional and moral issues related to sexuality and marriage, let alone parenting (Leppälä, 2014, pp. 136–141).

One further indication of changed attitudes was a discussion about the need to renew Finnish terminology. The term '*vajaamielinen*' (feeble-minded) was increasingly seen as derogatory, especially among parents of feeble-minded children. Vajaamielisten Tukiyhdistysten Liitto (the main parental advocacy association in the 1960s for persons with intellectual disability) argued that the term '*vajaamielisyys*' (feeble-mindedness) should be replaced with the concept of '*kehitysvammaisuus*' (developmental disability). However, '*vajaamielisyys*' should not be abandoned altogether, because of its preciseness – even though the term had become infected with negative connotations, at least everyone knew to what kinds of people it referred to. The main Finnish organisation promoting the cause of the feeble-minded, Vajaamielishuollon Keskusliitto changed its name to Kehitysvammaliitto (the Finnish

Association on Intellectual and Developmental Disabilities) in 1965 and recommended that same terminological change would be introduced in legal and academic use. It was even suggested that the term developmental disability (*kehitysvammaisuus*)[13] could be applied to all impairment groups. These suggestions received mixed responses. For example, Lääkäriliitto (the Finnish Medical Association) and Invalidiliitto (the Finnish Association of People with Physical Disabilities) pointed out the risk of conflating those with 'intellectual developmental disabilities' to those with physical disabilities and argued that such a confusion would be counterproductive for both groups. Despite various unfavourable criticism, the term '*kehitysvammaisuus*' gradually became established in the 1970s and referred specifically to people previously called '*vajaamielinen*' (feeble-minded) (Leppälä, 2014, pp. 121–125).

New mentality in terms of disability rights did not, however, challenge the status quo regarding institutionalisation. It was still generally agreed that the only suitable environment for people with profound intellectual disability was the institution. The number of residents in institutions kept increasing in the 1970s and the last large institutions were built at the end of the decade. In 1979, the number of people placed in intellectual disability institutions had risen (5,612 residents), whereas the number of residents with intellectual disability in mental hospitals and old people's homes had decreased (1,416 and 1,656, respectively). Simultaneously, the number of clients in day activity centres had increased steadily (at the end of 1970s, over 4,400). Although the first critiques of intellectual disability institutions, and their predominant status in the care system, started to appear in the late 1960s, the legitimacy of institutions as such remained unquestioned. Besides, at the time there were very few non-institutional residential homes for people with intellectual disability. One reality that maintained the dominance of institutions was the legal requirement that one should be

---

[13] Interestingly, a similar terminological change took place in the United States some 40 years later, when the term 'mental retardation' was replaced by 'intellectual and developmental disabilities', which is very similar to the Finnish term '*älyllinen kehitysvammaisuus*' (intellectual developmental disability).

placed in an institution before the age of 16. Many parents ended up placing their children in institutions just to secure their future, when the parents themselves would be too old to look after them (Vesala, 2003).

Increasingly, institutional care received criticism on the grounds of the new intellectual disability policy that emphasised individuals rights and needs. A situation where individuals had no genuine opportunities for living arrangements outside institutions was seen to be discriminatory (Vesala, 2003). This mentality was the result of the new guiding principle of disability policy in the Nordic countries, namely normalization. It was increasingly argued in the 1970s and 1980s that disability services should be provided as part of mainstream social services and that, accordingly, institutions and segregated teaching arrangements for persons with intellectual disability should be abolished (Leppälä, 2014, pp. 290–293; Tøssebro, Bonfils, Teittinen, Tideman, Traustadóttir & Vesala 2012). Such criticism resulted in heated debates in the intellectual disability field. It was argued that the normalisation principle, with an emphasis on integration, had ignored the views of families, and was, all in all, utopian. Why bring down brand-new, expensive institutions with qualified professionals who had long experience of working with people with intellectual disability? Many professionals in the institutions were offended by the normalisation and deinstitutionalisation critique, which was labelled as idealistic and biased. Nevertheless, the first group homes were established in the 1970s and the unquestioned dominance of institutions started to break in practice. At that time, the issue of adults with intellectual disability living with their ageing parents also received increasing attention. At the turn of the 1980s, approximately 60–70% of people with intellectual disability (ca. 5,000 individuals) still lived at their childhood homes (Leppälä, 2014, pp. 196–214; Vesala, 2003).

It was not until the 1990s that the number of people with intellectual disability living in institutions started to decrease rapidly as they were moved to group homes. Group homes have been a crucial part of the process of deinstitutionalisation, but they have also been seen to include characteristics similar to traditional institutions: in Finland, group homes are typically large units (several group homes in the same building unit) with dozens of residents, and they have not brought a change to the passive status of people with intellectual disability as service users ('*palvelunkäyttäjä*', a term widely used nowadays) or the relationship and the power imbalance between the residents and the staff. So, in practice, the move to community care has partly been just a matter of reclassifying existing institutions as group homes. In a somewhat similar way, in Denmark the concept of the institution was removed from regulations and statistics in 1998, which, on paper, made them disappear and the country had all at once completed the process of deinstitutionalisation. The move from institutionalisation in Finland has been slow compared to, for example, Sweden and Norway, and it is still an ongoing process. Norway closed all its intellectual disability institutions in the mid-1990s, Sweden by 2002 (Mietola, Teittinen & Vesala, 2013, pp. 10–11; Socialstyrelsen, 2018b; Tøssebro et al., 2012).

In Finland, the intellectual disability service system is not as regulated as it is, for example, in Sweden. Persons with PIMD in Sweden live in their own apartments with full-time personal assistance, in group homes, or with their parents (Socialstyrelsen 2018a, 2018b, p. 14). In Finland, most persons with PIMD live in group homes. These differ from their Swedish counterparts in size (group homes in Finland have usually five to eight residents but there can be several group homes in the same building) and their location (either in suburbs or outside residential areas). Many group homes in Finland are architecturally very institutional. They look and feel – both inside and outside – like small-scale hospitals rather than someone's home (see Chapter 7). This contrasts with Sweden, where (at least on paper) the design and building of apartments in group homes is controlled by the same regulations that apply to housing in general, and by the residents themselves. The aim of these regulations is to provide the residents with conditions through which they can actively take part in community life (Mietola et al., 2013, pp. 20–21). However, reports by the Swedish National Board of Health and Welfare (Socialstyrelsen, 2011, 2018, pp. 29–31) have concluded that reality does not always correspond with regulations. The size of group homes in Sweden is sometimes much larger than the recommended three to five apartments, and in some cases group homes have been placed in the same locations as service homes for the elderly, which inevitably creates an institutional feel.

This tendency seems to apply to all Nordic countries. As Tøssebro et al. (2012) conclude in their review of Nordic intellectual disability services, 'the ideology of community care and small group homes prevail in the Nordic region but, in reality, the implementation shows conflicting trends' (p. 139). In Finland, the government launched a national programme in 2010 with the aim of closing all intellectual disability institutions by 2020. However, at the end of 2019, there were still 452 persons with intellectual disability living in institutions, 131 of whom were under 18 (https://sotkanet.fi/sotkanet/fi/taulukko/).

Outline of the book

In the upcoming chapters, we will present our data and main findings and analyse some key theoretical issues that persons with PIMD have made us confront.

In Chapter 2, we explain how our research was carried out: the recruitment process of our research participants and the various practical problems related to it. Our research engages with the everyday lives of people who could not, themselves, give us the permission to observe and take part in their lives. Therefore, we need to clarify some ethical issues related to data collection as well as knowledge production with this group of people. The chapter also explains the complexities during the fieldwork regarding interpretation, field notes and research relationships: what did we see, how should we describe it, and in what ways should we engage with the everyday lives of our research participants?

In the beginning of our fieldwork, Reetta and Sonja mostly concentrated on making sense of our research participants: how would we know what particular sounds or expressions meant in particular contexts? How do we know what they know, or what they can? We soon realised that these kinds of questions perplexed the care workers as well, and played an important role in their professional practice. Chapter 3 presents the ways care workers describe the personalities and competencies of our research participants, and persons with PIMD in general. The chapter unpacks the conflict between the formal medical knowledge concerning persons with PIMD, and the knowledge that the care workers formed about our research participants. How did these conceptions affect the care work practices?

One individual asset that some of our research participants had, according to the care workers, is sociability; they enjoyed socialising and, in general, the company of other people. We discovered (in Chapter 4), however, that, while our research participants are constantly surrounded by other people (in that they live in group homes and participate in day activity centres), they have little genuine opportunities for social interaction. This is partly due to the care culture and scarce resources in many group homes, where the emphasis is one-sidedly on basic care tasks like dressing, feeding and toileting. But it is disability policy that ultimately directs the organisation of care work and what is prioritised in group homes. The policy is concerned about enhancing the social lives and inclusion of persons with PIMD outside the group homes and day centres – outside the disability service system. But the problem is that our research participants' lives take place almost exclusively within the disability service system, of which the policy texts say next to nothing as regards sociability.

Sociability is typically seen important to youth and young adults, who are expected to build various, possibly lifelong relationships. This raises the question of age, and its role in the lives of persons with PIMD. In Chapter 5, we focus on the life of Hugo, a young man in his early twenties, and how his care workers, teachers and mother think of what kind of life is appropriate for young people like Hugo.[14] We examine the reasons why Hugo has no possibility to lead such a life. The key issue in this context is the meaning of the principle of age-appropriateness: why do we think that people at a certain age should act in certain ways, and to what extent do these cultural conventions apply to persons with PIMD?

An obvious, and difficult issue related to age-appropriateness is sexuality. Chapter 6 asks[15] whether persons with PIMD have the right to sexual pleasure and whether their carers have the duty to facilitate their possibilities to flourish as sexual subjects.

---

[14] Chapter 5 is a revised version of Mietola and Vehmas (2019).
[15] This chapter is a revised version of Vehmas (2019).

And, if sexuality is seen as a right, should it be seen on a par, for example, with other dimensions of care, similar to nutrition or health care? What are the risks involved in facilitating sexual pleasure and would it be better to do nothing in order to nothing wrong? Sexuality is an important issue regarding well-being and a good life, but it is also symbolically significant because the way we grant (or not) sexual rights for certain people reveals how we perceive these individuals as human beings.

People with intellectual disability have a long history of being seen as animal-like and, therefore, they have been seen unfit to enjoy, for example, sexuality. In current philosophical ethics, it is not uncommon to see persons with intellectual disability as psychologically comparable to non-human animals. Such comparison is often seen to suggest a lower moral worth of persons with PIMD than the rest of us. But animality is no longer merely a negative signifier. It is increasingly seen in humanities and social sciences as something positive that does not necessarily deprive one of full moral status. Chapter 7 explores the potential benefits and risks related to the conceptualisation of persons with PIMD in terms of animality. What are the ethics of comparing human and non-human animals and their individual characteristics with one another? Is such an engagement epistemically helpful and ethically justified?

In Chapter 8, we summarise our main findings and theoretical reflections. The appendix returns to the philosophical starting points with which we began: the basics of moral status and moral worth of persons with PIMD. It explains and analyses the main theories and arguments used in philosophical debates on moral status. We use those debates to develop our own view that persons with PIMD share a moral status equal to other human beings and higher than non-human animals. We argue that the standard philosophical account that evaluates the moral worth of individual beings in terms of their cognitive capacities is flawed. In fact, we argue that no fully satisfactory account exists that would manage to take into account all relevant factors and provide theoretical considerations that would help to solve the issue.

Chapter 2: Ethnography: Recruitment, Interpretation and Ethics

It is an early spring afternoon and Hugo has just returned from school. As usual, he is received by a care worker, who suggests to Hugo that he should have a short rest in his bed before dinner. The care worker starts to open the straps on Hugo's wheelchair, while explaining to Hugo what she is doing: 'You have all this stuff here; let's open them a bit' ('*sulla on paljon näitä rensseleitä, otetaan näitä auki*'). She takes off one of the armrests on the chair and prepares to lift Hugo out of the wheelchair, telling Hugo – who is stretching himself – to remain in a sitting position so that she can lift him out of the chair and onto the bed. Reetta is aside observing what is happening, paying attention to the bodily movements of the care worker and Hugo, to the details of the care worker's talk and gestures, and to Hugo's responses.

After the care worker has tucked Hugo in and left the room, Reetta remains sitting on the sofa placed in front of the window, behind Hugo's bed head, writing down in her notebook notes about what just happened. For example, she writes down an exchange that took place between Hugo and the care worker:

> 'Do you want to listen to music?', care worker asks, leaning again closer to Hugo, 'No. Will I put an audio book on?'. Care worker waits. 'You're not sure.' Hugo has his chin up, raises it a bit, to the right, care worker asks whether Hugo wants to listen to the children's voices [from outside]. That she can leave the window open so that Hugo can listen to the voices, 'We don't need to turn [stereo] on. I'm not sure whether it is because of you [wanting]

---

or it is more our staff members' habit that it is always turned on.' The care worker walks away from Hugo's bed, explains to me that she is unable to interpret Hugo in a way that she would definitely know what he means.

While Reetta is still writing notes of the previous moments, she realises that Hugo is 'talking' to himself, and thus writes in her notes: 'Hugo starts to make sounds, "Ee-eee-uuu. Hrr [grunts]".' After listening to Hugo for a while, Reetta asks him 'What are you talking about there?' and when Hugo continues to 'talk' Reetta gets up from the sofa and walks over to bedside to say hello. Hugo has raised his hands up in front of him, laughs aloud by himself, and startles a little when Reetta starts talking to him. He turns his head towards Reetta, smiling. Reetta talks to Hugo for a while, then returns back to the sofa, telling him that she will now go and sit down to write.

This is what ethnography is by and large about: being present, participating in people's everyday lives, and recording one's observations. In our case, the notes consist of descriptions of action (movements, facial expressions, gestures) and discussions. Since the researcher participates in the observed situations, field notes often include descriptions of the researcher's actions and reflections of her first-hand experiences of activities and relationships in the field. The notes thus provide multilayered descriptions that comprise of different perspectives and 'voices' in situations in which the researcher takes part. Knowledge production like this may seem rather straightforward. In reality, however, it is (or at least *should* be) a result of careful thought process and multiple decisions concerning research practice and focus.

Just getting to the point where Reetta could sit on Hugo's sofa writing notes (which she also did when sitting with staff) had required thinking around research ethics, multiple negotiations with different parties, and the development of ethically sound research practice that is in line with organisational practices and Hugo's preferences. Reetta's actions in the situation are on the one hand based on conscious decisions made within the research team, for example on how the researcher should enter and be present in research participants' private spaces, or what kind of relationship it would be appropriate to develop during the fieldwork. On the other hand, these practices are based on Reetta's interpretation of Hugo's personality and personal preferences, and how they should be taken into account. Reetta had become to know Hugo as a person who enjoys socialising and the company of others. Being present in Hugo's room, where he spent most of his time at home, seemed ethically justified inasmuch as Reetta was attentive to Hugo's responses to her presence.

What Reetta wrote down in her notes was a result of the gradual development of focus and practice. Our research question – *what makes a good life for people with PIMD?* – does not generally provide a clear focus for observation. In order to be able to address such a large question, we had to ask first very basic questions about the lives of people with PIMD such as what happens in their lives, where it happens and why. Gradually we were able to sharpen our focus to things we became to consider significant in relation to 'living a good life'. For example, in the episode described above Reetta's attention was drawn to the efforts of the care worker to find out Hugo's preferences concerning pastimes, and how she immediately questioned her skill in interpreting Hugo accurately. This episode reminded Reetta about her previous observations on the ambivalence of interpretation with people like Hugo: how and what we know about their own perspective, and how we engage with them were constant sources of worry to the care workers, and played a crucial role in the ways the care work was carried out (see Chapter 3).

The practice of note writing is not just about what gets written down but also about how the researcher arrives at her observations. In order to record the ways Hugo responded to talk, being moved from his chair to his bed, or even just to sounds of the children in the playground, Reetta had to learn how to interpret him. The whole practice of note taking thus turned into a process of learning how to notice and capture movements, sounds, gestures and facial expressions that make up Hugo's 'talk' his 'voice'. This intertwined process of learning to interpret through writing led Reetta and Sonja not only to acquire new skills, such as writing observations in adequate detail, but also to profoundly rethink about how we observe, how we interpret, and ultimately how and what are we able to know.

This chapter is about our research practices and the ways they developed during the project. While our primary focus is on practical questions of what and how we actually did, the following discussion also aims to elucidate our thinking behind the acquired practices. Our account has been informed by previous qualitative studies, in particular ethnographies that have had people with intellectual disability as key participants (e.g. Davis et al., 2008; Komulainen, 2007; Simmons & Watson, 2014). This chapter does not have a specific section on research ethics, since ethics is a theme that runs through our discussion. The mere choice to do ethnography was based on the ethical commitment to see the lives of persons with PIMD as valuable and worthy of being understood. In our view, ethics is a crucial part of ethnographic understanding. To Paul Atkinson (2015), this ethical orientation manifests in ethnography's devotion to represent lives of research participants in their 'full complexity, with due regard for the rationality of social action, and with respect for the social actors involved' (p. 173). Don Kulick (2015) writes that, for him, being an anthropologist is about working in a way that 'extend[s] across boundaries, to listen to people whose language and culture one struggles to comprehend, and to represent others in a respectful and empathetic way' (p. 17). The views of Atkinson and Kulick resonate with our project's key ethical commitments and with the concerns that we faced when planning the execution of the project. Our starting point was to position people with PIMD as moral subjects, which implied that our research practice had to be designed in a way that acknowledged and supported our research participants' dignity. Ethnography provided the means to carry out our research accordingly.

For us, crucial aspects of ethnographic knowledge production are development and learning; one does not have to know the people and culture in question when entering the field. Rather, one learns about them throughout the research process. As we have learnt to know about our research participants, we also have learnt something about how to interact with them in ways that respect their personalities. We have learnt what is relevant in order to understand their lives and, to some extent, even to learn to understand them as persons.

Ethnography's roots are in anthropology, which has traditionally studied culture, especially non-Western cultures. Owing to criticism raised, for example, by post-colonialist perspectives, anthropology as a discipline has had to engage with discussions around politics and ethics of studying 'Others'. According to Kulick (2015), it is the premise and promise of anthropology 'that one not only can, but one *should* represent people who are very unlike oneself' (p. 31). In other words, studying a group that you do not belong to is not only a question about the right, but sometimes also an obligation to 'speak for' them.

Our research participants have very limited means to express their 'voice'. It therefore has been unquestionable to us that as researchers we have an obligation to try to make sense of and represent these 'voices' – however ambiguous these voices are; however insufficient our tools for 'capturing' them might prove to be. Part of this engagement is a conscious risk involved when one aims to 'speak for others' – the epistemic risk (and related ethical and political risk) of misrepresenting their lives and them as human beings. We have tried to see these challenges as something productive, as questions that push us to develop our thinking and methodological practices. Besides, if the 'don't speak for others' argument were taken to its logical conclusion, then persons with PIMD would never get represented by anyone.

Who and where are people with PIMD? Finding and recruiting research participants

The project was launched in September 2014. We instantly started to prepare documents for ethical review for the University of Helsinki Ethical Review Board, and, at the same time, made first contacts with service provider organisations (management level), to find out about their requirements for research permits and ethical review. We contacted municipal social welfare agencies and private sector service provider organisations in the Helsinki capital region. We had collaborated with some of the organisations previously, while others we acquired through municipal agencies. We inquired whether the organisations would be interested in participating in our study, and whether their service users would fit our research interest.

All relevant 'stakeholders', from managers of provider organisations to family members, were happy to take part in our research. In fact, they repeatedly emphasised in different stages of the project how important in their view research on the lives of persons with PIMD is. Two key factors probably explain this enthusiasm: the disability politics in Finland at the time, and the various expectations these stakeholders had for our project.

Our project started in a situation where intellectual disability services were finally made to bring the deinstitionalisation process to a conclusion; governmental programmes allocated money for new housing solutions (i.e. group homes to replace institutions) and forced municipalities to implement a transfer from institutional care to community care (Mietola et al., 2013). This situation most likely had an effect on our negotiations with different parties. The managers of service provider organisations thought that participating in our study would give them knowledge of whether their services reached the policy aims, especially in relation to people with complex needs. One middle manager-level actor even asked to get information from our observations to be used in their organisation's internal evaluation. One service provider unit actually took our research question (what is a good life and how it materialises) and has been using it to analyse the experiences of their service users (i.e. interviewing their group home residents).

As for family members, their interests seemed to be both personal and political. They wanted information about their family member's living conditions, but also to express their concern over the quality of the services and everyday care (e.g. the effects of the high turnover of staff). They emphasised, however, how things had improved and that they were, in general, satisfied with the current situation. Some of the care workers, on their part, hoped that our study would give visibility to the important work they do in the changing context of intellectual disability services. They repeatedly talked about the lack of knowledge regarding this specific group of people, even among the staff who work with them. Alongside visibility, they hoped for appreciation for their work, which in their view still suffers from a stigma of being a substandard form of institutional care.

During the initial discussions with different service provider organisations, the ambiguity of the term 'profound intellectual and
multiple disabilities' became evident. One key challenge related
to providing a clear definition of who we wanted to recruit was
that we were ourselves uncertain about the matter. While all of
us had worked with people with intellectual disability, our contacts had almost exclusively been with people with milder intellectual disability. This is hardly surprising since individuals with
severe or profound intellectual disability still live their lives tightly
within the disability service system and thus largely hidden from
our everyday surroundings.

After initial discussions with one service provider organisation,
our research team sat down to rethink how to proceed with these
negotiations. The manager of that organisation was enthusiastic about our study and wanted us to start working with service
users, who in their organisation were seen as puzzling and challenging. However, the individuals the manager had in mind were
persons with milder intellectual disability. It was apparent that we
needed to be clearer about the key criteria for our research participants, and find a way to communicate the criteria in a more intelligible way to the professionals. In order to gain access and build
trust with the service provider organisations and staff members,
we needed to hear their concerns in relation to which individuals
were marginalised in and by the service system, and find ways of
taking these views into consideration in the recruitment process.

Around the time of these initial discussions with the service
providers, we also visited the Communication and Technology
Centre Tikoteekki at the Finnish Association on Intellectual
and Developmental Disabilities. With two experts in the field
of intensive interaction, Kaisa Martikainen and Kaisa Laine,
we discussed expedient terminology. They argued that the term
'profound intellectual disability' is not an established term in
Finland. Accordingly, they recommended that we use the term
'persons with most severe intellectual disability' ('*vaikeimmin
kehitysvammaiset*') in our recruitment process, and also specify
that we are interested in people who do not have spoken language
and are capable of only very rudimentary forms of non-verbal
communication. We followed their advice as it seemed to reflect
the more metaphorical definition and a criterion that we had in

mind; we were looking for people who remain mysteries to people close to them in much more profound ways than usually is the case with people close to us. This conceptualisation arose from our previous discussions with some parents who described their children in those terms (some care workers in our data also referred to our research participants as 'mysteries'). They had learnt to understand their children and their communication but were still puzzled on a regular basis regarding what their children wanted to communicate.

All of the management-level negotiations were very positive; the managers immediately recognised the importance of the project; some even cheered that finally someone was interested in people with PIMD. They were eager to have us doing fieldwork in their organisations. Managers gave us contact persons (heads of day and housing services) who could help us to identify possible research contexts/units and participants. Our research participants had different kinds of service combinations: living in public or private services and going to a public day centre, or living in private services and also going to private day centre. Services for people with intellectual disability are often produced in public–private partnerships, which means that ethnography in these services requires multiple review processes and negotiations in different contexts.

An important part of this process was discussions with specific units and group homes where we asked them to identify potential research participants for us. Often these early contacts meant that we got to meet service users, including our intended research participants. After finding an agreement with the care workers on suitable individuals for our research, we sent letters to their next of kin via the units, informing the family members about the project and more specifically what participation in the project would mean. All contacts were positive, and, after more detailed discussions with family members or close care workers, proxy consent was given on behalf of our participants (each of our research participants had a guardian or family member who was legally empowered to make decisions for them).

While these discussions proceeded smoothly, in some cases it was somewhat difficult to judge who should give consent on behalf of the research participant. While in most cases our participant's parent was also his or her legal guardian, we also had participants whose family ties were very fragmented (older participants who had been institutionalised since early childhood), and who had been appointed a public legal guardian (who only monitored their financial matters and typically did not know them personally). In the case of Ella, for example, the initial negotiations to include her as a participant involved an extra round of discussions about proxy consent and who should give it on her behalf. After talking with her group home's care workers, her brother and her legal guardian, it became obvious that neither a family member nor her legal guardian would know her and her life well enough to assess her will in this matter. As a result, all parties agreed that written proxy consent should be given by the housing unit care worker who coordinated her care.

The care workers in our research contexts were in a key position to finally open doors for us but were the last ones to be asked for consent. We invited ourselves to staff/team meetings in the group homes and day centres, where we introduced the project and practices of fieldwork (what our participation means in practice) and asked for the staff members' (verbal) consent. The atmosphere in these meetings differed: in some contexts, reception was very enthusiastic, with lots of questions about the aims of the project, whereas in other contexts the staff members seemed more cautious. Only one person among all of those we contacted declined to participate (a care worker in one of the research contexts). In this particular case, we carried out our fieldwork in the unit during times when that person was not working. When we had gained access to our fieldwork contexts, we informed other care users in these contexts and their family members (by letter) about the project and our fieldwork's possible impact on them. Also, should they refuse to take part in the research, they could do that by either informing the care workers or contacting us directly.

With one of the organisations we also negotiated the possibility of doing a short pilot observation in one of their group homes. Since we were in the middle of the process of ethical review by the University of Helsinki Review Board, and did not have research permits or agreements, it was agreed that we would visit the unit as visitors, and that the data produced would be only for our own use with the aim of defining how we would proceed with our fieldwork in this particular organisation (who would participate in the research; in which unit the fieldwork would take place). The aim of our pilot study was to get some understanding on the specific issues involved in the fieldwork with people with PIMD. The three-day pilot was carried out in November 2014.

We recruited six key participants, who were in their twenties, thirties and forties, with varied physical, cognitive and emotional characteristics: Anna was in her early 20s, Ella her late 40s, Frida her early 30s, Hugo his early 20s, Leo his early 40s, and Sebastian his early 20s. We considered writing biographies of each individual but decided not to do so because we wanted to secure our research participants' anonymity; after all, they represent a very small group of people. However, we have included information about each individual in different parts of the book to contextualise the issue under discussion.

Fieldwork took place in five group homes, two day centres and one vocational school during 2015–2016. We observed one research participant at a time, by one researcher, usually two days a week for a period of three to four months. In practice, this means that we spent more or less a hundred hours observing each participant. Our data consisted of field notes, 19 interviews with family members and care workers, and written materials such as personal treatment and activity plans. During the fieldwork, we met dozens of professionals and service users. We also had frequent contact with the family members of those research participants who had close relationships with their families. All in all, we had contact with hundreds of people in our research contexts – care users, professionals, care workers and family members. The nature of these contacts varied; some became important informants through repeated contact and mutual rapport, while others remained more or less distant.

Developing research practices and research relationships

The recruitment process described above included plenty of ethical consideration and decision-making. One key question that had to be resolved early on had to do with the principle of informed consent, which, in the case of persons with very limited cognitive and communicative capacities, is highly problematic. Our research participants were most likely not able to understand the information provided (what they were supposed to consent to) or have the means to communicate their will in the matter. There are very few official guidelines for conducting research with a group of people like this. For example, the General Research Ethics Guidelines for Humanities and Social Sciences (Finnish Advisory Board on Research Integrity, 2009) did not address the issue of how to proceed with consent in cases where participants of age have significant cognitive limitations. In order to find some starting points to our thinking in relation to consent, we turned to ethical guidelines in medical research, more specifically the Medical Research Act (488/1999).

To our surprise, the medical research legislation not only addresses the issue of research with participants with significant cognitive impairments but also provides a more holistic perspective to informed consent than was the case in the social science guidelines in Finland at the time. The Act states that written consent is required from the next of kin or other representative close to the participant. Furthermore, consent should also be evaluated from the point of view of the possible stress or harm caused to the research participants.

Our approach to consent was based on a view that combines proxy consent with a strong emphasis on the constant monitoring of the research participants' well-being. Following examples of previous international studies (e.g. Cameron & Murphy, 2007; Cocks, 2006), our solution was to combine proxy consent with a continuous process of assent. This meant keeping the well-being of our research participants the major concern during the fieldwork; we were prepared to withdraw at any time should it seem that a participant was disturbed by our presence. This approach resonates well with both our general approach to ethics, which has been influenced by feminist ethics of care (e.g. Kittay, 1999) and the related ethical commitment to recognise the personhood and inalienable value of people with PIMD as fellow humans (Kittay, 2005; Nussbaum, 2006). But how could we be sure that our presence did not cause harm and stress to our research participants? How does one build research relationships based on mutual recognition and respect with persons with PIMD?

For us it is self-evident that the recognition of personhood and worth of our research participants can only be achieved through the recognition of the profound difference between them and us. Rather than treating the undeniable difference(s) related to cognitive impairments as a risk that closes opportunities to connect with people and interpret them, these differences should be 'engaged with' (Kulick, 2015). As Kulick (2015, p. 28) points out, '[t]he space between that familiar sameness and the in many ways unknowable difference is the space of ethics'. Part of our engagement with this space of ethics was a conscious awareness of our accountability, as well as of the significance of our choices and practices during the fieldwork.

In her account of 'asymmetrical reciprocity', the American philosopher Iris Marion Young (1997) argues that ideal communication starts with mutual recognition, where the other person is seen to have equal moral worth and irreducible perspective that ought to be taken into account. However, moral respect also entails recognition of the differences between communicative subjects. According to Young (1997), the relationship between participants of a communication situation is always asymmetrical as each of them is distinguished by a particular history and social position: 'when privileged people put themselves in the position of those who are less privileged, the assumptions derived from their privilege often allow them unknowingly to misrepresent the other's situation' (Young, 1997, p. 48). Acknowledging the irreversibility of the perspectives of communicating subjects is therefore an essential element of moral respect. Young, however, seems to 'assume an "other" who can talk, or who can express himself or herself clearly through some other medium, such as sign language' (Kulick, 2015, p. 25). The risks and obligations involved in 'speaking for others' are intensified when we are talking about people who have very limited means to express themselves (ibid.). Kittay (2010) challenges academics who study and write about people with significant cognitive impairments – people who cannot speak for themselves – to know those people they are writing about (epistemic responsibility) and to acknowledge what they do not know (epistemic modesty). Translating these ideas into practice has meant that our research process has involved constant critical reflection. While we have made various interpretations about our research participants, we have simultaneously had to challenge our knowledge about them: why do we think we know, and what are, the limit(ation)s of our knowledge?

As early as the initial negotiations with the care workers, we emphasised that we must rely on their experience and guidance regarding the ways our research participants should be approached and what their preferred ways of interacting with others were (see also Boxall & Ralph, 2010; Simmons & Watson, 2014). We had some general principles concerning interaction; for example, we always greeted our key participants verbally (and with touch if they preferred) when arriving at the context, and interacted with them (verbally or by touch), thus respecting their right to be included in ordinary interaction and communicative community. Instead of relying on predetermined, unchallenged diagnostic categorisations that lump together people with the same diagnosis, we aimed to develop our practices according to what we learnt about the individual preferences of our participants in the course of getting acquainted with them (see Christensen & Prout, 2002; Klotz, 2004).

> I go to Ella to say hello, kneel down next to her on the floor, touch her hand and say 'Hi Ella, how are you?'. Ella turns her face towards me, takes hold of my hands and claps my hands together. Then takes my hand to her lips, and from there to her face, pressing my palm against her face. She then lifts her gaze towards me and smiles. Starts clapping with my hands again, then lets go. (Field notes, with Ella)

In order to further enhance our ability to communicate and interact sensitively with our profoundly disabled, non-verbal participants, we also consulted with experts from the Finnish Association on Intellectual and Developmental Disabilities concerning intensive interaction methods. We found these methods useful particularly with those research participants whose means and initiatives concerning interaction were most difficult to interpret. For example, with Anna, one of our first research participants, finding a momentary interactive connection required that Sonja learnt to attend and respond to Anna's subtle and unique, and often transient, interaction initiatives (such as brief eye contact or when she reached to touch Sonja's arm). Anna's and Sonja's research relationship had to be built on and through these brief moments of connection. However, some of our research participants were very skilled in communicating their preferences and they responded to people and activities around them with gestures, expressions and sounds that were easier to interpret. For example, it would have been difficult to miss or misinterpret Sebastian's excitement when anyone suggested a game of ball throwing. After few weeks, we learnt to know our research participants and were able to start building one-to-one relationships with them, thereby becoming less dependent on the care worker's interpretation assistance.

Previous studies with non-verbal persons have underlined how understanding about individual modes and preferences of communication can only be built over time, through sustained presence and participation (e.g. Pockney, 2006; Davis et al., 2008; Simmons & Watson, 2014; Björnsdóttir et al., 2015). By observing the interaction of our participants with other people in different situations, we gradually learnt to develop dialogical relations with them (cf. Klotz, 2004). Some of the participants seemed to want to keep distance to us, which we respected; hence, we stayed in the background, and participated in their activities only minimally. However, others seemed clearly to enjoy close, even physical contact, such as clapping hands, sitting on our lap, or hugging. At the same time as we tried to be sensitive to our participants' preferences, we also paid attention to how these changed situationally or over time. For example, Frida, who at first seemed very reserved, eventually had long 'chats' with Reetta and was clearly delighted when Reetta arrived to her group home. We responded to the participants' interaction initiatives whenever we could, and interacted with them in ways they preferred.

> I'm sitting on a sofa in the living room and writing notes. Sebastian rolls his wheelchair towards me, stopping in front of me. He sits there a while making repeatedly some of his characteristic utterings, slapping his thigh with his hand, his gaze wandering around,

sweeping over me occasionally. I start echoing his utterings. He then grasps my hand firmly, and takes my notebook and throws it to the floor. I rise to pick up the notebook, then return to the sofa. Putting the notebook aside, I bend slightly towards Sebastian and look at him. His head jerks slightly and he lifts his eyebrows, looking enlivened. He rolls a bit closer still in order to pat my thigh with one hand. I pat him back, and on we go, patting each other in turns a long while. In the midst of this patting game Sebastian smiles cheerily and smacks his mouth as if giving me a flying kiss. (Field notes, with Sebastian)

It was crucial for us to learn to recognise our participants' initiatives, and how they signalled different physical states (e.g. being tired or agitated). Interpreting some of our participants felt easy (like with Sebastian) since they actively made contact with other people. But the process of learning to interpret the expressions and gestures of some other research participants took months. Despite the experience we gained during the fieldwork of our participants' means of expressing themselves, our interpretations remained partial and situational. We also repeatedly confronted moments when we felt uncertainty over how to interpret our participants' action (see Boxall & Ralph, 2010). For example, interaction with Ella, who often sought physical contact with people around her, sometimes turned into action that could be seen as a form of self-harming.

I go and sit down next to Ella. Ella moves herself so that she sits right next to me, takes hold of my hand, slipping her fingers in between mine. She's looking at our hands, but doesn't turn to look at me. She suddenly raises her hand (and mine) and hits her forehead with my hand. I tell her 'No, I don't want to hit you Ella', let go of her hand and stroke her hair, but she repeatedly takes hold of my hand and tries to hit herself again. I try to move bit away from her, but she follows right after me, sitting again glued to my side. (Field notes, with Ella)

Incidents like this kept us aware of the complexity of building ethical fieldwork practice and interpretations. In particular, situations that involved crying, yelling, biting, scratching or hitting, which in the care contexts were often interpreted as signs of distress or anxiety, were troubling for us. We wanted to respect our participants' right to express wide range of feelings, but at the same time we also wanted to feel as certain as possible that our participants were not expressing displeasure towards our presence with these behaviours.

Respecting participants as moral subjects also involved their right to privacy. As Kulick and Rydström (2015, p. 6) note, 'for many disabled people, especially those who live in group homes, or who need assistance to do things like bathe and dress, the line between public and private is blurred, and often it is neither acknowledged nor respected'. We raised the issue of respect for the privacy of our key participants and their housemates early, during the negotiations with the care workers. We asked them to explain 'house rules' concerning privacy (e.g. knocking on door when entering a private room) and to explain how our participants expressed their desire to be left alone. In these discussions, we also defined clear limits to our participation, for example not entering toilet, dressing or other private activities. We mostly stayed in the shared rooms and exercised special caution when we entered participants' rooms. Their rooms were private spaces and we needed to think about the justification for entering them. Therefore, we paid attention to their reactions (typically bodily expressions) in order to get a confirmation of some kind that they were happy to have us in their rooms.

However, while we accepted respect for privacy as a general rule, we also took into account individual differences and contextual complexities. For example, Frida seemed to enjoy spending time alone in her room, listening to music or resting in bed. Both Frida's parents and the care workers explained that this was because Frida had shared a room with two other residents when she lived in an intellectual disability hospital. For Reetta, Frida's 'own little home' (her father's expression) seemed a very private space, and in a sense this privacy was something that had been defined, at least partially, by Frida herself. However, since Frida's room was so important for her, it was important to spend time there with her. Reetta reasoned that her presence there would be justified as long as she could do it in ways that Frida accepted.

Since our research participants lived in group homes, we entered not only our key research participants' private spaces but their housemates' homes as well. Group homes are, or at least should be, first and foremost homes, but they are also workplaces for people who support and assist the residents in their everyday lives. In order to do research in an ethical and considerate manner, we had to consider in advance how our presence in these contexts would affect the residents and the staff.

Gradually, we realised that the effect that our presence had in these everyday contexts depended on how the care was generally organised. In contexts that were stable in terms of who and how many people (in a team) worked with service users, it was relatively easy for us to find ways to participate that suited the staff and respected the social conventions of the unit. In some contexts, change was more a rule than an exception, with care workers changing continuously (due to the rota, the way work was organised, and replacement workers covering absent staff members). In these contexts we needed more time to internalise their conventions, structures and rules but we also felt that our presence there did not raise as many questions and as much attention as in more stable contexts. As people were constantly coming and going in these contexts, we researchers were not the only new faces asking about the 'house rules' and everyday practices, or just trying to work out a way to 'fit in'.

Almost all the daily activities of our research participants were organised in groups (group home, day activity centre), where, due to limited staff resources, the service users got only a very limited amount of one-to-one time with the care workers. Since our participants had very high support needs, they spent long periods of time waiting for care workers to involve them in activities. Our presence made it possible for the participants to have someone there during these times to watch TV with, to communicate with, or just to 'hang out' with. In some contexts and with some participants it was easier for us to find ways of being 'useful' (the extra pair of hands that enabled their participation in surrounding activities) and thus do fieldwork in a more participatory manner. This, however, required that we already were aware of the general institutional practices, how they were applied individually with our research participants, and also what our participants' preferences were concerning support.

Frida's group in the day centre is decorating gingerbreads for the upcoming Christmas party. When others are already finishing, there are still two gingerbreads on Frida's plate. I talk to Frida, ask whether we should still decorate these two. I take a gingerbread in my hand and a tube of sugarpaste in the other, and hold my hands in front of Frida. Frida's eyes are fixed on the gingerbread while I squeeze the tube. I ask Frida did it turn out ok, she reaches her hand out and touches the gingerbread quickly. I take another gingerbread, once again bring it and the tube close to Frida. Frida reaches her right hand forward, stretches her fingers and takes hold of the tube. We stay holding the tube for about a minute together, until she lets go of the tube. I continue by squeezing some sugarpaste on the gingerbread. (Field notes, with Frida)

Our relationships to the staff members in different contexts varied. Typically, the coordinating care workers of our research participants were eager to tell us their interpretations about the participants and their behaviour. Some of them seemed to regard our project and our presence in the field as a chance to reflect on their own work. They shared their knowledge about the history and rationale of current practices: why, for example, Ella's life looked the way it did, and what kinds of change had taken place in her life during the past years. While some care workers remained reserved and distant, most of them engaged with us in discussions, and reported to us the everyday comings and goings of our participants.

Don Kulick (2015) argues that researchers take not only political and epistemological risks (for getting it all wrong) but personal risks as well when engaging with difference respectfully: fieldwork is 'a transformative experience that renders one a different person by the end than one was when one started' (p. 31). The obligation to make sense of our research participants (e.g. how they communicated, what kind of interaction they preferred) pushed us into very intensive form of fieldwork. In order to find an ethically sound way of being in the field with our research participants, we needed to learn to understand their communication. From the point of view of a researcher, this meant that we immersed ourselves into the process of making sense: we had to tune ourselves to note even the smallest gesture or facial expression, even breaths, in the moments.

We were delighted, and also somewhat overwhelmed, about the close and meaningful relationships we were able to build with some of our research participants during the fieldwork. These relationships also meant that we could not emotionally remain mere bystanders. While we experienced many moments of shared joy in the field, we were also distressed by the shortcomings of the care system and its practices. Being present in situations where, in our view, the care was substandard, felt painful – situations, where, for example, the care workers ignored the residents' need for sociability and acted as if they did not even exist. In all fairness, these moments were mostly matters of the culture of some group homes rather than conscious neglect or mistreatment.

Embodied ethnography in practice: writing field notes, constructing interpretation

The issue of sufficient time for ethnographic fieldwork has been a source of various methodological debates. Some have argued that, in order to make any sense of people and culture(s) in a specific context, one should stay in that context for years.[16] This view has, however, become questioned as the focus of ethnographic inquiry and our understanding of what makes an ethnographic field have become more diverse (e.g. Marcus, 1995). But, often, the standards of one's discipline and practical concerns (what is actually possible within frames set by funding, one's research context, and the participants) determine how the research is carried out (Honkasalo, 2008).

One of our main concerns was how much time we would need in the field in order to get a grasp of the everyday lives of our research participants – where they take place, with whom, and what kind of aspects in these contexts and relationships are important regarding a good life, as well as how much time would be required to make sense of the individual means and preferences of our research participants regarding communication and interaction. Could we learn to interpret our research participants in the

---

[16] When Simo was writing the funding proposal for the project, he asked Eva Kittay how long one should observe persons with PIMD to understand them properly. Eva replied: 'A few decades would do.'

timeframe provided by the research funding (considering that one criterion for the recruitment of our participants was people who had been in their lives for years and experienced difficulties with interpreting their communication)?

We found out relatively soon that it did not take very long to build a general picture of the research participants' lives. This re-alisation formed one of our key findings, namely that our partici-pants lived generally very 'narrow' lives. Each of our participants had only a few places where they spent time, typically group home and day activity centre. Almost all of their social contacts were with people in these contexts. Additionally, our participants' days could be described as repetitive. The pace and content of their lives were typically determined by care routines, and only very seldom did something break this routine. We learnt soon that four hours in a group home or in a day activity centre can actually be a very long time, filled with slowly passing moments, only to be interrupted by short moments of interaction with staff members (or sometimes family members). Our decision to experience these everyday comings and goings alongside our research participants meant that we also had to slow down our pace and adjust to their time. In fact, we were often the only non-disabled people in their surroundings who were able to take this kind of time. The staff members' time was limited and they mostly focused on completing tasks related to basic care such as eating, toileting and dressing.

Unlike most people close to our research participants, we had access to (all) settings of their lives. The various professionals who worked with them, on the other hand, only knew what was going on regarding their particular realm of expertise. This divide was most obvious between our research participants' home lives and their activities in the day activity centre. Staff members of group homes and day centres had yearly meetings to discuss whether the services met the needs of the service users. The units kept contact in-between these meetings by exchanging latest happenings with a notebook that moved between home and day centre with the care user, or occasionally by email. In the case of Anna, for example, whose health was a topical issue during the fieldwork, these me-etings and exchange between group home and day centre focused on her health. However, the professionals did not seem to have a sense of the everyday practices in the other context. After only few weeks in the field, we found ourselves in a situation where we were the ones who were asked detailed questions in the group home about the ways some aspects of Anna's and Ella's care were handled in the day centre, and the other way round. Similarly, family members used us to get a fuller picture of the everyday lives of our research participants, asking us questions about their daily activities, routines and well-being.

Another concern had to do with interpretation, and this proved to be trickier. We have consciously aimed at being modest in depicting our research participants' views or experiences. Rather, our aim was make the kinds of detailed notes that would provide us means to build interpretations about their everyday lives and to some extent even about their lived experiences. Our epistemological approach was already based on the acknowledgement of our positionality as producers of data and the impossibility of producing 'objective' representations. In other words, our observations were produced from a particular perspective, and formed by our academic as well as personal interests and understandings. Our pilot study, however, made us realise how profoundly infused our observations were with assumptions about human action – we were inclined to automatically assume what gestures or utterances meant. Accordingly, we needed to write our notes in a way that would make visible – to ourselves and others – how we had made our interpretations.

During our first visit to the group home in our pilot study, one staff member told Ella that she and Ella would soon go to the swimming pool. Reetta and Sonja both had written down this incident in their notes, and later on agreed that Ella reacted to this positively, that she looked 'delighted'. However, they realised that neither one of them was able to describe in detail Ella's facial expression or gestures, and what was it in them that made her look 'delighted'. A similar realisation occurred when they talked about Ella's laughter; Reetta and Sonja had both noticed how Ella was making laughter-like sounds, and both had initially described this in their notes as 'laughing'. However, Ella also made these sounds in other situations (for example, when she was sitting quietly alone), when she did not seem particularly joyful, which made us doubt whether her 'laughter' actually counted as laughter. Reetta and Sonja realised that they needed to step back and slow down, ask what they actually had observed and write the notes in ways that captured both the details of observed actions as well as their primary interpretations about those actions.

Reetta's and Sonja's efforts and techniques of writing in detail also developed their abilities to note the details of embodied action. For Reetta, the process of typing the notes sometimes involved physical imitation of her research participant's gestures and expressions. With Frida, Reetta was at first confused when trying to make sense of her facial expressions and bodily gestures. For example, Frida had a habit of pushing her body up and forcefully against the back of her wheelchair. Her body seemed very tense and her care workers saw that to signal that she was either scared or excited about something. As Reetta sat down to type her notes on such moments, imitating Frida's gestures helped her to recall details in her posture, breathing and movement. It also gave her an opportunity to explore with her own body what Frida's expressions and gestures might have meant. This kind of embodied practice provided her with new means to conceptualise and reflect on the translation of her embodied, situated experiences into field notes (see Aromaa & Tiili, 2018; Pink, 2009).

Another aspect of our fieldwork that forced us to be reflexive about our observation (what they captured and what not) was the fact that our participants' lives were filled with moments when nothing much seemed to happen. This presented us with a methodological challenge; even though we were (as ethnographers typically are) eager to define a clear focus during the fieldwork (what would be worth observing and writing down), had we focused only on those moments that involved lots of activity we would have written only few notes during every visit. Additionally, this kind of focus would have lost something essential about the lives of our research participants. We were aware that action and sound can draw one's attention away from people and situations when nothing much seems to happen (Gordon, Holland, Lahelma, & Tolonen, 2005). We were nevertheless surprised how difficult it was to settle down and tune our gaze in order to see interesting elements in the seemingly inactive moments.

During the first leg of the fieldwork, the confusion about what was 'worth' writing down intertwined with questions about focus – questions about how and what. Our research question was not very helpful as regards what we were supposed to see; the question of 'a good life' seemed rather obscure during those first weeks in the field, when we just tried to make sense of our research participants' gestures and expressions. Our field notes started to fill with descriptions of Ella's and Anna's behaviour, descriptions of activities taking place with and around them, notes recording care workers' talk to our research participants, to each other, or explaining to us what and why they were doing what they were doing.

As we kept on writing notes and typing them afterwards, we felt uncertain whether they had anything to do with 'a good life'. Our notes were anything but tidy; they did not produce neat 'episodes' or 'vignettes' that would capture 'the essence' of a specific moment or practice. Rather, the notes often described simultaneous things with no clear 'plot' or an idea what was the meaning or purpose of the episode in question. For example, Ella spent a lot of time rocking herself – both when she was sitting alone and in moments with social interaction. As a result, Reetta's notes were filled with descriptions of Ella rocking herself, in different contexts and situations, and what happened around her while she rocked herself. Reetta also recorded in her notes discussions about Ella's rocking, how Ella's rocking was interpreted by different people in different situations. While Reetta struggled to see the relevance of rocking had as regards the issue of a good life, whether it was at all important to capture this activity, she could see no reason either to exclude such descriptions from her notes.

During the fieldwork, we had to tolerate the uncomfortable experience of uncertainty and to keep our minds open. Reetta found it difficult to accept the explanation made by some staff members of Ella's rocking – namely that it was just a symptom of her impairment, and as such unintentional and even uninteresting, and signalled nothing but boredom. As the fieldwork with Ella continued, Reetta started paying attention to the variety of interpretations and responses that rocking got: in some moments it was interpreted as dancing, in some moments as an invitation to interact with Ella. If Reetta had just accepted the first interpretation, that it was just stereotypical behaviour, she probably would not have noted all these interpretations that approached rocking in a more positive way.

Similarly, Leo's self-harming behaviour (biting and hitting himself, banging his head on hard surfaces) was seen by many care workers to be unintentional, a mere symptom of his condition. Sonja, however, noticed that Leo often started to hurt himself when he seemed to find a situation uncomfortable in one way or another. This made Sonja wonder whether Leo's self-harming behaviour was a way for Leo to express his own will. Our way of holding back our interpretations, and to engage with the 'inexplicable', can be seen as *ethnographic practice of unforgetting* (Stewart, 1996) that pushes the researcher to concentrate on that which refuses to make sense (see also MacLure, 2013). It was a process in which we intentionally resisted the easy option of pushing aside behaviours that are hard to grasp.

While we learnt during the fieldwork to note different qualities of behaviour and make interpretations about their meaning, our somewhat messy data inevitably includes episodes that do not 'make sense' in an unquestioned manner. During the writing process, we returned to aspects in our data that eluded us, which our interpretations and representations failed to grasp. After the first leg of fieldwork, our research assistant Johanna created a code named 'nothing happens', alongside codes that we had already recognised as interesting and 'code-able' (MacLure, 2013), such as social engagement and sexuality. The 'nothing happens' code aimed to capture moments in our data that seemed interesting and meaningful but were hard to categorise under some specific concept.

> Ella is sitting on her bed. Sun is shining into the room through slatted blinds. Ella is rocking herself, lifting her gaze to the window every now and then. Morning discussion program starts on the radio. Ella rocks herself a little, her gaze lifted forward, utters some sounds. She stops rocking, bends her legs, turns slightly towards the wall next to her bed and softly knocks her forehead against the wall. Radio starts playing music. Ella straightens her legs, rocks herself deeply couple of times, laughing aloud, then lifts one leg over another and claps her hands together, then against her tights, repeats – together and on tights. She blows raspberries a couple of

times, then gently leans her forehead against the wall. (Field notes, with Ella)

The above data extract was coded with the 'nothing happens' code. It represents a serene and a rare early-morning moment in Ella's room; typically she preferred to spend time in rooms busy with social interaction, in particular the kitchen rather than in her own room. In this episode, Ella is again rocking herself, but gently. For Reetta, who sat in the room writing down notes, this moment was about peacefulness: Ella sitting on her bed, perhaps listening to the radio and noting the rays of sunlight shining through the blinds.

In our view, moments like these, where seemingly nothing happened, may well have represented episodes of a good life. When Ella lived in an institution, she was considered to be severely autistic and highly problematic as regards her behaviour (such as smearing her faeces or damaging furniture). Now, many years later, she was clearly feeling well and, generally speaking, was in a good place in her life. A place that enabled her to enjoy silent, morning moments.

On the analysis

In line with the conventions of ethnography, we have used a multiple set of analytical strategies to unpack our data. We began by coding the data (and using the Atlas.ti program) with a predefined code list. Some of the codes were based on our observations during the fieldwork; some were based on theoretical discussions in the research literature. For example, in Chapter 3 the analytical focus was directed by a contradiction we recognised during the fieldwork: the care workers depicted our research participants as people with unique personalities, but their care work routines seemed to assume a homogenous group of people. In order to focus our analysis on details of what the care workers said and what the care practices signified about people with PIMD, we coded our field notes with codes 'staff explains person/behaviour' and 'staff explains/describes practice'.

In comparison, social interaction and social relations (discussed in Chapter 4) were already among our objects of interest during the preparation stage of the fieldwork, inspired by the capabilities approach, where affiliation is conceptualised as one crucial element of human lives and well-being. The code 'social interaction' allowed us to specify the analysis of the data, and it enabled us to focus on differences, details and nuances in interaction. For example, whom did interaction take place with (participant – care user; participant – care worker)? When, how often and where did it take place? The process of coding also challenged us to think critically about the meaning of interaction and communication: what amounts to and what should be coded as interaction and communication, and what different kinds of form do they take with people with PIMD?

Similarly, our choices concerning methods were based on our analytical interests. In Chapters 3 and 5 the focus is on meanings. We were interested in how our research participants were seen by the care workers and what kind of understanding about them prevailed within the care services. In order to focus our analysis on the processes and boundaries of sense making, we utilised discourse analysis. Our interest was in particular in how 'people with PIMD' were talked about in the Finnish context, where the disability service system was in the midst of a deinstitutionalisation process. What kinds of discourses (medical, human rights etc.) were present in the care practices and policy and how did these affect the ways that care workers approached the care users? Thus, we were interested in not only what the care workers actually said but also what could be said or made sense within the Finnish intellectual disability policy context.

Discourse analysis often focuses just on language, but in our analysis the focus was on knowledge and the ways it was produced and used (see Bacchi & Bonham, 2014). This means that words as well as actions, practices and policies are all discursive. Our analysis of the care practices in Chapter 3, for example, enlightens how care practices are guided by medical discourse, with a focus on diagnostics and rehabilitation. We will argue that discursive hegemony explains, at least partly, the conflict between the ways care workers recognise the individuality of people with PIMD, and the ways care practices often do not.

Theory played an important role in our analysis, which can be described as dialectically entwined (Beach, 2010) or theory-informed (Willis & Trondman, 2000). This means that during the process of data analysis we moved between data and theory, forming a dialogue between the two (e.g. Paju, 2013). Theoretical insights have sensitised us to particular aspects of the data, enabled us to see things we would not have seen otherwise, and helped us to see beyond the obvious and push our understanding of the lives of persons with PIMD a bit deeper (or at least, so we would like to think). For example, in Chapter 5 we employ the sociology of age, in particular in relation to the principle of age-appropriateness in intellectual disability services. The sociology of age provided us with useful 'sensitising concepts' (Willis & Trondman, 2000) such as the accountability of age (Laz, 1998; Nikander, 2000), which helped us to articulate the relevance of age in relation to the identity and everyday lives of our research participants. In Chapter 4, on the other hand, the capabilities approach helps us to focus analysis on the capacities of our research participants as well as on the care practices, and how they enabled or denied opportunities for social engagement.

However, the function of theory in our research was not only to work as a tool in the data analysis. Theoretical discussions also guided us to look at our data in certain ways. Sexuality, let alone animality, are the kinds of issues that were not present in our data as evidently as, for example, affiliation and age. Theoretical interests motivated us to also look at the data deductively, and analyse sexuality (Chapter 6), animality (Chapter 7) and moral status (Appendix). One reason for this is that arguments that are in conflict with our own intuitions and values (e.g. philosophical arguments that grant lower moral worth to people with PIMD than to so-called normal people) challenge us to evaluate, rethink and sharpen our arguments. But mainly we have engaged with these issues because of their importance to persons with PIMD – issues that are often silenced, like sexuality, or analysed inappropriately, like moral status. Through such theoretical engagement we have aimed at producing a fuller picture of the lives and identities of people with PIMD.

Chapter 3: Conceptions of Competence

A person versus F73

F73 Profound mental retardation

> The IQ in this category is estimated to be under 20, which means in practice that affected individuals are severely limited in their ability to understand or comply with requests or instructions. Most such individuals are immobile or severely restricted in mobility, incontinent, and capable at most of only very rudimentary forms of nonverbal communication. They possess little or no ability to care for their own basic needs, and require constant help and supervision. (The ICD-10 Classification of Mental and Behavioural Disorders, WHO, 2004)

The definition of 'profound mental retardation', cited above, captures one key challenge that both the service system and our research project were confronted with when working with people with profound intellectual disability: this group of people has been, and still often is, defined by deficiencies – by abilities they do not possess, by capacities they lack.

The emptiness of the PIMD category stands in stark contrast with the heterogeneity of people who are labelled with the category. When we began looking for research participants, we found ourselves entangled in discussions about who can be defined as a person with PIMD – who is 'disabled enough'? To what extent are these kinds of definitions contextual? In our initial discussions with the care provider organisations and care workers, we also encountered descriptions that strongly challenged the idea of the incapacity of individuals with PIMD: even though they needed

How to cite this book chapter:
Vehmas, S. and Mietola, R. 2021. *Narrowed Lives: Meaning, Moral Value, and Profound Intellectual Disability*. Pp. 57–85. Stockholm: Stockholm University Press. DOI: https://doi.org/10.16993/bbl.c. License: CC-BY 4.0.

constant support and care, they were also acknowledged as people who were capable of expressing their wishes, as sociable and affectionate, and in possession of a sense of humour.

This contradiction that we encountered reflects a problem often recognised by people who are either professionally or privately engaged with people with PIMD: the key formal knowledge used within the service system about individuals is still primarily medical, consisting of diagnostic definitions that lay out a long list of needs that the service system is supposed to meet. This knowledge tells us only very little about particular individuals, their interests, likes, dislikes and, perhaps more importantly, their abilities. Philip and Dianne Ferguson (2001), when writing about their adult son with multiple disabilities, describe this knowledge in the following way:

> Predictably, the educational and adult service systems involved in his life have given labels only to his perceived limitations; there have been no clinical diagnoses for his mixture of odd talents and personal quirks that are the main images we share of him now. ... When does he get graded for the terrific laugh he shows along with a warped sense of humor? The scary stereotypes and diagnostic categories that lie behind the official labels can easily swallow up our son's individuality. (Ferguson & Ferguson, 2001, p. 71)

While personal experience with people with PIMD only has an informal position in the service system, it might be exactly the kind of knowledge that is needed to develop the system and the care it provides. In order to support the self-determination of the service users, especially in the case of those who have difficulty expressing their views and wishes, the care provider organisations need knowledge that facilitates a fuller picture of the people they care for. This kind of knowledge would also affect how these individuals are approached in the services, how the professionals construct understanding of the service users, and how this knowledge is transmitted within the system. The information provided by the personal experiences of care workers together with medical knowledge would have the potential to transform dominant cultural conceptions concerning people with PIMD, and provide a more balanced picture of them.

This chapter focuses on the cultural knowledge that is formed and transmitted within the service system in the context of

everyday work. We are particularly interested in the cultural conceptions concerning people with profound intellectual disability.
Our analysis examines the descriptions and definitions provided
by care workers of our research participants, and of people with
PIMD at large. What are the wider discourses that frame knowledge concerning people with PIMD? What kinds of attributes
and personalities are attached to them?

Persons 'behind impairments'

We noted from early on that care workers' descriptions of our
research participants conflicted with a stereotypical understanding of people with PIMD. While the care workers were happy
to share vivid descriptions about the personalities of our research
participants, at the same time they emphasised difficulties related to interpretation. In the case of Ella, for example, the care
workers described in detail what kinds of activities she liked,
what kind of music or food she loved, how she expressed her
own will (e.g. by staying put on the floor when she did not want
to cooperate), and how she was a sociable person who enjoyed
the company of other people. However, even the care workers
who had worked with Ella for years emphasised that making sense of her viewpoint was always complicated and uncertain, especially in relation to virtually anything that is not directly connected
to the ongoing activity.

There were differences in ways the care workers described communication with different people – some were considered easy,
and some difficult to interpret.

Reetta: How do you see Hugo, what is he like?

Care worker: Good question. Usually Hugo is cheerful and cu-
rious. Like a really easy-going [rento] guy. And he is really skilled
[osaa tosi hyvin] at expressing if he doesn't like [something] or if
he's not feeling good.

Reetta: And how about the other side, those things that are pleasant? How clearly does Hugo express those?

Care worker: Of course also that, like, that he laughs really loudly
and happily. Like you can see when Hugo is feeling good and when
not. And like it is a really, really good and wonderful thing, since

there are also some guys who don't [express], like there is a big difference. It is good to work with Hugo, you can make sense of him. What's good and what's not.

Despite difficulties concerning interpretation, the care workers in fact constantly interpreted our research participants' communication simply because they had to. Interpretation is a necessity in care work with people with PIMD, building knowledge about their characteristics and needs. This knowledge often concerns direct interpretation about the primary needs of the care users, which they usually express with a particular sound or facial expression. This ability to interpret provides a foundation for care work – as the care worker above says, it is 'good to work' with Hugo because it is easy to make sense of him. Also, in order to meet the requirements for self-determination, the care workers needed to assess an individual's likes and dislikes. Such information was routinely shared among care staff through informal discussions. However, the care workers' descriptions were not limited to listing likes and dislikes, and how our participants expressed them.

> The care worker says [to Sonja] that Sebastian is a colourful fellow, a real man [äijä], loves swimming on top of playing ball. (Field notes, with Sebastian)

Care workers often described our research participants' personalities in general, abstract terms, such as being sociable and 'easygoing' (rento), or having a good sense of humour. These kinds of description construct a more complete picture of persons with PIMD, one that underlines their oneness with other humans. As the care worker above describes Sebastian as 'äijä', a Finnish expression referring to a particularly masculine man, he recognises Sebastian as belonging to a specific cultural category, with a recognised cultural status. Sebastian, and his behaviour (his obsession to play ball), is thus made culturally intelligible and even affirmative.

While rich descriptions of the personalities of our research participants were used to normalise them, and to challenge stereotypical conceptions about PIMD, they also worked to rearrange the relationship between personalities and impairments.

I think that there is a strong own personality in Frida, or like own character. That you can see it from behind the impairment, like you can see Frida, I think. (Interview with Frida's care worker)

Care workers consistently described important features of our research participants' personalities as something separate from their impairments, things that could be found 'behind the impairment', as explained by Frida's care worker above. Mostly, the distinction between personality and impairment was done implicitly. The care workers passed over our research participants' impairments when discussing their personalities. Thus, Hugo would be described as a 'really easy-going guy' rather than as a 'really easy-going guy who needs constant assistance due to his cerebral palsy and cognitive impairment'. Thus, the personalities of our research participants were described as something that was 'in the background' ('there is a person with a great sense of humour in the background'/'*siellähän on hirveen huumorintajuinen persoona taustalla*') – they needed to be 'dug up' ('*siellä on kaivettavaa*').

While these kinds of expressions construct a relationship between a personality and impairments (and that the person is not the same as her impairments), they can also be seen to underline the effort, skill and time required to recognise the person behind impairments. As one care worker said, one needs time and space to 'read' a person in different situations.

Views about the personalities of some of our research participants were widely shared by the care workers, and considered to be self-evident. Sebastian, for example, was described as sociable by almost everyone working with him. His sociability was evident, for example, when he sought contact with others by moving himself with his wheelchair. Frida was also described by some of the care workers as sociable, but in her case this characteristic was more difficult to detect: while Frida often expressed unhappiness when she was left alone (by crying aloud), she could also get visibly anxious in situations where she was surrounded by other people. When Reetta started to do fieldwork with Frida, she thought that Frida was anything but sociable: it seemed to her that Frida's dominant response to other people's social initiatives was either to 'freeze' or startle.

One of Frida's care workers emphasised that getting to know Frida was a long process, where both parties need the time and space for Frida's personality to disclose. Similarly, Anna's care workers described how her 'own funny humour' (*'oma hauska huumori'*) became visible in situations where she would wheel herself in the opposite direction to where she was meant to go, and this way would 'play tricks' (*'jekuttaa'*) with the care workers. To notice this kind of playfulness requires the care workers' ability to note and make sense of the little differences in Anna's demeanour: sometimes she wheeled away from other people in order to 'play tricks'; sometimes she did that because of anxiety caused by loud voices or sounds.

The idea of personality lying 'behind the impairment' can also be seen to suggest that profound impairments of our research participants are seen to be so impassable that they cover their personalities from other people. Impairments may be the only things one sees in people with PIMD. In our view, the ways the care workers described and emphasised the individuality of our research participants epitomises an epistemic and ethical motivation to recognise people with PIMD as individual persons. Making sense of their personalities might be complicated, and it is ultimately the result of subjective interpretation – the care worker above cautiously added 'I think' after having emphasised Frida's individuality. But, still, it is, in their view, the right thing to do.

Hesitation around cognitive capacity

Care workers' accounts of people with PIMD are in conflict with a stereotypical conception that concentrates on deficits and fails to appreciate their individuality. However, while the care workers repeatedly talked about our participants' personalities and highlighted how skilled they were in their own ways (for example, expressing their own will), they hardly ever talked about our research participants' cognitive capacities. There were only a few remarks where a care worker suddenly pointed out how 'intelligent' (*'älykäs'*) Sebastian is or how Leo really is a 'clever guy' (*'fiksu tyyppi'*).

So the question of cognitive capacity was not often directly addressed. However, the care workers repeatedly told the kind of stories about our research participants that built an image of persons with more extensive cognitive capacities that the diagnostic category PIMD would allow one to expect. For example, all of Anna's care workers agreed that she was very difficult to understand, but they also said that she is a person who could 'make her wishes very clear' (*'tekee tahtonsa hyvin selväksi'*) and be both cooperative and uncooperative depending on her preferences. Also, sometimes she drew attention back to herself and burst out crying if she felt that someone was stealing attention from her. However, the care workers said that, due to her cognitive impairment, Anna had only a very limited capacity for self-determination – even a choice between milk and buttermilk would be too demanding for her, and the decision would be made on her behalf.

Our participants were described as being 'jealous' (*'kateellinen'*) or 'dramatic' (*'olla dramaattinen'*), having 'a sense of humour' (*'huumorintajuinen'*) or 'sense of discretion' (*'tilannetajuinen'*), or they might act 'mischievously' (*'ilkikurinen'*) or 'protest' (*'osoittaa mieltään'*). These kinds of expressions suggest that the person in question has cognitive capacity that enables him or her to make sense of the ongoing activity or situation, and to act intentionally in relation to it (e.g. Frida understands that someone else is going out, gets jealous, and therefore protests by crying). Also, our research participant's gesture or response (a laugh, a sigh) often became interpreted as a comment, as fitting to the particular context and thus intelligible.

In our view these kinds of stories and expressions implied cognitive capacity. Therefore, we thought it was important to address the issue with the care workers, and ask them directly what they thought about our research participants' cognitive capacities. The care workers usually did not want completely to rule out the possibility of some cognitive capacity or potential, but they were nevertheless very careful in their responses. Frida's coordinating care worker explained that, in her view, it was always worth trying different things that might make visible some hidden potential. She also said that, with children with intellectual disability, 'lots of different things' are tried out, but later in life the focus in care work is on maintaining the current level of competence, with the addition of providing 'enrichment with comings and goings and activities'.

While this care worker thought that people with PIMD can learn and develop, she said firmly that she is a 'realist' in relation to expectations that she sets for Frida's development. But, while she hesitated when being asked about Frida's cognitive capacity and her potential to develop and learn, care workers working with Frida repeatedly told stories about changes that they had noticed in her behaviour. These changes were often discussed in relation to her recent move to a new housing unit, after having lived a long period in an institution. In her coordinating care worker's view, this transition opened a totally new life for Frida: she finally had a private room, which everyone thought was something that Frida had longed for, she had received a new wheelchair that had been designed to her individual needs, and on weekdays she attended a day centre, where she participated in different kinds of activity groups. And, most importantly, after the move Frida had also re-established close relationships with her parents.

Changes that the care workers had noted concerned both Frida's physical capacity and her personality. One care worker said that Frida moved a lot more than she previously had, for example when lying in her bed, and she was able to change her posture in her wheelchair by lifting her hips, as well as using her hands to scratch her nose or to reach for things. All these movements were new, even surprising for the care workers. Also, the care worker mentioned that Frida seemed more alert and took part in social situations, not only showing interest by following what is happening around her but also taking part in social interaction by uttering sounds.

As Frida and Reetta got to know each other, they had chats by taking turns: when Reetta joined Frida's company, she turned to face Reetta and kept looking at her attentively, and responded to Reetta's speech by uttering sounds. These kinds of exchanges could take several minutes, with Frida and Reetta taking turns. Similarly, during his visits to the group home Frida's father helped Frida to phone her mother. Her father held his mobile in Frida's hand while she uttered sounds at the phone (interpreted by her father as Frida telling her mother about recent happenings). These new features in Frida's behaviour supported the notion of her being a sociable person. What these observations also suggest is that Frida has the capacity to understand some dynamics of social interaction – taking turns in making utterances, listening and participating.

When making sense of the care workers' conflicting views about Frida's potential and capacities, and the changes in her behaviour, we realised that the way these perspectives differ is in terms of the significance of interpretation and speculation. Care workers' estimation concerning (hidden) capacity steps away from the everyday knowing – the kind of knowledge they use, transmit and build collaboratively. This kind of knowledge is also built through interpretation, but the everyday nature of this knowledge masks the process through which it is produced – how observations in different situations and discussions with colleagues are the material for the knowledge production of persons with PIMD. Our question concerning capacity and potential, however, positions the knowing in the forefront. It again makes visible the uncertain nature of interpretation, and the subjective nature of knowing.

While continuous interpretations about the needs and wants of persons with PIMD are ethically compulsory in everyday practice, interpretations about their potential for personal development are clearly considered to be ethically precarious. The care workers seemed to be comfortable reporting their observations concerning changes that had already taken place but they were more reluctant to speculate on those that may happen in future. They especially avoided making overly far-reaching, optimistic interpretations. Additionally, these interpretations concerning change were again constructed and confirmed collectively, supported by the views of, for example, family members (like in the above extract by Frida's parents).

However, some of the care workers did mention how some of the capacities of our research participants remained hidden. One reason for this was the complexity of their impairments. As one of Frida's care workers said, 'for certain there are more things going on than you might think, in the head. ... That there clearly is such understanding. And ability to act in the right places. But it's just that one is a prisoner of one's body in a way, that when your hands don't move, your hands don't move.'

But sometimes hidden capacities materialised. Leo had acquired new skills such as supported walking, and Frida's communication and social skills had improved (as discussed above) after having moved to a group home from an institution. One care worker suggested that the current understanding about the capability of people with PIMD is profoundly influenced by the service system – whether it enables or prevents opportunities for development and change. As the service culture and practices change, our understanding and expectations of people with PIMD change as well. One staff member in Ella's day centre said:

> So individuals with intellectual disability, who are now small schoolchildren, probably have the equipment and aids and all the support they can get when you compare them to those who are now in their fifties or sixties, who have lived in institutions for a long time and didn't have the kind of activity.

Production of knowledge and re-minding persons

While knowledge about our participants' personalities and capacities was clearly crucial from the point of view of everyday care work, this type of information seemed to have only a secondary position in the formal systems of the care units. Instead of gathering and transmitting knowledge that would support care workers in interpreting the care users, the formal practices and structures of knowledge production were primarily reserved for transmission of more medical and unnuanced information about everyday care practices:

> [Reetta asked Hugo's care worker how knowledge concerning residents is transmitted in the unit, whether new care workers get an introduction about the residents, how to interpret them and how to work with them] No, like that is really. Like I might have been lucky, since the care worker who is here today, like she has really familiarised herself with Hugo, she has told me lots about Hugo. And unfortunately we do not have any kind of introductory file [concerning the residents]. And transmitting that kind of knowledge is really difficult, and in bad shape. This is just how it is. And even if we have for example this info notebook, where we write down things, it's not definite that all care workers read this. [Reetta continues, asking what kind of things are discussed in the daily meetings] Well, like since we have residents who have epilepsy, then if there have been any seizures. How has the eating been, whether everyone has eaten ok. And like physical needs,

whether these have been met. And also psychological, like has someone been tearful, or in a good mood. And whether there are any special events for the day, someone going to visit [the family] home or excursions or like. (Reetta's field notes)

The above extract makes visible how the information systems of the care units are concerned with serving the basic care work by recording details concerning physical well-being of the care users and how their basic needs have been responded to (e.g. toileting, sleeping, eating).

Current disability and social service policies emphasise self-determination as the guiding principle in care work, and thus direct the services to approach every care user as a person with individual interests and means to communicate them. In the context of PIMD, this means that even services directed at this group need to find new approaches and new tools for self-determination. And, while in all of our research contexts this principle was acknowledged, in our view their knowledge systems did not support realisation of self-determination. For example, the daily records in most group homes consisted almost exclusively of scant remarks of basic care and bodily functions (whether someone had eaten, taken their medication, been washed etc.), and quite a bit of time was spent daily on writing them. The individual care plans, on the other hand, which aimed to provide more holistic view of the care user and their needs, seemed to exist mainly for administrative purposes rather than to inform the daily care work, as few care workers ever read them, anyway.

All group homes and day centres kept daily records (*kirjaaminen, raportointi*) and individual care plans (*ohjaussuunnitelma, hoitosuunnitelma*), but in all units they seemed to have different functions. The daily records focused on the basic care work and the daily well-being of the care user, whereas the care plans reported each care user's services and therapies and his or her individual targets of care. The individual care plans were written by the coordinating care workers (each care user had one care worker who monitored their services and care in the unit), and they were updated twice a year, or even more seldom, depending on the unit. All of these documents were stored in the office spaces or on the unit's computers, and they were accessible for all staff for use. However, as Hugo's care worker commented above, in some contexts it was uncertain whether the care plans played any role in the daily care work. In one context, however, the care workers unanimously stated that they had established ties between everyday care work and care plans. In this organisation, all new staff members were required to familiarise themselves with the care plans since they provided relevant information about the care users.

All the interviewed care workers emphasised the importance of collegial discussions as regards the transmission of information and knowledge production. These kinds of discussions took place during the everyday work, during coffee breaks, or in the unit's staff meetings. Alongside sharing information about daily affairs, key points from the individual care plans were discussed in these meetings, especially when changes in care plans concerned the whole staff (e.g. a new activity was introduced to a care user's daily or weekly routine). All our interviewees described these verbal exchanges as an important and natural part of the everyday care work. Reetta and Sonja, however, were not convinced that all care workers took part in these discussions, in particular in units that had lots of staff turnover, or staff working in three shifts.

However, sharing and documenting knowledge was not seen to be a simple matter. Care workers in Ella's group home, for example, underlined that the way to learn to understand Ella was to spend time and work with her. But they also emphasised that existing knowledge and documents included basic information that was necessary for ensuring good care. For example, when Ella is in pain it is absolutely essential that the people working with her understand how she expresses pain and are able to respond to her distress.

Knowledge production practices are not, however, only about documentation and transmission of knowledge. They also form the work cultures of the group homes and day centres. We noticed that keeping records was an important part of the daily routines of care work: the care workers would sit down at the computer to type records every day, in some contexts even multiple times during their work shift. Considering that this information mostly concerns basic care tasks related to nutrition, personal hygiene and so on, one cannot help but wonder whether such focus maintains or challenges care work practices.

Our data also provides examples of how knowledge production practices can actually support care work that focuses on individual personalities and aims to actualise self-determination. The coordinating care workers wrote care plans, and saw them as highly relevant for their work. The process of writing care plans gave them the time and space to think about the care users and their lives, as well as the service system, from multiple perspectives. On the one hand, the process forced them to focus on the service users' individual characteristics such as their needs, abilities and impairments. On the other hand, the process of writing care plans made them consider the bigger picture of the care users' lives in the service system, whether the current services met their needs, and what could be done to make things better for them. In Frida's case, such process materialised in a plan to apply for a support person for her leisure time activities, speech therapy assessment and physiotherapy.

Bruce Jennings (2010) argues, with reference to dementia, that dementia care is about 're-minding', or reconstructing the person, which takes place against the background of the erosion of the mind or the person prior to the effects of dementia. He sees re-minding as a process that involves the care user, those providing the care, and the environment where the caring takes place. While Jennings's account is about dementia care, it is applicable to the care of people with PIMD as well. The concept of re-minding highlights both the collective knowledge production process and the importance of the type of knowledge that aims to preserve and develop a more holistic view of the person. From this point of view, the descriptions and stories concerning our research participants can be seen as a key part of the kind of re-minding process that Jennings analyses. They work in dialogue with the observations of individual care workers, providing a base where the fragmentary information they have gathered construct an understanding of the person's narrative and personality. The process of building a mutually shared, full conception of individuals with PIMD requires environments that acknowledge the importance of transmitting re-minding information to others included in the process.

We noted instances where this kind of collaborative re-minding was implemented and actively supported, but also contexts where this type of knowledge was missing or had been lost. In Frida's case, for example, forming a coherent narrative of her life was difficult due to her move from an institution to the group home. The institution where Frida had lived refused requests to deliver existing documents and information to the group home about her life in the institution. As a result, the care workers in Frida's new home tried to build an understanding of Frida and her life history through a few medical documents, and by the testimonies of the staff members that had worked with Frida in that institution. Frida's parents took an active part in providing knowledge about her childhood: what she had been like as a child, what kind of changes they had noted in her personality, and what kind of characteristics in their view best described Frida's personality. This information provided the care workers with continuity regarding Frida's life story and her personality.

The conflict between the knowledge produced within the service system and the kind of knowledge the care workers consider important in their work will continue to exist unless there is a conscious effort to produce, document and transmit 're-minding knowledge'. In the worst case, the collectively built understanding of the care users, their personalities and their 'personal quirks' disappears with the care workers that possess this quiet knowledge. Guaranteeing that individuals' personalities are recognised in the care system requires, in our view, that the importance of this type of knowledge is recognised, and that knowledge systems are developed in a way that supports the construction and use of it.

The care workers descriptions drew a picture about our research participants as a heterogeneous group of people, with different kinds of personalities and individual capacities. They do not, however, challenge the view in which people with PIMD are seen purely in terms of their limited cognitive and physical capacities. Rather, a view that conceptualises them in terms of deficiency continues to direct the everyday care work and the service system in general. In the following section, we will analyse the care work practices, and how views about the cognitive competence of persons with PIMD explain the way that good care and a good life for them are understood. While persons with PIMD are increasingly described and seen as a heterogeneous group of people possessing different kinds of abilities, the cultural conception of them having extremely low cognitive capacity still directs what kind of services, resources and activities are made available to them.

Profound intellectual disability formed by care practices

[I'm reading through documents written about Frida, sitting at the kitchen table in Frida's group home, with Frida sitting next to me]. Last I look at TOIMI-form [used widely in Finnish intellectual disability services to measure a person's ability to function] which has been filled about Frida. My attention is drawn to how in almost every section estimation concerning Frida is set in the lower end of the scale – sometimes it has even been estimated that she is totally unable to function. For example, social interaction has been defined in a way that represents Frida as totally incapable to interact. I ask from the care worker about the TOIMI, at the same time telling her that I'm wondering whether this is useful, since Frida seems to score really low in everything. The care worker responds that it works really poorly 'with our customers', doesn't really work and thus is not really useful. (Field notes, with Frida)

People with profound intellectual and multiple disabilities are a small population, and in Finland have been until recently placed mostly outside community care services. The service system has been designed from the point of view of those with 'mild' or 'moderate' intellectual disability. The above field note from a discussion Reetta had with a care worker concerns the TOIMI (Seppälä & Sundin, 2011), a tool widely used in Finnish intellectual disability services to measure the care user's ability to function in order to adjust the provided services to the individual care user's capacity and needs. The care worker notes how the tool works 'really poorly' with people with severe or profound intellectual disability but has nevertheless been mechanically used in the evaluation of each care user (including Frida).

These types of tool, which are supposed to help us to build a full picture of particular persons with PIMD, allow no space to recognise their 'odd talents and personal quirks' (Ferguson & Ferguson, 2001). In fact, the tools and practices used in the services can carry a very restricted understanding of capacities, as well as defining what is recognised as a capacity. For example, the way that Frida interacts with others does not qualify as social interaction in the TOIMI tool (Seppälä & Sundin, 2011, pp. 18–19, 29), and can thus go unnoticed and undocumented in the service system. On the other hand, those practices that have been designed particularly for people with profound intellectual disability have also been planned with a specific conception or image of them in mind. This can also lead to practices where the heterogeneity of this group – including those 'odd talents and personal quirks' – is left unnoticed.

Finding fitting practices for our research participants seemed to cause different kinds of challenges to different kinds of services. In the group homes, the practices revolved around everyday living and household tasks, with only limited space for one-to-one interaction and leisure time activities. Considerations about suitable activities often involved the question of accessibility, for example how there were only few TV programmes that were directed to adults and were at the same time accessible to people with intellectual disability. One of the group homes had included rehabilitative practices in the everyday routine, and thus had relevant equipment available (e.g. physio-acoustic chair, Motomed), as well as staff resource allocated for individualised activities. The suitability of such activities and equipment was explained in terms of rehabilitation rather than as a way of providing meaningful activities for those with PIMD.

In all of the group homes, emphasis was on everyday tasks of eating, hygiene and sleeping/resting. In some group homes, walks outdoors or visits to local shops were part of the weekly routine. Residents' participation and self-determination were enhanced by routinised practices. For example, they were given simple choices concerning what to drink with their dinner (between two options, e.g. milk or buttermilk), or what coloured shirt they wanted to wear. When we asked why the residents did not have any hobbies and why there was so little activity in their lives, the typical answer was their extensive needs and limited capacities. 'This is such a care-intensive group' ('*hoidollinen porukka*'), as one of the care workers said, in comparison to residents with milder intellectual disability, who, unlike our research participants, lived reasonably active lives. This kind of discourse risk reducing persons with PIMD primarily as objects of treatments and care rather than seeing them as individual human beings entitled to a good life.

The question of finding suitable activities for people with PIMD seemed to be more pronounced in the day activity centres. The two day activity centres participating in our study had both been profiled as providing services to people with profound intellectual disability. One of the centres only had care users with PIMD; the other had a more varied user profile, and also provided services for persons with mild, moderate and severe intellectual disability. However, the latter unit had organised their activities so that they had multiple activity groups, with some specifically directed for care users with PIMD.

In both of the centres, lots of multisensory activities were used. The care users were introduced to different scents and sensations, as well as visual and auditory stimuli. Some of these sessions were designed around specific equipment (e.g. physio-acoustic chair, neon lights or black light/dark room); some were based on one-to-one interaction with the care user (like massage or positioning therapy). Both of the day centres also provided music sessions combined with gymnastics or dancing. While the two centres differed in many ways, they seemed to have a similar view regarding suitable and accessible activities for care users with PIMD – what this group of people would benefit from and what would they enjoy.

According to one instructor, who had worked in day activity services since the late 1990s, almost all activities and tools at the time were designed for people with milder intellectual disability. Therefore, the activities for those with PIMD had to be planned and implemented from scratch by the staff in each day centre. Current similarities between the two day centres can be seen to reflect the dramatic change in the field since the 1990s, with a more established and commonly shared view of suitable activities and approaches emerging, even with particular programmes designed specifically for people with PIMD.

The instructor keeps reading a book for the group for 25 minutes. She stops, comments that she doesn't feel up to reading further. Tells me that she's happy that they found this particular book

Ruusun aika [a Finnish novel about a stepfamily] from the library, since Eemil and also some other care users are that kind of age that they would have watched it [a TV series based on the book] on TV. Continues explaining how it doesn't really matter what they are reading, the important aspect is the language, rhythm, how you are reading. Like you don't even have to continue reading from where you were left the last time. (Field notes, with Ella)

During the fieldwork our attention was already being drawn by practices and activities in the day activity centres that seemed to reflect a very specific conception of people with PIMD. While the descriptions and definitions discussed above produced an image of a heterogeneous group of people with different kinds of interests, capacities and personalities, the dominant activities and practices, however, reproduced a homogenous group of people with PIMD. The words of an instructor in a day centre sums up this notion well: this group of people differ from care users with milder intellectual disability as being 'more like a sense-and-body-group'.

The notion of people with PIMD being the kinds of persons to whom the sensory world is more important than the world of cognition and imagination was manifested in the activities offered to them. First of all, the activities were based on an underlying expectation of a (maximum) level of (cognitive) capacity, and what kind of activities and practices people with this level of capacity would benefit from. This mentality manifests in the extract above: while it is recognised that people with PIMD enjoy listening to stories, it is assumed that they do not possess sufficient cognitive capacity to follow and understand the actual storyline. Secondly, these practices and activities seemed to be based on a behaviourist (pedagogical) approach, where the care users were introduced to different kinds of sensory stimuli, with the expectation of inducing a reaction in the recipient (see Simmons & Watson, 2014).

In practice this meant repetitive activities consisting of different kinds of stimuli, with the expectations of the care users reacting to these stimuli, preferably with expressions of enjoyment. In her field journal, Reetta named these processes 'teasing out responses', thus referring to activities that seemed to have no other purpose than to get some kind of a response from the care user. These activities operated purely at the stimulus–reaction dimension, with low cognitive expectations: they were expected to 'work' (to keep people happy and active), even if the person was not capable of making sense of the purpose of the activity. This kind of framing of the activities also became visible in the way how one of the day activity centres had named a group of care users with mild and moderate intellectual disability 'the academics'. The division between 'the academics' and non-academics referred to the difference in the substance and focus of the activities: the activities for 'the academics' were hardly ever limited just to physical and/or sensory exercises. Even during positioning treatment sessions, the care users with milder intellectual disability were involved in other tasks, like reading magazines. 'The academics' took part, for example, in the drama and café group, whereas the non-academic group's activities involved mostly sensory-motor content, sometimes with emphasis on communication skills (intensive interaction sessions).

The emphasis on sensory activities in day centres is not surprising as it is a continuation of the long tradition of sensationalism in the pedagogics of individuals with intellectual disability. Sensationalism is a theory that all human knowledge and understanding is acquired from sensory experiences, not from innate ideas of the mind (Stainton, 2018). Its applications to the care and tuition of people with intellectual disability were based initially on the sensationalist theory of John Locke, who thought that the human mind at birth is a blank slate (*tabula rasa*), 'upon which experience and reflection derived from sensation leave their impression, and from which ideas or knowledge are eventually derived' (Stainton, 2018, p. 131). The sources of knowledge based on experience are sensation and reflection. Since the latter is out of reach for 'idiots', as their minds are devoid of ideas, all one can do is to make the best of what nature has given to them.

Locke's theory worked as a basis for educational theorists like Rousseau, who concluded that human beings are malleable and that sensory education was essential in the making of free and equal citizens. Rousseau, however, had very little interest in 'ill-constituted' children, whereas his fellow Frenchman Jean-Marc-Gaspard Itard (1774–1838) attempted to verify Locke's and Etienne Bonnot de Condillac's (1714–1780) sensationalist theory empirically through his observations and experiences with Victor, the 'Wild Boy of Aveyron'. Condillac, in particular, had argued that sensory processes were the basis of all knowledge and that different sensations (smell, hearing, taste, sight, touch) improve understanding and memory (Stainton, 2018).

Itard did exactly this with Victor by giving him very hot and very cold baths for two to three hours a day, or just by rubbing or tickling Victor with the hope that these stimulants would enhance his receptivity to sensations (Itard, 1972, pp. 105–111). Since sensory processes were crucial in the acquisition of knowledge, the body became the primary site of education. Stainton (2018, p. 143) argues that the sensationalist tradition set the stage for the emergence of psychology, especially behaviourism, which remains the dominant stream concerned with intellectual disability. Sensationalism and behaviourism both focused on controlling the stimuli (or sensations) to effect behavioural change: 'The intellectually disabled subject is essentially the malleable clay to be crafted into moral man (if possible) through control of his sensory experience by external agents' (Stainton, 2018, p. 143).

The tradition of sensationalism has materialised in various current therapies, such as Snoezelen, where sensory stimuli is offered through light, sound, touch and smell for people with profound intellectual disability. The aim of these multisensory interventions is to provide an opportunity for restoration and refreshment, as well as to reduce challenging or stereotypic behaviour, and advance adaptive behaviour (Fava & Strauss, 2010; Lancioni, Cuvo, & O'Reilly, 2002; Lotan & Gold, 2009). Our intention is neither to criticise nor to endorse multisensory therapies. We have merely made an observation that emphasis on multisensory activities plays a central role in the rehabilitative activities offered for persons with PIMD. Arguably, these practices maintain the idea that persons with PIMD are a group of people whose lives are primarily directed by their senses. Whether such notion would be inaccurate is a separate issue and we have no competence to evaluate it.

While the emphasis on sensory activities seems to produce a homogenous group of people with PIMD – as having very low cognitive capacities, and who need and enjoy strong sensory stimuli – it could well be the case that these activities respond to their individual needs. For example, the activities that Sebastian took part in at the day activity centre were very stereotypical, but at the same time they did look like Sebastian, as it were. He often participated in activity groups that concentrated on physical activities, for example gymnastics accompanied by loud and energetic music or one-to-one sessions with a care worker throwing ball to one another. After having observed Sebastian, we felt that these kinds of activities would probably be the ones he would choose himself, anyway. Also, focus on accessibility at the day centres is naturally a crucial consideration. Ella, for example, had earlier been at a day centre where activities were designed mainly from the viewpoint of those with milder intellectual disability. Ella, currently described as a 'basic-happy' person, had been reported to be constantly anxious at the day centre, with very limited possibilities to participate in the activities. Additionally, the premises of the previous day centre were not accessible, which made it impossible for Ella to move around unattended. In the current day centre Ella was able to participate in all of the activities, and seemed to enjoy many of them.

'Teasing out responses' can be seen as a useful approach in the process by which the care workers get to know the care user, finding activities that he or she particularly enjoys. The challenges with interpretation discussed above are particularly pronounced when a new care user starts with the service. In practice this means a process of mapping the care user's preferences and interests, trying out different sorts of activities and stimuli and simultaneously learning to interpret what their reactions and expressions may mean.

[I've asked the interviewees what they consider the best in their work] And that there is some kind of change in the basic expression [on the care users face], whether it is like sad or happy thing, and that you see that this what we have just done has somehow touched this person. So maybe this is the moment that you go like yes! Wonderful that she [the care user] expressed herself somehow. Or like, this is our interpretation. But of course when this happens multiple times and when you learn to know the person, then you will be able to say that this is what this [expression] meant. That now she is saying that I was having fun! [Laughs]

However, we also witnessed moments where care users participated in activities that did not seem responsive to their individual needs or interests. Anna, for example, who was one of the
most complex ones of our participants in terms of interpreting her
expression, often seemed to get very uncomfortable with strong
sensory stimuli. The day centre's staff members expressed similar
thoughts about Anna's response to these types of activities: they
were aware of Anna's discomfort, and said that she would enjoy
more the kinds of activities where she could spend one-to-one
time with an instructor, 'just babbling something and anything
and tickling every once in a while, that's what she likes'. Despite
Anna's repetitive expressions of anxiety, she was often expected to
participate in activities where she was seemingly uncomfortable.
The staff members explained that the unit did not have necessary
staff resource to organise activities in a more individualised manner, since the activities were expected to be organised in groups.
Having said that, they emphasised that within a group-based activity they tried to find time to engage each day with each service
user individually, if even just for a moment.

The staff in group homes and day centres often talked about our
research participants as being cognitively able in multiple ways.
Their descriptions typically underlined how our research participants were individuals, rather than stereotypical persons with
PIMD. However, there seems to be a gap between these views and
the current practices in the Finnish intellectual disability service
system, which is by and large arranged for groups under a certain diagnostic category rather than for individuals. The services
are resourced accordingly, thus not allowing sufficient resource
for sustaining one-to-one interaction for a long time. In both of
the day activity centres that participated in our research, the staff
members emphasised that they took into consideration the individual preferences and needs of the care users. In practice, however,
only seldom did these units have activities that were designed to
meet a specific care user's needs. The most individualised activities
that reflected the user's particular needs, interests or initiatives
took place as part of 'therapy' (e.g. physiotherapy) or 'intensive
interaction'. These were often the only activities that required,
and allowed, one-to-one contact.

This incongruity between staff accounts and institutional practices resembles findings from special education research, which show how special support, which by definition should be individualised in order to meet the specific needs of individual students, in reality often merely meets the needs of 'average students' with a certain type of diagnosis (e.g. Hjörne, 2004; Mietola, 2014). Because the services are planned with a certain group of people with assumed characteristics in mind, the diagnostic knowledge starts to define the practice rather than the re-minding knowledge about individuals.

In our view, the gap between principles and practice is significant in relation to thinking about the politics and ethics of care. Our analysis above suggests that, while the staff members, both in group homes and in day activity services, continuously face challenges related to interpretation, they are also capable of making sense of the initiatives and expressions of our research participants. Also, the staff have a key position and responsibility in the 're-minding work', of building a full picture of the care user. The challenge is thus not one of interpretation and knowledge but of putting this knowledge about individuals into practice. The current practices are effective in taking care of basic needs, but seem to be inefficient in terms of providing individualised service – making possible everyday lives that reflect the service users' personalities. The critical question then is not only what kinds of conceptions about people with PIMD are dominant in the services but what follows from these perspectives, how these conceptions are put into practice (see Kulick, 2015).

There is an uncomfortable discrepancy in a situation where Hugo is described as a charming, humorous and very sociable young man, while his everyday life at group home is characterised by lack of social engagement. The right to, say, full participation is not duly recognised until the manner and context of participation reflect that particular individual's personality and are in line with his interests. When claiming for personalised services, it is important to note that (as the care workers emphasise in our data) people with PIMD are continuously changing subjects, just like everybody else (see Chapter 4). Recognition of this element

of change in persons, their personalities and interests, requires 're-minding work'. Without knowledge about the needs and
wants of persons with PIMD, we cannot provide them with space
and opportunity for change.

Enabling change

Our data also includes some examples of practices that radically
extend thinking about who our research participants, and people
with PIMD in general, can be, and what kinds of activities and
experiences might broaden their lives and bring new aspects to
their personalities.

> Next task is about blowing bubbles. Instructor shows everyone a
> card with a picture of a soap bubble. She suggests that Nina and
> Mark would come and blow some soap bubbles for Frida. While
> Nina blows bubbles the supporting care worker makes sure that
> the bubbles don't go directly on Frida, but so that Frida sees what
> happens. Care worker points at the bubbles, 'Look Frida, bubb-
> les!'. Also Nina speaks to Frida. Nina blows couple more bubbles,
> then passes the jar to Mark who blows once, then passes the jar
> to the care worker. Care worker blows some more bubbles, calls
> Frida to look at the bubbles. Frida is blinking her eyes fiercely,
> she hums a bit, her body tenses so that she pushes herself up in
> the chair, also pushes her hands out and then again draws these
> tightly against her body. She pinches her lips, and some foam is
> coming out of her mouth. The care worker stops blowing bubb-
> les, watches Frida for a second, then touches her arm and calls
> 'Frida, hey Frida'. Frida is still very tense, pinched lips, blinking
> her eyes. The care worker takes hold of the wheel chair, starts pus-
> hing, whispers to me 'Are you coming with us? I'm going to check
> whether this is a [epilepsy] seizure.' While passing the instructor,
> gestures to her that she's going to out to check if Frida is ok, and
> just then the instructor says that 'Now there comes a smile' [Frida
> smiling]. (Field notes, drama group, day activity centre)

The example above is from Frida's day centre session that focused on working with different drama methods and assignments.
While in this particular day activity centre care users with PIMD
mostly participated in their own activity sessions with a focus
on motor-sensory work, Frida's personal schedule also included

activity groups where most participants were service users with milder intellectual disability. So, Frida participated in intensive interaction sessions, the café group (a cooking and baking group that held a café once a month), and the drama group. The head of the day activity centre explained this variation in Frida's schedule with the process of finding appropriate activities for her:

> all that advance information that we got [when Frida started at the centre], like for example that it is really important to do physical exercises with Frida, and positioning treatment and all these kinds of assumptions, based on that she is profoundly disabled, thus needing these [kinds of activities], were then quite quickly proven, that Frida doesn't like that kind of stuff. That she rather wants to stay in the big groups, than exercising one-to-one with an instructor there – And as we have learned to know her, we have strengthened those things that Frida likes – and still Frida sometimes surprises us, like new things come up.

This was the head person's answer when Reetta asked her what kind of information they had received about Frida before she started at the day centre. During her answer, she simultaneously looked up the initial 'arrival evaluation' in which the starting points for Frida's personal plan were set. In the evaluation, familiar activities were emphasised: sensory activation, body perception, exercise to keep up her mobility, stretches and massage to alleviate her spasticity. After having read through the document aloud, the head person commented immediately that, 'even if all of these aspects are still valid, I would not say that these are Frida's own targets'. She also noted that they had difficulties interpreting Frida's interests, her 'own targets'. Frida's way of expressing interest or lack of interest was different from most of the other service users. She did not always show interest in a very visible way (e.g. by laughing). Rather, one could notice a change in her state of alertness – in the way she related to the surrounding activities. Frida's lack of interest would mean that the instructors were unable to create contact with her and she would be immersed in her own world. During activities that Frida found interesting, she was alert and carefully followed the actions of the instructor and the other group members.

The head person continued to explain how lately they had aimed to break down the division between people with milder and severe/profound intellectual disability, since they had realised that 'sensory things' are important for all of them and because Frida enjoyed being part of the other groups as well. She felt that, especially in the case of Frida, it was important to 'break the pattern that she would only be amongst people of her own kind'.

The head person's account makes visible those underlying and intriguing assumptions that are often the basis for the practices directed to people with PIMD. While the services emphasise the heterogeneity of the group and individualised practices, there is still a general assumption of appropriate practices, of what would work with people with PIMD in general. These practices are sometimes applied with a logic of self-evident truths where it is assumed what these people naturally like, without questioning whether these assumptions actually represent the care user's personal interests. Another implication of this self-evident way of framing the activities is that it leaves very little room for the care user to surprise, or to challenge the predefined conceptions about her capacities, and the capacities of people with PIMD in general. In this kind of institutional culture, the idea of the appropriateness of provided activities, and the expected maximum level of capacity among care users, does not get easily challenged.

Consider the incident described in the first extract of this section, from a drama group where the group members were blowing bubbles, and Frida seemed to have a seizure but started to smile instead. When Reetta talked about this incident with the care worker concerned, we agreed that this was a situation where Frida surprised, as it were, both of us. Our shared interpretation about what happened in the situation was that Frida was focused on the assignment of blowing bubbles, instead of having a seizure. When Reetta discussed this particular incident with the instructor after the drama session, it became clear that she, unlike us, was not surprised. Frida had already surprised her during the earlier sessions, with her ability to make sense of the task at hand and to participate.

We want to highlight two aspects of the previous incident that are important in relation to conceptions and practices. Firstly, Frida's presence in a session that was not particularly designed to meet her assumed impairment-related needs opened totally new forms of participation and experiences for her. Frida's presence challenged the group to form new, inclusive ways of working, so that Frida could participate in her own way (for example, when Frida was being interviewed as part of one drama exercise, the sounds she made on her turn were considered to be answers to the interview questions). These changes and observations can in the future open up new opportunities for participation to other persons with PIMD, and challenge the division between 'academics' and others. Secondly, Frida's participation opened up space for 'surprise'. It made visible a capacity that the staff members were not yet aware of (this is not the only case in our data – there are similar stories, for example, of Sebastian, how a care worker describes that he is a 'totally different personality' at the swimming pool, and how in this particular context one 'can see what kind of things Sebastian actually is able to do'). These experiences importantly changed the staff members' conceptions about Frida's capacities in that she was offered similar assignments as other 'academics' within her capacity (e.g. kneading the dough with a mixer in the bakery group). However, in the long run these kinds of experiences can also change conceptions concerning the capacities of people with PIMD in general. As the head of the unit expressed, Frida's participation has made visible that she 'clearly has that kind of understanding. And ability to act according to the situation, in the right moment. She's got that kind of talents, that we are not like even aware of, as do many others in here.'

In terms of providing change in the lives of persons with PIMD, the care system needs practices that make it rethink and reconceptualise people with PIMD and the kinds of lives they can have. In our data, one good example of this kind of practice was personal assistance. While at the time of our fieldwork the specific Act about personal assistance in Finland (Finlex 3.4.1987/380) was defined in a way that excluded people with PIMD (since they are seen not to possess the required capacity for self-determination in relation to personal assistance), one of our research participants (Ella) had a personal assistant (PA) for leisure time activities.

It was interesting how this extra resource made it possible and necessary for the staff members to engage in a new way in the 're-minding work'. Since the PA had a predefined number of hours per month to use with Ella, use of these hours had to be planned ahead. Both the PA and Ella's coordinating care worker regularly sat down to talk about how these hours should be used. These negotiations would include both talking about experiences that the PA had of trying out new activities with Ella and thinking about activities that had not been tried yet, and which Ella might enjoy. This kind of thinking would consider Ella's personality – her preferences – as well as accessibility. While Ella had some regular hobbies that she would participate in weekly with the PA (dance lessons, gymnastics), there was always some time left to experiment with new things. The PA as an extra resource opened up new space for imagining Ella and her life. Instead of settling with Ella for her everyday routines, the mere existence of the PA pushed the system to think what could be added to her life – what kinds of experiences (e.g. taking Ella to events) or social bonds (e.g. visiting Ella's parents, hanging out with the PA) would improve Ella's life. Additionally, through gaining new experiences with Ella, in new environments and situations, and sharing these experiences, the care workers gained new knowledge concerning Ella, which helped again to build a fuller picture of her as a person. In these two ways, by providing concrete extra resources and a new space for imagining, the PA provided a major step towards building a life that reflects Ella's personality.

Conclusion

This chapter has analysed the ways that care workers balance medical, policy and their own professional discourses that portray people with PIMD in a very different manner. The tension between the dominant medico-diagnostic conception, which sees PIMD through deficits, and policy, which emphasises self-determination and individualisation, has made care workers question the homogeneity of the PIMD category, and focus on each individual's personality instead. However, while care workers emphasise the individuality of the people they care for, and how the diagnostic category misses many of the crucial elements of each individual and their capacities, the institutional and therapeutic practices very much produce a static, homogenous group of people who are handled mainly in terms of their limitations.

At the heart of the matter are epistemic and ethical issues related to interpretation. Interaction with non-verbal people necessarily requires constant interpretation, which the care workers saw as a natural and necessary part of their work but which also includes a risk of misjudgement, especially regarding evaluations of the cognitive capacities of persons with PIMD that were too optimistic. The uncertainty the care workers felt about interpretation, and the sincerity which they talked about it, can be seen as part of their ethical awareness. It can also be seen as a commitment to be open to surprises and unforeseen changes in the lives and personalities of the people they care for instead of holding on to a fixed view about them.

Care work in the case of persons with PIMD requires an imagination of what this particular person may become, how he or she may want to change. A here-and-now mentality easily leads to care practices whose sole purpose is to keep the service users content, particularly in the case of adults. But it also requires backward-looking stories that enable those currently working with the person with PIMD to build a more defined, holistic view of her. Understanding who this person is, and providing the support that enables her to live a life that is in line with her individuality, requires her carers to be able to access the knowledge about her past. Stories that capture the essential aspects of life path (stories of Frida being a busy and bright baby, of Hugo crawling under a bookshelf as a child), what kind of life events and changes they have experienced (stories of schooldays, of moving to intellectual disability institutions), and how these have affected their personalities. Dignified care thus needs to approach also people with PIMD as persons with a full life-histories – a past, present and future.

Chapter 4: Social Lives

Introduction

In 2010, the Finnish government launched a national programme for the development of community care services for people with intellectual disability (KEHAS programme, 2010–2020). A key target of the programme was to close intellectual disability institutions and to build community housing for people with intellectual disability, thus to conclude the process of deinstitutionalisation that had been the goal of disability policy since the 1970s. The focus, especially in the first stage of the programme, was on housing arrangements (form of housing, number of habitants in a housing unit etc.), with a strong emphasis on newly built housing services in ordinary neighbourhoods. The existing national and international policies that emphasised community living and participation in public sphere, specifically with regard to issues such as paid work and independent living, supported such development (Clifford Simplican, Leader, Kosciulek, & Leahy, 2015; Hall, 2010).

We found that the targets of community living and participation were in stark contrast with the everyday lives of our research participants. While we did not expect residence in mainstream community to automatically lead to community participation (Clement & Bigby, 2009), we were overwhelmed by the fact that our participants lives were so socially isolated – despite being continuously surrounded by others (housemates and care workers). This was the case in some contexts despite the fact that the care workers recognised our research participants' capacity and desire for social interaction and relationships.

In this chapter, we will analyse how the goals concerning community living and participation are defined in policy documents in Finland, and how these goals are fulfilled in the disability services (in particular in housing services). In addition, we will reflect upon ways to understand and conceptualise inclusion and social relations in order to make them available to this group of people.

Social participation and persons with PIMD

Most of the research discussing people with intellectual disability is focused on persons with low support needs. This means that research on social participation and inclusion of people with PIMD is scarce (Boxall & Ralph, 2010; Mietola, Miettinen, & Vehmas, 2017; Verdonschot, de Witte, Buntinx, & Curfs, 2009). The existing body of research approaches these themes from multiple perspectives. Some focus on the micro-processes of interaction and communication (such as the variety of expressions displayed in interactions) that are considered necessary for building social relations and participation (e.g. Brigg et al., 2016; Watson, Jones, & Potter, 2018). Others have adopted a sociological perspective, and examine the social relations, community participation and inclusion of persons with PIMD (e.g. Kamstra, van der Putten, Post, & Vlaskamp, 2015; Qian, Tichá, Larson, & Wuorio, 2015).

These differences in perspectives can be seen to represent the overall complexity of defining social inclusion. As several authors have noted, there seems to be a general confusion over what inclusion and other related concepts, such as participation, mean, and whether people with PIMD have genuine possibilities to achieve them (e.g. Hanzen, van Nispen, van der Putten, & Waninge, 2017; Verdonschot et al., 2009). Definitions of inclusion range in their scope, setting and depth, with some focusing only on particular dimensions of social inclusion, whereas others approach inclusion from a broader perspective (Clifford Simplican et al., 2015). Both approaches are somewhat problematic: 'Narrow definitions undercut the social and political purposes of social inclusion, whereas vast definitions threaten to become too demanding, thus inviting some stakeholders to conclude that social inclusion may be for some people with disabilities, but not all' (Clifford Simplican et al., 2015, p. 27).

It seems reasonable to argue that the focus of mainstream research on the inclusion and participation of people with intellectual disability is problematic from the point of view of people with PIMD. First of all, inclusion and participation are mostly 'measured' through the frequency and type of social contacts (Emerson & Hatton, 2008), the width of social networks (Kamstra et al., 2015) and participation in activities outside one's home (Emerson & Hatton, 2008; Clement & Bigby, 2009). These studies undoubtedly provide important insights into the social lives of people with PIMD, especially in relation to the scarcity of social contacts and narrowness of social life. However, they do not unpack the processes of inclusion and participation, let alone provide explanations of what is required for participation to materialise in the lives of persons with PIMD. Secondly, the body of research that focuses on the micro-processes of communication and interaction argues that problems in the way communication is conceived and approached is the key barrier to social relations. However, this kind of research rarely includes discussion of how successful communication can make social participation and inclusion come true.

Some authors have pointed out how conventional conceptions on persons with PIMD, which emphasise the lack of basic abilities required in interaction, are difficult to combine with policy goals such as community participation (Clement & Bigby, 2009; Mansell, 2010; Parry Hughes, Redley & Ring, 2011). Also, empirical studies that focus on the views of care workers or family members have revealed how even those closest to people with PIMD sometimes consider community participation to be an unrealistic aim (Bigby et al., 2009; Clegg, Elizabeth, Kathryn, & Harvey, 2008; Clement & Bigby, 2009; Simmons & Watson, 2014). 'Low expectations' (Mansell, 2010) may imply that the social initiatives and expressions of persons with PIMD can go unrecognised and lead to practices that do not support the formation of social relations.

Individual empirical studies have challenged the view of people with PIMD as emotionally and socially incompetent, and represented them as being able to build and maintain social relations, as well as to grieve loss of these relations (Brigg et al., 2016; Simmons & Watson, 2014; Young & Garrard, 2015). Some studies have underlined the specific qualities of interaction (such as adjusting communication to meet the preferred communication style of a person with PIMD), aspects of care work that support participation (Forster & Iacono, 2008; Johnson, Douglas, Bigby, & Iacono, 2012a), and how these may contradict organisational and professional policies (Forster & Iacono, 2008).

Some scholars have argued that, when the targets of policy (such as participation and inclusion) are left undefined, and the tensions and complexities entailed in these policy targets are met with silence, the result is a state of ambiguity that inevitably leads to a failure in the implementation of policy recommendations (Bigby et al., 2009; Hall, 2010; Parry Hughes et al., 2011). The research community unanimously calls for clear definitions and a realistic operationalisation of concepts and policy targets. However, some scholars have questioned the status of inclusion and community participation as the sole policy targets for people with PIMD. Also, a number of young people with intellectual disability and their parents have questioned policies that position social relationships only as a secondary objective – as a means for attaining inclusion or as a by-product of inclusive policies (Clegg et al., 2008). The family members of people with intellectual disability interviewed by Clegg et al. (2008) did not totally abandon inclusion as a policy target. They underscored the importance of the means for attaining inclusion such as skills of the staff in facilitating social relationships, as well as the availability of participatory activities and communities.

Previous research suggests that we need to define and operationalise participation and inclusion as policy objectives clearly so that we know what they mean in practice for persons with PIMD. Research that focuses on deinstitutionalisation has underlined the problems connected to the 'residential relocation' of people with intellectual disability, and it has made visible how community presence does not automatically lead to community participation (e.g. Clement & Bigby, 2009, 2010). The focus of development work and research has been on participation in mainstream society, while special contexts, like group homes, and relationships with disabled peers within these contexts have been overlooked (Clement & Bigby, 2009; Clifford Simplican et al., 2015; Hall, 2010).

Community living and participation in the policy texts

A variety of Finnish policy documents address the deinstitutionalisation of intellectual disability services. The top policy documents analysed here, *government resolutions* (Finnish government, 2010, 2012) and *the steering letter targeted to municipalities* (Ministry of Social and Health & Ministry of the Environment, 2010), are primarily targeted at the public sector, municipalities and joint municipal authorities. Their function is to set a general framework for the local planning and execution of the transition to community care. Another category of documents is *the evaluation report of the programme* (Ministry of Social and Health, 2016), which also sets measures for the final stage of the programme.

We have also included in the analysis some documents and general guidelines that, in our view, are part of the national information steering of community care development and housing services for disabled people (Ministry of Social and Health, 2003), as well as two documents produced by the national Intellectual Disability Services' Advisory Committee for Housing (IDSACH, 2010, 2011). The above-mentioned policy documents, which are tightly connected to the KEHAS programme, systematically refer to these guideline documents as providing criteria that should be taken into consideration in the local planning and transition processes. Also, organisations that apply public funding provided by the Housing Finance and Development Centre of Finland (ARA) are expected to follow these criteria in their plans.[17]

> The housing program for people with intellectual disabilities aims at making possible individualized housing which strengthens inclusion and equality of people with intellectual disabilities in the community and society. (Finnish Government, 2010, p. 1)

---

[17] Financial steering has had a key position in the national steering of the KEHAS programme. This has been implemented through the public funding allocated for construction of new community housing for people with intellectual disabilities (up to 50% of the total costs). We have excluded documents provided by the Housing Finance and Development Centre of Finland from the analysed dataset since these are stricly focused on the steering of the physical structures of housing (Mietola, Teittinen & Vesala, 2013).

The extract above makes visible both the key terms used and the policy emphases in the current intellectual disability policy in Finland. Primary emphasis is placed on the individuality of housing and services. In the analysed documents, individuality is approached from two perspectives. Firstly, it is discussed in relation to personalisation of services, with a focus on individually tailored housing solutions and support services that meet 'individual needs' (IDSACH, 2010, p. 3). This means that services should 'respect persons' life choices' (IDSACH, 2010, p. 4) and make possible their 'own looking life' (*'oman näköinen elämä'*) (IDSACH, 2011, p. 2). Across the documents, individuality is discussed mostly as a question of the right of persons with intellectual disability to participate in the process of planning. Secondly, individuality is brought up in relation to privacy, as a right to have one's own private room or apartment.

The extract above from the government resolution works as a good example of the unspecified way terms such as 'inclusion' and 'community' are repeatedly used in the documents. The concepts remain abstract and obscure and sometimes interchangeable (see Parry Hughes et al., 2011). For example, we found only a few individual sentences about the possibility of a multitude of communities in a person's life, but no suggestions about what those communities might be and where they might be found.

'Participation', 'inclusion' and 'local community' (*'osallistuminen'*, *'osallisuus'* and *'lähiyhteisö'*) in these documents refer specifically to participation in the public domain, outside one's home – inclusion has to take place in mainstream society in order to be inclusion proper (e.g. Hall, 2010). The policy emphasis on 'ordinary living' (*'tavallinen asuminen'*) in 'ordinary neighbourhoods' (*'tavallinen asuinalue'*), as well as on the physical structures (size of units, size of a private space/apartment) and the location of housing, directs the focus onto the local community and physical accessibility of public spaces. Even when the development of services is discussed, the focus is on mainstream services (e.g. private and public health care) and not on the specialised services and support that persons with PIMD typically need: 'Through this resolution, the Government commits itself to continue the structural reform of the services for persons with intellectual disabilities and to develop services that enable people with the most severe disabilities to live in the local community' (Government resolution, 2012, p. 5).

Two documents take a somewhat different perspective. Both the Ministry of Social Affairs and Health in 2003 and IDSACH in 2011 aim to provide guidelines for support and services, which have remained on the margins of the general development work in the programme. While these documents emphasise participation in the public sphere, outside one's home, they also imply that communities can be formed within specialised intellectual disability services. The 2003 document uses phrases such as 'sense of community' ('*yhteisöllisyys*') and 'communal housing' ('*yhteisöllinen asuminen*'). These are, however, discussed in terms of spatial planning (how to separate private and communal space within a group home) rather than in terms of forming communities or enhancing social lives: 'All housing solutions have to provide people with possibilities for private life, domestic peace and sense of community' (Ministry of Social and Health, 2003, p. 23).

The guidelines for support and service provided by IDSACH (2011) specifically discuss the role of support in inclusion and participation. It is, for example, stated that 'the person receives the necessary help to interact with people who are important to her' (IDSACH, 2011, p. 8), and that 'Supporting societal participation and social affiliation is defined as part of [a care worker's] job description' (IDSACH, 2011, p. 24). However, even here participation outside one's home is emphasised over the community at home: when discussing support, the focus is on the access, not on how receptive a given community is or what kind of assistance a person might need in order to be included or to participate.

Possible communities formed within group homes or within specialised services (e.g. day activities, work) are not generally visible in the policy texts. For example, the aforementioned quality recommendations of support (IDSACH, 2011) state that 'I [the individual service user] get support for meeting my friends and family who live outside the living/housing community' (p. 23). While this statement suggests a possibility of also forming friendships in the housing community, the assumed social world exists, nevertheless, outside one's (group) home. This kind of mentality may support the notion that social inclusion is an unrealistic

option for persons with PIMD who need extensive support to access social world outside the service system, and to form and maintain social relationships. To arrange such support would be very
difficult, if not unrealistic, in the current service structures (as we
will discuss below). And pursuing something unrealistic can be
seen as a waste of time (e.g. Bigby et al., 2009).

The way policy emphasises the right to privacy (private
space: 'home is more than a room'), and participation in outside-
the-home activities (location of housing, accessibility of mainstream community services), makes sense when these texts are placed
in the context of deinstitutionalisation. The identification of institutional characteristics, and the definition of strict guidelines
that have the goal of avoiding such characteristics, is relatively
straightforward in relation to the physical structures of services
– for example, not housing people in shared rooms. In relation
to services, the policy emphasises individualisation: individualised
services and self-determination in the planning and implementation of the services.

Policy documents like these have marginalised group homes and intellectual disability services like day activity centres
as places for social participation (see Clifford Simplican et al.,
2015; Hall, 2010). Similarly, the strong emphasis on individualisation has marginalised participation. The individualised focus
thus tends to displace the social realm. Policy documents discuss
homes as if they were things that come about in the interaction
between an individual service user and the care workers. In reality, however, the homes of persons with intellectual disability are
mostly group homes, where support is shared by a group of residents and provided in accordance with the institutional order of a
group home. This means that social interaction between a resident
and a care worker will be affected by the needs of other residents,
the available staff resources, and how care work is organised
in the unit (as will be discussed below). Our research makes visible
how the everyday lives of people with PIMD take place almost exclusively within intellectual disability services. The contexts that
these services provide are virtually the sole available arenas for
social participation for people with PIMD. However, the current
intellectual disability policy discourse does not provide any clear

suggestions of how to create inclusive communities *within* group homes and other disability service contexts.

While some policy texts use terms such as 'housing community', such communities mean in practice and self-evidently group homes. However, policy discourse does not engage with practical issues such as how to support the formation of communities, and how participation among them could be enabled. Such an engagement is needed since group homes, as the following analysis highlights, do not automatically imply access to social relations, or the formation of a social community.

The social communities of the research participants

All our research participants live in group homes located in regular neighbourhoods. The homes are part of service units with several separate group homes within the same housing complex. Between five and nine inhabitants live in each group home. According to current Finnish policy guidelines, each inhabitant should have their own apartment within the group home. In reality, their apartments are more like en suite private rooms. Our participants' rooms differed in size and furnishing. Those who lived in older units had smaller apartments, approximately 10 square metres (bathroom excluded), while in the newer group homes the apartments were a bit bigger. All our participants had some personal decoration in the room, like photographs, posters or paintings.

Four of our research participants had moved to their current group homes from long-term institutions: Ella moved years ago; Frida, Hugo and Leo only recently. The two other participants (Anna and Sebastian) moved to a group home from the homes where they grew up with their parents and siblings. Five of our six participants had still contact with their childhood families. Hugo's, Frida's, Anna's and Sebastian's parents visited them regularly. Sebastian's, Anna's and Frida's parents also sometimes came to pick them up for a visit in their home. Ella paid occasional visits to her parents' house, supported by her personal assistant. Leo had had no contact with his family ever since he had been placed in an institution as a child.

Only one of our participants, Ella, had a personal assistant, which her municipality had granted her. This service has in recent years become a statutory right in Finland for persons with significant disabilities. Eligibility criteria for this service also involve the capacity to express one's will – verbally or otherwise. How to determine who has such a capacity is left unclear. In our view, Ella did not differ significantly from our other research participants in her ability to communicate. Like the rest of them, she did not have any other communication method except non-verbal communication, and her way of communicating without words was equally (un)intelligible. Her eligibility for this service was due to the efforts of her care staff in the group home, who had applied for this service on her behalf. Persons who are ineligible for personal assistance can get a support person for 20 hours a month.

Having a personal assistant provided Ella with more possibilities to attend activities outside her home. The young man working as Ella's PA had clearly become an important person for her: she greeted him enthusiastically when they met and was clearly happy to go out on excursions with him. Sebastian and Anna had been granted a support person, which is not the same as PA; the latter is a form of regular employment, whereas the former get a fee for their work, but no other benefits related to employment. Being a support person comes closer to voluntary work and recruiting people for such positions is more difficult than employment to PA positions. However, even several months after the fieldwork, Sebastian's and Anna's housing units had not been successful in finding the right persons.

All research participants were provided with publicly funded day activities on weekdays. Care workers talked about these activities as our participants' 'work'. The day activities were mainly provided in different service units located outside their group homes. Hugo was not in day activities at the time of the fieldwork since he was in post-compulsory education, in a pre-vocational training programme directed at people with profound disabilities, which prepared them for independent living and work. However, the expectation was that, after he had finished school, he would return to day activities. Sebastian, Anna, Leo and Hugo had been granted publicly funded personal rehabilitation. While the rehabilitation sessions were sometimes organised in locations outside their group homes and day activity centres, such as public swimming pools, they typically only involved contact with a professional therapist.

The social worlds of our research participants were constituted almost exclusively by the intellectual disability services. Even though day activities and rehabilitation functioned as contexts for participation, the group homes were the primary social communities for persons with PIMD because the bulk of their everyday lives was located there. They spent their nights, mornings, evenings, weekends and holidays in their group homes, apart from the occasional visits to their parents' house (in the case of Anna and Sebastian) or excursions to the outside world (rare except for Ella). In other words, the group homes are not a means for persons with PIMD to live in a community – group homes are *the* community in which they live their social lives.

Persons with PIMD as social beings

One may be tempted to think that persons with PIMD do not have the capacity to be sociable beings, that their cognitive impairments would automatically lead to socially isolated lives, and that a meaningful connection with such people would require immense amount of work and specialised methods. These kinds of stereotypes were not shared by the people who worked closely with our research participants. Our research participants were without exception described as sociable persons who enjoyed social interaction. Some of them were even seen as capable of initiating social interaction, even if these initiatives were often idiosyncratic and intelligible only to those who knew them well.

Naturally, our research participants' preferences regarding social interaction varied (how much and in what way to take part), as did their capacity to initiate and sustain social interaction. For example, Sebastian, who was capable of wheeling himself over to others, often initiated interaction by touching or 'patting' the person he wanted to interact with. He sustained, and clearly enjoyed, long moments of one-to-one interaction by taking turns in patting, vocalising, or just giving hugs. Ella sought company by walking to the common spaces of her group home, in particular the kitchen, which was the busiest spot of the house. Sometimes she walked up to the person she wanted to spend time with, touched him or her, or just stayed standing right at that person's side. Occasionally, being small, she climbed to sit on their lap.

While there were similarities in ways Sebastian and Ella pursued social participation, the responses to their initiatives differed dramatically in their group homes. Sebastian often steered his wheelchair to the kitchen where the care workers usually spent time when they were not busy with their work. However, in his group home the inhabitants were not allowed to go to inside the kitchen for 'safety reasons' (it never became clear to us what those safety reasons were exactly), which meant that the kitchen door was often closed when care workers were preparing food or cleaning up after meal. Sometimes Sebastian was allowed to stay in the doorway, where he sat listening the care workers chatting and observing their activities quietly. In Ella's group home, by contrast, residents could move freely in the common areas where care workers and residents spent time together – including the kitchen. The floor plan in the group home was open, with no doors between the common areas and the kitchen space. Thus, the care workers and residents were able to socialise while working in the kitchen. Ella typically sat on the kitchen floor and rocked herself in the middle of all the social activity, and was only occasionally, due to safety reasons (when someone carried a hot pan or pot across the room), led to sit next to the kitchen table.

Anna and Frida, in contrast, became often distressed in environments with the hubbub of social activities, such as those that occurred in their day activity centres. Anna expressed her discontent through moaning, restless hand movements, and by turning her wheelchair away from others. Frida often 'froze' in the interaction situations where she was expected to engage in one-to-one interaction, which had made some of the tutors in the day centre think at first that she was not a particularly sociable person. However, the care workers in Frida's group home did not share the view of Frida as being 'unsociable'. Quite the opposite: they talked of her as a person who did not like to be alone. She enjoyed moments of one-to-one interaction at home, as long as they were with persons she knew well, as well as activities at the day activity centre that involved social interaction between other group members. She did not necessarily actively take part in the interaction, but she followed it intently.

Our research participants also differed in their interactive and communicative capacities. While none of them spoke any intelligible verbal language, they had different means of communicating: mainly gestures, facial expressions and utterances. And, as we discussed in the previous chapter, the care workers considered some of our participants to be very transparent, able to express their opinion, and also able to initiate interaction. Sebastian and Ella were able to move to others and seek contact this way, which other participants could not, owing to restricted mobility or restricted capacity (or motivation) to interaction. Anna, on the other hand, appeared to most people around her to be a socially complex person; finding the means and right moments for a connection with her was very difficult. According to her care workers, Anna's alertness varied greatly, and sometimes it was very difficult to get through to her as she seemed to be immersed in her own world. Some of the care workers also pondered whether Anna's health was deteriorating, and caused her states of pain that further closed her in her own world (because some days Anna responded to almost any initiative by crying). However, Anna's mother told Sonja that Anna had learnt only recently to make interaction initiatives after having participated with her coordinating care worker in intensive interaction methods training.

Thus, the capacities of our research participants not only varied but constantly developed in relation to their environments. Some had the ability to initiate interaction but not a capacity to sustain interaction, or vice versa. Frida, for example, seemed to understand the idea of turn-taking in interaction. She demonstrated this by making sounds in response to other's talk, 'chatting' in this way in turns. This happened especially when she was addressed directly and asked to comment on an ongoing happening or discussion. While she sometimes also took the initiative by taking part in discussions around her, these initiatives were rare and often difficult to detect. Hugo's capacities can be described similarly; while he responded to interaction initiatives in a visibly delighted manner and could sustain interaction for a long time, he hardly ever initiated interaction himself.

Leo, on the other hand, was a person whose interactive repertoire consisted mostly of very strong responses, often considered challenging behaviour in his group home and day centre. Sometimes Leo responded violently to other people's interaction initiatives: when talked to, he often responded by shouting, hitting or biting himself, or kicking while sitting in his wheelchair. While his care workers showed skill in interpreting his moods, Leo's communication appeared to us to be extremely confusing. However, as the fieldwork progressed, we began to think whether Leo's shouting, kicking, biting – and to some extent his self-harming behaviour too – might not, at least partly, be interaction initiatives. We witnessed situations where he straightened his leg (while sitting in his wheelchair) and blocked a care worker's way with his leg. What was his intention for doing this – did he mean to fool around, injure himself or the worker, or simply seek attention? Sometimes care workers interpreted these kinds of 'gestures' as attempts to harm others, but sometimes the care workers responded to Leo's loud distress and violent behaviour by offering him an opportunity to take a short, supported walk, or just to move out of the room. When this happened, Leo notably calmed down.

All in all, our research participants were clearly able to develop social interaction and reciprocity in their own individual ways. However, since they needed support in virtually any activity, they were unable to create social lives on their own. Their interest and capacity to relate to others was possible only through other people's recognition and active measures.

Care practices and social lives in group homes

The care workers saw our research participants as capable and willing to have social interaction and relationships. These beliefs did not, however, materialise in all our research contexts. In some contexts, moments of mutual recognition and affection between the research participants and their care workers were not common. Time and support provided for social interaction depended on individual care workers and their motivation. In these contexts,

the contact between our research participants and their care workers was mostly limited to the daily routines of eating, dressing,
washing and toileting. The description of the structure of Hugo's
daily life provided by his care worker in the following extract
represents the rationale and prioritisation of care work in many
of the group homes.

> The physiotherapist asks the care worker 'Is it ok if I first ask
> you a couple of questions concerning how Hugo's days are here
> at home?' The care worker answers to this 'They are fine.' The
> physiotherapist goes on to clarify that she meant to ask what his
> days consist of. The care worker starts to explain – how in the
> morning Hugo is lifted off his bed into his wheelchair and then he
> eats his breakfast 'in the chair', and then after breakfast sits in his
> wheelchair, but 'might get tired already before lunch' and then gets
> lifted into his bed to rest. 'And will be lifted back to his wheelchair
> to eat [lunch]'. After lunch he sits in his wheelchair until he gets
> tired, and gets lifted into his bed to rest. The care worker keeps on
> explaining Hugo's daily 'schedule' this way, until she gets to the
> point when Hugo is put to bed for night's sleep – with eating ('gets
> fed in his chair'), sitting and resting as the only activities of the day.
> (Field notes, with Hugo)

The extract above pictures Hugo's life through the lens of care
work, with nothing worth mentioning rather than eating and resting. This is undoubtedly a caricature description of Hugo's life in
his group home. However, it is also accurate in the sense that it
exemplifies the way basic care work was prioritised, and how this
prioritisation dictated care work in general in this group home.
As the staff members focused on managing basic care tasks, they
would only make contact with Hugo during the moments of eating, dressing, washing or toileting. This way of organising and
prioritising care work was visible in many of our research contexts.

  There were significant differences between our research
contexts in relation to what kind of social existence was enabled
for our research participants. These differences had to do with the
values and organisation of care work: whether social lives were
valued and considered possible for persons with PIMD, and
whether the everyday routines were arranged in ways that supported their realisation. So, the lack of sociability was partly a
matter of care culture, but, importantly, it was a matter of limited

resources as well. In particular, group homes with only residents with extensive needs had very few resources for anything but basic care work.

However, some of the interviewed care workers explained the lack of practices to support social lives by individual care workers' 'attitude': care workers differ in their commitment to interact with care users as well as in their attentiveness to the needs of the care users. These care workers suggested that the marginalisation of social needs could be challenged, and changed by focusing on the quality of interaction between care workers and service users, 'so that [when working with a care user] you are touching, you're talking, you're present and listening', as one unit manager told us in interview.

We agree that the quality of interaction and 'attitude' of the care workers matter. Having said that, it became poignantly clear during the fieldwork that moments of care provision constituted only a very small part of the everyday routines of our research participants. Many of our research participants spent a lot of time alone in-between the care activities, either in their apartments or in the communal spaces. For the long solitary moments in their apartments, they were usually provided with some kind of entertainment. For example, Hugo was often left in his bed to listen to music or audiobooks and Sebastian, a man in his early twenties, was given some toys he liked to play with when he lay on the mat in his room. Both Hugo and Sebastian seemed to enjoy these activities – Hugo chuckled while listening to his favourite stories and Sebastian was seemingly focused in playing on his own. However, considering that both of these young men were described as very social persons, leaving them alone in their rooms for long periods of time perplexed us.

Even those care workers who explained the lack of engagement with social lives by 'attitude' provided different kind of explanations when asked whether they themselves were able to allocate time to activities other than just basic care. With some hesitation, they talked about the ways the rotas were arranged, which times of the day should be reserved to support social interaction, and how last-minute changes and shortage of staff limited possibilities to do different activities. The concern over limited resources was especially apparent in those repeated situations where the care workers apologetically explained to a resident directly (and to Reetta and Sonja indirectly) when they needed to move immediately after having finished a care task, and to take care of someone else. In these moments, they openly said how they wished that they would have more time to spend with each resident, and how they hoped that our research participants would not be bored.

In Hugo's, Leo's, Sebastian's and Frida's group homes there were usually one care worker per three to four residents at daytimes (at nights this imbalance was significantly higher). All the residents in these group homes required a great deal of care. Consequently, time spent with one resident constantly competed with the demand to complete care for others. The busy care workers often complained how the scarce personnel resources affected the focus of their work. For example, Frida's care worker explained how on weekdays there was very limited time for anything but basic care work, whereas at weekends they had time for walks, or just spend time in the living room sitting, talking, reading newspapers or watching TV together. These kinds of moments of relaxing and spending time together were rare in these particular contexts.

Also, the way in which the care work was organised in group homes was a central aspect of the context in which the relationships between the staff and the residents developed. In Hugo's, Leo's, Sebastian's and Frida's group homes, the care workers were expected to work with all the inhabitants within the group home in question. Consequently, the care workers negotiated among themselves their assignments with the residents in the beginning of each shift; there were no fixed assignments. In addition, the care workers were occasionally expected to do shifts in other group homes in the same service unit. This was apparently thought to ease the substitution of staff members. A result of this was constant changes in care relationships. Leo's coordinating care worker, for example, problematised these practices; she emphasised how Leo does not trust just anybody and becomes often emotionally distressed when an unfamiliar care worker approaches him. She said that the inhabitants should have regular care workers, but that there was very little she could do about it since her view was not shared by other staff members of the unit.

Some care workers expressed similar concerns. They told us that our research participants had different kinds of relationships with different care workers, and notable preferences as regards who worked with them. For example, Frida's coordinating care worker explained that they had established a close relationship, and Frida was quite picky about care workers. Also, in Frida's housing unit work tasks had been rearranged to ensure their equal distribution between care workers. This rearrangement meant that Frida's coordinating care worker had recently not been able to work with Frida at all. While the coordinating care worker appreciated the worry over an equal share of workload, she critically commented how this arrangement did not meet care users' needs ('*ei oo asukaslähtöstä*').

In comparison, in Anna's and Ella's group homes, care workers were organised into teams so that each resident had four to five permanent care workers. This enabled stable care relations and mutual interaction between care workers and the persons they cared for. In addition, while the staff–resident ratio in Anna's and Ella's group homes was otherwise similar to other group homes, the residents were very different in terms of their need for assistance. This reduced the workload of the staff and opened up possibilities for interaction with the residents. Furthermore, many residents in Ella's group home had personal assistants who accompanied them to leisure time activities and helped them to have social interactions outside the care unit. This extra resource supported social interaction because it gave the group home's staff more time with the remaining residents.

Ella's group home was socially very lively, and that was, at least partly, boosted by residents' heterogeneity. The residents had the habit of talking casually about their day at the day centre, about their plans for the evening, or talking about television programmes, music, sports events or whatever was of interest to them. This kind of social interaction was a natural part of that group home's everyday life that took place when the residents were, for example, preparing and eating dinner, or getting ready for hobbies. This group home was busy with everyday talk and action – the way homes often are. For Ella this meant that she could listen to daily discussions, follow residents and care workers to the kitchen or living room, and in this way connect to the social activities around her. The contrast with contexts where most residents were non-verbal and had extensive support needs was huge. Quotidian discussions were limited in those group homes to the care workers' interactions with each other. Interestingly, one of Frida's care workers had noted how Frida enjoyed following other people's discussions and activities. Since Frida's housemates were mostly non-verbal, care workers sometimes took her to another group home in the same building, where the residents were younger, verbal and able to move independently. These visits offered Frida opportunities to enjoy social life in ways that were not possible in her own group home.

More than half of Ella's housemates were verbal, and some were quite independent in many everyday tasks, like preparing their own meals or using independently public transport. This heterogeneity opened up new possibilities for Ella's social interactions: while she still had her limitations in relation to communication, some of the housemates were able to interact and communicate with her momentarily through fleeting verbal exchanges and touches (like Paul stroking Ella's hair while she leaned against his shoulder). Sometimes these moments of interaction were supported or supervised by a care worker, who explained Ella's intentions to her housemates and guided them, like in the following extract, where Senja, a new resident in the group home, meets Ella:

> Ella walks across the kitchen over to Senja. Care worker notices this, 'Look, Ella came to say hi.' Senja pulls Ella over to her, gives her a hug with one hand, Ella raises her gaze, smiles with a wrinkled face, pushing her tongue out. Senja lets go of Ella, moves away a little bit, Ella follows her, then leans her head against Senja's arm, apparently tries to take hold of her arm with her teeth since Senja cries out laughingly 'Help, don't eat me Ella!'. The care worker walks over to Ella, gives her a big hug by standing behind her, 'What are you up to Ella?' Walks over to the kitchen table with Ella. Senja comments: 'Thanks for saving me.' (Field notes, with Ella)

The care workers told that sometimes they consciously paid special attention to Ella, just to make sure that she got her share of their time. In a heterogeneous group, residents who were more capable in expressing their needs could demand more attention, and it was the care workers' responsibility to stand up for Ella. The time reserved for Ella consisted typically of one-to-one interaction, like sitting together in a swing or sofa (in the common spaces), with Ella sitting on a care worker's lap, singing songs or nursery rhymes and clapping together, which was Ella's favourite activity. Ella would also regularly spend one-to-one time with her care workers during walks in the neighbourhood, or trips to the swimming pool.

Other group homes were less successful in securing social opportunities for their residents. Especially in group homes with only people with severe or profound intellectual disability, interaction between the residents was rare, even when they spent time together in common areas. In Frida's, Hugo's and Leo's group homes it was common practice to bring residents together to watch TV in the common spaces. This was an unsuccessful attempt to initiate social interaction between the residents. In our view, fostering interaction in such moments would have required that a care worker had taken part in the activity, and engaged the residents in interaction, for example by talking about the TV programmes.

On some occasions, the care workers made attempts to encourage friendships between the residents. For example, Frida's care workers placed her and another young lady living in her group home close to each other as often as possible. While the two sometimes briefly interacted, the interactions (which consisted of short exchanges of utterances while watching cartoons) appeared to us to be vague and somewhat random in nature: the presence of her housemate did not seem make Frida as delighted and excited as the company of persons she particularly seemed to enjoy. Similarly, Frida was not keeping up 'the conversation' in the way that she often did with care workers, her parents and Reetta.

In contexts that had mostly non-verbal residents, the lack of social interaction was not strongly problematised. While some care workers talked critically about the lack of opportunities, their criticism was steered towards small details of the organisation of work, and the non-social lives of the residents remained unchallenged. One explanation for this was the care workers' conceptions about persons with PIMD. Some of the residents were seen to be predetermined to an impoverished social existence due to their profound impairments.

> I ask the care worker about Sebastian's schedule for the rest of the evening. She answers that she is not sure because she is only temporarily working in this group home, and that I should ask the other care worker. As I repeat the question to the other care worker, Vera, she says that there is nothing else in plans but hanging around. The other care worker says that this is what she would have said as well, but didn't have the courage to do so. Vera explains Sebastian's evening schedule – or lack of it – by saying that 'this lot needs so much care after all'. The other care worker adds that the other group homes of the unit are 'completely different'. When I ask how, she gives a description of the individual abilities of the inhabitants of these group homes – they have fewer limitations in functioning than the inhabitants of Sebastian's group home. (Field notes, with Sebastian)

In this extract, the care workers explain the differences between the two group homes with differences in the degree of support these two groups of residents require. The focus and content of the care work in the discussed group homes are determined by the individual qualities (i.e. impairments and support needs) of the residents. The needs of Sebastian and his housemates are seen as so extensive that there is no possibility to do much else than meet those immediate needs. That the substitute care worker did not have 'the courage' to say that they had no other plans for the evening except just hang around suggests that she, at least, did not see this as an ideal state of affairs.

But it became clear to us that in some group homes, and for many care workers, facilitating residents' social interaction was something marginal; the residents were not considered social beings who had a right to be included in everyday social activities. Disheartening manifestations of this kind of dismissal were situations where, for example, Frida was placed sitting alone, back towards others, peeking over her shoulder towards others, while the care workers talked about the private affairs of other residents (such as their care or medication) over a cup of coffee, as if Frida did not even exist. It is hard to explain this kind of dismissal by anything other than a conception that for people like Frida it did not really matter. She could not understand or take part in the discussion, so why bother?

Thus, differing opportunities for social lives in different group homes reflect differing views about the competence of people with PIMD, as well as differing views about care culture: to what extent persons with PIMD are seen to be able to enjoy social relationships, and to what extent existing practices and resources at group homes enable such relationships. What was considered to be possible determined what was normal and acceptable in these contexts. In Frida's and Hugo's group home it was only normal that everyday interaction revolved around care tasks, which were initiated by care workers, and only very rarely was the sole focus of action socialising, just spending time together. But in Ella's group home lively social interaction that included all residents, irrespective of their capacities, was considered to be normal. When asked, Ella's care worker said that she could not imagine it in any other way.

Conclusion

On the whole, our research participants had different kinds of opportunities for social interaction in their everyday lives. The care workers of the group homes were their primary social contacts and it was mostly up to them whether persons with PIMD could develop social lives of any kind. Keeping company with the residents, however, was not among the central responsibilities of the care workers in most of the group homes in our study, despite the fact that the care workers said that all our research participants enjoyed social interaction. This conflict was explained by limited resources and work cultures that forced the staff to prioritise basic care tasks. As a result, social interaction was limited mostly to constricted moments of care provision.

These kinds of practice in group homes are clearly a by-product of the deinstitutionalisation policy that has failed to address the realities of the lives of persons with PIMD and to ask what a social life in their community in reality requires from social services. In the current Finnish intellectual disability policy, social inclusion and participation are something that should take place outside the service system, in mainstream society. Yet, the primary social relations of persons with PIMD are within disability services, outside mainstream society. The problem is that these services lack the necessary resources and a clear vision of how to enable the social lives of people with PIMD.

The emphasis on social relations outside the intellectual disability services is understandable on a policy level. But this emphasis ignores and devalues the social relations formed within group homes. The relations between the staff and residents of group homes have the potential to improve the social lives of those with PIMD and offer them a sense of affiliation. This would require a conceptualisation of interpersonal relations to be valuable as such, as a crucial part of a good professional practice. Sensitive and empathetic care work requires emotional involvement in any case, so being professional with persons with PIMD does not imply emotional and social detachment (Kittay, 1999). The care workers in the group homes we talked to would agree, at least in word. But their actions or, perhaps more accurately, their care practices did not always agree with their words.

Providing homes for people with intellectual disability is a central goal of deinstitutionalisation policy. However, home is understood in current disability policy mainly in terms of privacy and self-determination, for example as the right to one's own room in a group home. Having a private space is undeniably also important for persons with PIMD. However, it can also mean loneliness if they are simply left alone and isolated in their own rooms.

The practices of some of the group homes positioned social interaction at the margins of care work, whereas in some other contexts social relations and interaction were valued and care work was conducted accordingly. These were group homes where just hanging out and having fun (see Johnson, Douglas, Bigby, & Iacono, 2012b) were seen valuable, and all inhabitants, regardless of their impairments, were encouraged to relate to other people. The staff engaged with each person's individual way of communicating and acting, no matter how quirky they might have seemed.

The differences between group homes cannot be explained merely by different resources. The differences have to do more with a care culture that either ensures or does not that the resources are used in ways that enable social relationships. If the value of social life for people with PIMD is not recognised, it is unlikely to materialise. Interestingly, when Reetta asked the care workers in Ella's group home about the central values and aims of their work, they immediately provided well-thought-out and well-articulated answers in which, for example, the need for social interactions was acknowledged. But care workers in Hugo's and Frida's groups had difficulties engaging with the question. We do not, however, wish to suggest that the differences between group home care cultures depends solely on individual care workers and their 'attitudes' or awareness of the aims and values guiding their work. One possibility would be to explain the differences regarding care culture as matters of leadership. In their study, Clement and Bigby (2010) underline the importance of the way each individual group home is managed. Leadership is undoubtedly important in the process of implementing the values and aims of the care work, but leadership as such rarely explains the differences in group home care cultures. After all, managers and house supervisors work in organisational structures that force them to prioritise different work tasks (Clement & Bigby, 2010).

Epilogue: Ella at a rock concert

What might social inclusion look like and what would it require in the case of persons with PIMD? Consider the following episode from our ethnographic data. This episode took place in a park in the middle of a city, in a busy open-air concert. After having carefully thought through Ella's preferences (she very much enjoys rhythmic music) and the activities accessible to her (she has a substantial visual impairment), Ella's PA decided to take her to a rock concert in a park, to enjoy the music and the outdoors.

Ella and her PA (as well as Reetta) are sitting on a lawn; Ella is rocking herself along with the music, surrounded by other people. This episode represents how the intimate and public layers of social participation intertwine: Ella's and her PA's mostly non-verbal interaction and closeness, and how the emotional and physical support provided by the PA enables Ella to take part in this event, enjoy the presence of others, different sounds and noises, the breeze of the wind and the warmth of the sunshine.

> We are sitting on a lawn, surrounded by people, some distance away from the stage but still close enough to hear the music clearly. PA moves his rucksack behind him and lies down, head on the rucksack, next to Ella. Ella is sitting and rocking herself in a low pace, PA touches Ella every now and then, Ella takes hold of PA's hand and claps the ground and/or PA's belly with his hand. Sometimes Ella stops rocking, gaze lifted up, smiling. [Wind is blowing to the spot where we are sitting; it seems that Ella stops to feel the breeze in her hair.] After a while Ella grabs some grass and sticks of the ground to take them into her mouth [as she had done previously], I take these off her hand, and finally the PA draws Ella back to lie against him [in order to stop Ella from eating grass and soil]. Ella stays leaning her elbows against PA and her head to her hands, sometimes clapping PA's hand with her own hand, but otherwise looking very peaceful, listening to music, smiling.

This moment of inclusion in a park can be read as an end product of a long process that required the kind of culture in Ella's housing unit that has nurtured social interaction and belonging, acknowledged Ella as a social being, and worked insistently with her to develop the means to strengthen her social life. It also required financial resources in the form of personal assistance (which is very uncommon in Finland for people with PIMD) and, finally, a PA who is personally committed to working with Ella, to trying new activities, surroundings and events so that Ella can develop new areas of interest, and new spheres of inclusion.

Chapter 5: Age-Appropriate Lives

Introduction

In this chapter, we will analyse cultural conceptions about youth in relation to young adults with profound intellectual and multiple disabilities. Our starting point is a realisation that took place during the fieldwork: while our research participants were of different ages, it seemed that their chronological age had only a little, if any, significance in their lives. This was especially apparent in relation to the ways their support, services and everyday lives in general had been organised. But, while the service *system* did not appear to be sensitive to age, our data included numerous comments and thoughts related to chronological age by staff and family members. This contradiction seemed most poignant when looking at the youngest participants of our study, who were in their early twenties during the fieldwork.

The research literature has repeatedly highlighted how most people with intellectual disability still face barriers in the pursuit of full adult status; they have commonly been conceptualised as eternal children, and are often subjected to infantilising practices (e.g. Baron, Riddell, & Wilson, 1999; Bjarnason, 2002; Johnson & Walmsley, 2010). Additionally, research focusing on transitions of young people with severe or profound intellectual disability has highlighted the problems arising from the lack of forms of support and services that meet the specific needs of this group of young people (e.g. Clegg et al., 2008; Gauthier-Boudreault, Gallagher, & Couture, 2017).

While the existing research on young people with intellectual disability has produced valuable observations concerning the

How to cite this book chapter:
Vehmas, S. and Mietola, R. 2021. *Narrowed Lives: Meaning, Moral Value, and Profound Intellectual Disability*. Pp. 113–133. Stockholm: Stockholm University Press. DOI: https://doi.org/10.16993/bbl.e. License: CC-BY 4.0.

inequalities that they face, the notion of youth (like any other age category) seems to be treated as self-evident truth in this body of research. We would argue that concepts like 'adult status' or 'age-specific-needs' are unintelligible in the case of young persons with PIMD unless the qualities and cultural meanings attached to different age categories are unpacked properly. Age categories need to be analysed in order to make visible the cultural ideals and norms linked to them. Thus, in order to make sense of accounts such as 'he is, after all, a young man', as one care worker referred to Hugo, we need to unpack meanings attached to 'being young', and how they relate to the young person in question.

Our analysis here focuses on data produced with one participant, Hugo, a young man in his early twenties. In Hugo's life the question of youth was especially pronounced: while Hugo lived quite an active life during the fieldwork due to his current status as a student, his life in general was described by people close to him as 'narrow' and lacking the qualities that Hugo 'as a young man' should be able to access. We felt that these arguments resonated with the focus of our study, the question of a good life, because these kinds of statements seem to assume that young people should be able to pursue certain things in order to flourish.

What difference does age make?

What caused us to pay attention to how age was addressed in our data and to wonder the (in)significance of age in this context was most likely the tradition of normalisation that we as Nordic academics have absorbed since student days. Normalisation in its different forms has had a profound impact on intellectual disability service systems around the world, especially in the Nordic countries (e.g. Culham & Nind, 2003; Simpson, 2018). It is based upon the conviction that persons with intellectual disability should have access to 'patterns and conditions of everyday life which are as close as possible to the norms and patterns of the mainstream of society' (Nirje, 1970, p. 62), and that they should be able to, as much as possible, establish and/or maintain personal behaviours and characteristics that are typical in the culture they happen to live (Wolfensberger, 1972, p. 28). One crucial demand that normalisation entails is respect for age-appropriateness in all areas of life that affect one's status and identity in a given culture. In short, people with intellectual disability should have the opportunity 'to undergo normal developmental experiences of the life cycle' (Nirje, 1969, p. 182) and do what members of their peer group of the same age are doing; adults with intellectual disability should be recognised as adults with the same expectations, demands, liberties and responsibilities as other adults (Wolfensberger, 1972, pp. 180–181).

In practice, as William Bronston (1976, pp. 508–511) advises, this all means that adults with intellectual disability should live like adults in general do; in apartments that are not furnished like nurseries but in ways that are typical for people of their age. Ordinary life rhythm means that they do not necessarily need midday naps and that they can study and work according to an ordinary schedule. Persons with intellectual disability should also be able to enjoy similar rights as their peers regarding mundane things such as health care, movement, privacy, work, leisure, socialising, drink, smoking and sexuality. Finally, since appearance is a powerful interpreter of age, it is important that one's clothing, accessories, hairdos, cosmetics and so on are in line with one's age. If the previous considerations are violated, 'a dehumanizing cycle evolves: A handicapped adult is seen and treated as a child' (Bronston, 1976, p. 510).

While age-appropriateness has achieved an established position in the services as an important instrument for achieving equality for the service users with intellectual disability, it has also been criticised for resulting in the kinds of practices that restrict people's agency when their preferences and behaviour have been interpreted as being inappropriate in relation to their chronological age (e.g. Forster, 2010). It has also been argued that the normalisation principle has lost relevance in the services during the past decades, as other concepts such as inclusion, empowerment and citizenship have taken a firm position as guiding principles in disability services (Vesala, 2010).

Our discussion here returns to the arguments concerning age-appropriateness raised by the normalisation principle. As mentioned above, our data suggest that age still has relevance for the professionals when making sense of the quality of services, and, ultimately, of the lives of the service users. We focus in

particular on the possibilities and restrictions that the applica-
tion of the principle of age-appropriateness might produce to the
lives of people with PIMD (Forster, 2010). Additionally, our aim
here is to contribute to the academic discussion concerning complexities and tensions faced in the implementation of policy recommendations in relation to people with PIMD (e.g. Bigby et al.,
2009; Parry Hughes et al., 2011).

Hugo

Hugo lives in a group home, where he has his own room with a
bathroom. Four other men, all older (some considerably older),
also reside there. The group home is part of a larger housing unit
that consists of four group homes altogether. Hugo moved to his
current home a few years ago from an intellectual disability institution, where he had lived since he was 11 years old. Moving
to the group home and getting his own private room presented a
major transition in Hugo's life. He was also studying in a vocational special education school at the time of the fieldwork, which
provided Hugo with lots of new activities and social contacts.

Hugo does not speak or use any alternative (formal) communication method. Interaction with him is based on gestures, facial
expressions and touch. The people who work with Hugo think
that he is quite easy to interpret: he clearly expresses when he is
content and when he is not. The interviewed care workers also
described Hugo as a determined person who indicates (for example, by shouting) when he is in need of attention or help. Hugo
has cognitive, physical and visual impairments. He has cerebral
palsy and uses a wheelchair. He requires help in feeding, dressing, and caring for his personal hygiene. He is unable to move
his wheelchair on his own, but he can lift his hands and point
at things. When sitting up, Hugo is able to hold his head up and
turn his head. Controlling his body does, however, require lots of
effort, and he gets exhausted easily. Hugo's physical well-being
was a repeated topic during the fieldwork and the professionals
who worked with him felt that it had been neglected ever since his
transition from school to adult services. He had had no therapy of
any kind for his spasticity, which made him very tense and tired,

and which made even his dressing difficult. However, during the fieldwork, Hugo began physiotherapy with the aim of relaxing his body and increasing his mobility.

Reetta conducted a three-month period fieldwork, spending two days a week at Hugo's group home and at the school that he attended every weekday. At that time, these constituted the only contexts of Hugo's everyday life: since Hugo had no additional support (e.g. personal assistance) or hobbies, he had practically no opportunity to engage in activities outside these contexts. While major changes had taken place in Hugo's life recently in terms of housing and education, his life was generally characterised as 'narrow'; he had a very limited social network and only occasionally did he have the chance for leisure time outside the housing unit. At home, Hugo spent a lot of time alone. Hugo needed help and support to initiate and maintain social interaction. Other residents in his group home also had extensive support needs and multiple impairments that affected their capacity to communicate. Staff resources in the group home were very limited, and the staff who were there were primarily allocated to basic care tasks. As a result, while Hugo was repeatedly described as being sociable, in practice he had very limited opportunities to socialise. Hugo's leisure time was filled with activities that he could do on his own: he enjoyed listening to music and audiobooks lying in his bed and was engaged with this activity for hours, every day.

The data analysed in this chapter consists of four interviews discussing Hugo and his life: interviews with Hugo's mother, two care workers working in his group home and his teacher in the vocational school. The care workers and the teacher were in charge of Hugo's individual care and educational plans, as well as being involved in the everyday care work.

In our analysis, we draw from analytical perspectives developed in the field of sociology of age. Our analysis has been particularly inspired by notions concerning the naturalisation of age: at the same time as age is something that is always accomplished (by acting in ways that conventionally signal age), it also is something that becomes invisible when it is 'done' appropriately – when we 'act our age' (Laz, 1998). We only become conscious about age when someone 'fails' to act according to normative expectations related to, say, adulthood. In these moments, age suddenly requires explanation. Our analysis was motivated by the notion of the accountability of age (Laz, 1998; Nikander, 2000); we wondered why our interviewees needed to account for age, and what is done with these accounts – what kind of arguments are built around the notion of youth.

The meaning of youth

[Reetta asks from the care worker what has school brought into Hugo's life] Well, now he's got a normal everyday life. Like leaving for school or work. Young person. He used to go to the day centre, as a half-day [client], but that did not meet Hugo's needs at all. There [at school] they have, lots of activities since Hugo comes home tired. And it's good when you are tired after work or school day. And I feel that there are a lot less of those yelling attacks. Which he had at one point. It could have been that the young person was bored, here in the middle of the 'fossils'. Since it is quiet, the upstairs gang is quite old, the downstairs group is younger. So it [school] has really brought lots of substance into Hugo's life.

The conception of youth appears culturally very particular in our interviewees' talk. In the extract above, for example, being a young person is directly associated with 'normal everyday life': a life in line with Western societal conventions of an individual who is active, who goes to school or to work. This kind of image of 'normal youth' also resonates with current youth policies, where young people not going to school or work (so-called NEET youth) are immediately problematised. In our data, the notion of being active, however, includes any activity that takes place outside one's home. Thus, leisure activities taking place outside one's home would be considered a sign of a normal, active life. The interviewees also conceptualise the ideal of 'being active' in relation to passivity and lack of activities: a state of being that very much characterised Hugo's life before he started his current studies.

[Reetta asks about a good life, whether Hugo is living a good life] 'Well the good thing is that he is currently studying, that he got into this school. And at home, like a good life. Um. Well, what I would like to happen, I'm not sure, it might be a struggle, but that Hugo would have some more, like hobbies, or like, activities.

And some, like friends. That Hugo's life at home is like quite stereotypical, like same all over again. Like the good thing probably
is that the basic needs are met every day, of course, not talking
about that. ... But, well. Like those social skills and the psychological ones. That Hugo's life is pretty basic, quite narrow like,
nothing really happens.'

When analysing these representations of youth and good life,
our thinking was immediately drawn to questions concerning
age-appropriateness and its usage in the services for people with
intellectual disability. While age-appropriateness has worked in
the services as an important tool for enhancing equality of the
service users, it has also been noted that the services have adopted a very particular interpretation of age-appropriateness – one
that emphasises cultural normativity of action (e.g. Forster, 2010;
Vesala, 2010). This notion seems to also be relevant in relation to
our data. The care workers' accounts draw on a culturally specific, normative conception of youth. Additionally, these accounts
can be interpreted to suggest that this conception can and should
be applied to Hugo in an unfiltered fashion. Firstly, according
to these arguments a young person should live an active life, go to
school or work, and have friends and hobbies, and, since Hugo is
a young person, his life should be measured against these normative expectations regarding youth. Secondly, in the care workers'
accounts, certain needs are connected to 'being young'. It is not
just an active life that Hugo needs – he has also specific psychological and social needs that are part of 'being young' (see Gauthier-
Boudreault et al., 2017).

   Should we think that people of Hugo's age ought to live an active life, according to the prevalent normative conception of youth
in all areas of life in the spirit of normalisation (Wolfensberger,
1972, pp. 180–181), the principle of age-appropriateness faces problems. As Forster (2010, p. 129) has argued, age-appropriateness
'could be used to deprive an individual of activities others
consider inconsistent with the person's chronological age'. This
would be particularly harmful in the case of people with PIMD
since the vast majority of their practical needs do not have age-
equivalent corollaries because their 'comprehension of the social world, and in turn the person's social interaction needs, are
quite distinct from that of age-equivalent peers' (Forster, 2010,

p. 130). Thus, if strict age-appropriateness were applied, we would have to take away from adults with profound intellectual disability their precious teethers, dolls and bedtime toys, and we would have to prevent Hugo from listening to his favourite fairy tales or watching his favourite cartoons. That would be a way to suppress the little self-determination he has the chance to practise in his life.

Perhaps, then, limited use of age-appropriateness would be feasible, meaning it would be used 'as a principle for opening up opportunit[ies] in a person's life' (Forster, 2010, p. 131). This kind of policy would, in fact, be in line with the care workers' way of thinking as well. In our interpretation, they use age-appropriateness to highlight the inequality Hugo experiences, to stress his *right* to lead a more active life, and to have better access to the kinds of experiences that young people of his age usually have. In addition, when the interviewees talked about youth and active life, they were calling for more activities, friends and hobbies without taking a stance as to what they should look like (e.g. what counts as friendship). This is the kind of mentality that takes into account both objective ideals (e.g. active life) and Hugo's subjective preferences. These arguments are, however, based on notions concerning Hugo and his life circumstances: how he enjoys socialising, but still spends lots of time alone; how his everyday life has included long periods with very little activities available to him.

When we continued to analyse the above extracts in more detail and focused specifically on what kinds of qualities were attached to Hugo and PIMD in general, and how the differences between Hugo's life and an 'active life' are explained, we noticed that the accounts were critical of the service system. In the second extract, the care worker explicitly associates the 'stereotypic' nature of Hugo's life to the way his life has been organised, not to Hugo himself: stereotypic life is not the result of profound intellectual disability as such; it is the result of insufficient and inappropriate services (lack of activities, hobbies and friends). Consequently, accounts that emphasise activeness also challenge dominant understandings of PIMD as a passive state, characterised by deficiencies and limitations. 'Being active' is represented as congruent with Hugo's needs, as beneficial to him, and, most importantly, as something a person with PIMD can also be. By suggesting that there are some age-specific needs, attention is turned away from Hugo's impairments. With the youth talk, the care workers thus point out how Hugo is not just a person with profound intellectual and multiple disabilities but also, and perhaps more importantly, a young person.

Youth talk and the post-institutional care system

Hugo's age was mentioned early on during the first days of the fieldwork when Reetta talked about Hugo's interests and preferences with the group home's personnel. They explained that Hugo loves to listen to audiobooks, especially a particular CD of fairy tales, which was almost worn out due to its repeated use. Similar discussions occurred when the care workers looked for television programmes that would interest Hugo. Usually, Hugo watched children's programmes. According to the care workers, this was because there was only a limited number of programmes directed to grown-ups that were accessible (e.g. plain language). It seemed that the care workers felt they had to explain and justify these choices, and openly stated their awareness that these programmes were not age-appropriate. At the same time, the care workers emphasised how these programmes, books and music were the ones Hugo enjoyed and the ones that were accessible to him.

Age thus was a concern for the care workers – an issue they were aware of and sensitive to. We made similar observations with our other research participants: the professionals working with them repeatedly discussed our participants' preferences in terms of music, clothing and activities, and how these related to their chronological age. While we immediately interpreted these accounts as making visible how age-appropriateness is still used by the care workers as a central way to make sense of the values and targets of their work, we were however somewhat confused why this topic had to be repeatedly raised with us. It seemed that age had to be accounted for in these moments where the practices did not follow the (unwritten) rule of age-appropriate behaviour.

The concept of age is ultimately normative: 'When we say "act your age" we press for behaviour that conforms to norms' (Laz,

1998, p. 86). And, when we fail to act our age, we need to account for our action (Laz, 1998; Nikander, 2000). In the intellectual disability service system, however, this accountability is placed on the care workers: it is not Hugo who 'fails' to 'act his age', but instead it is the care system – and ultimately the care workers – that fail to provide him a life that parallels his chronological age. This is why age needs to be addressed. And, indeed, in the interviews Hugo's age was mainly discussed in relation to the wider question of how the care system is able to respond to needs of care users, of different ages:

> [I ask the care worker how does good life materialise in Hugo's life] We listen to Hugo when he's got something to say. And we try to find means of expression so that Hugo can express what is [the matter]. And of course, if we had better resources, going outside the house more during weekends. He is anyhow, well, he's not like middle-aged yet. And well, the middle-aged do go [out] too (laughs).

The Finnish intellectual disability system is still going through de-institutionalisation of services: while transition to and development of community care has been the primary policy emphasis since the 1970s, some individuals with intellectual disability are still living in intellectual disability institutions. Deinstitutionalisation is also strongly present in our data: four out of six of our research participants had moved out of these hospitals, three only recently, and many of the care workers participating in our study had also at some point worked in these institutions. While our research participants' homes were located in ordinary neighbourhoods, they lived in large housing units, with little or no influence over where and how they live. The aim of these services is to provide service users opportunities to live ordinary lives in ordinary surroundings. However, the limited availability of support and staff often means that the service users, who have extensive needs for support, actually have very limited possibilities to participate in activities outside their living units.

Bearing in mind the history of the disability service system, the care workers' comments concerning age can be conceptualised as moral accounts (see Bergmann, 1998). With references to Hugo's age, the interviewees make visible their critical stance in relation to the current state of the services. These accounts form a counter-narrative that challenges the dominant policy discourse and exposes the institutional qualities of care still present in intellectual disability services. Thus, when the interviewees point out the narrowness of Hugo's life, or the limited opportunities of the care users to take part in activities outside one's home, as in the extract above, the interviewees produce concrete and critical examples of how the services do not live up to the values and targets of the current policy.

The above extract makes visible also how the youth talk can be used in the services, and why there is a need for these types of argument. Hugo's age can be used as an argument in negotiations concerning the use of limited (staff) resources in the unit. While on a general level Hugo's right to self-determination ('to be heard') and social inclusion ('get out of the house') is recognised by the care workers, in everyday care work the use of resources is considered from the viewpoint of all the residents in group homes. When time and support are distributed from a shared 'pot' of limited resources, care users' interests might collide. Thus, references to age and related needs can be used to emphasise the special importance of Hugo having opportunities to live an 'active life'. Since the principle of age-appropriateness is still acknowledged, age also makes a powerful argument within the service system.

Youth lost in the service system

Earlier research has highlighted how there is a general lack of specific services targeted to young persons and young adults with profound intellectual disability; in the transition from children's services to adult services, activities and support tend to decrease (e.g. Gauthier-Boudreault et al., 2017; Hudson, 2006; Morris, 1999). Similarly, the availability of different types of rehabilitative services, such as physiotherapy or speech therapy, tends to decrease after paediatric services, and the criteria for entitlement for these services become more stringent. Usually, young people and their families have only limited post-school options to choose from. In Finland, the typical option offered is a placement in a day activity centre. These units, however, cater for service users of very different needs and ages and have a high user-to-staff ratio.

In Hugo's life this lack of suitable support and service had actualised in all the major transitions: in his move from childhood home to intellectual disability institution (which was at the time offered as the only available option), and also in the transition from comprehensive school to day activity centre (Mietola, 2018). While the interviewees felt that major positive changes had taken place in Hugo's life recently since he moved to the group home and started school, general worry and criticism towards the service system is still present in the data:

> Teacher: Well, I've understood that there is a background of multiple years, that Hugo had transferred to the day activity centre, kind of directly from the comprehensive school. So like, multiple years, have gone kind of down a pit. That has been a young man's active time like many years have gone in a way that there might not have been active support there so that Hugo could bring out his own expression and such.

In the above extract, the teacher describes how after comprehensive school Hugo's path has ended up in 'a pit'. With this metaphor, the teacher refers to the void between children's and adult services (Morris, 1999). While the metaphor points out the lack of specific services targeted to youth, the teacher's account also underlines how this fall into the pit has materialised as a break in Hugo's life course and development. The lack of active support in the critical years of young person's life has not only deprived Hugo of learning but also questioned the efforts of maintaining the already acquired skills (Gauthier-Boudreault et al., 2017). The teacher's account does not merely emphasise the specificity of young people's needs but also highlights how the service system ignores youth as a specific phase of life, as a time of change, development and learning (see Priestley, 2003). This builds a harsh contrast between the ways young people are approached in Western societies in general, as a future resource, and youth as a state of becoming (see Honkatukia, 2017).

During the interview, Hugo's teacher also verbalised the key differences between school and day activity services; it is not only a matter of resources but the target of the services. In schools, all activities are planned and evaluated with learning and development in mind (as required by the national curriculum), whereas the social services lack a similar binding goal. Thus, the transition from school to day activity services also means a significant change in terms of expectations and goals: what is expected from an individual and what kinds of future plans are made for him or her. Instead of making future plans by supporting and making use of existing skills (and setting new goals for learning and development on top of them), the services might not even recognise these skills – or even approach the young person as an individual with the potential for learning and development in the first place.

> Teacher: Like here [at school] we are now using loads of resources on that one student, for one to three years, and do lots of work, and have quite intensive time. But does that carry, if there are no services later on? Or that it [resources] falls into a total minimum. And then, there are no resources, like there in the group home, or elsewhere. So like, where does it lead to.

> [I ask Hugo's mother what her thoughts and hopes are concerning Hugo's future, after school] Well they don't have anything similar then, like where Hugo could continue, there isn't. Where they would still [train] the communication skills and such, like would in a similar manner train, but other than that, I don't really know. … The danger is of course that those skills acquired when you don't keep them up, then they will decline. And there will not be available any learning [of] new [skills], you need to support learning. So it's like really sad, I think.

In the above accounts, the teacher and mother express their worries regarding Hugo's future. While lifelong learning has an established position in education and disability policy internationally, our data suggests that the right to lifelong learning is not recognised in the case of persons with PIMD. Rather, the lives of our research participants were characterised by stagnation. Even with the youngest research participants in their twenties, there was a notable lack of discussion among the care workers about their future plans or personal life objectives. It seems that there is no need for such planning or visioning when the service user is placed into appropriate housing and day activity services. While there might be a discussion concerning different types of rehabilitative services or possibilities of getting support person for leisure activities, the bigger picture remains unchallenged.

This type of stagnation is most poignant in the case of a young person, like Hugo. Everyone working with Hugo emphasised the positive impacts of going back to school, and some expressed concerns about his post-school options. However, there seemed to be very little consideration of how the service system could provide Hugo lifelong opportunities to develop to his fullest potential. Instead of expecting a transition that would provide him with more opportunities, the interviewees expect another fall into a pit.

Returning to our discussion about the parallels between the lives of Hugo and his non-disabled peers, the most poignant difference for us is the way youth as a stage of planning and visioning is not present in Hugo's life. The fact that his life course deviates from the normative life course seems to mean that there is a lack of '"horizon" for orientation and planning of life' (Kohli, 2007, p. 256). There is no plan B, an established narrative for visioning and forming a dignified life plan for a young person with PIMD. It is not only youth that might get lost in the system but also a vision of the future.

Conclusion

We have discussed in this chapter the ways professionals in the care system talk about youth in order to highlight and promote young care users' rights. This kind of tactical use of the principle of age-appropriateness allows the care workers to discuss problematic aspects of the current services, and make concrete claims for change in a service system that already recognises the worth of the principle. The youth talk provides the interviewees also a means for 'indirect mode of moralising' (Bergmann, 1998); by addressing Hugo's age, the interviewees draw attention to urgent problems present in the care service system, or even in the service unit they work themselves. With the youth talk, they make us researchers aware of their critical views, and about their personal and professional values and targets, even if these contradict the everyday realities of the services.

The existing body of research has shown how people with intellectual disability have traditionally been deprived of recognition of their adulthood. We have, however, paid attention in this chapter to how Hugo, and other persons with PIMD, may not even be recognised as young people, with the interests, needs and rights young people tend to have. Our analysis suggests that, in the case of young people with profound intellectual disability, youth as a phase of life gets lost in the intellectual disability service system.

Admittedly, the general policy of lifelong learning or reaching 'one's full potential' might seem abstract and difficult to put into practice in relation to people with profound intellectual disability (see Kauppila, Mietola, & Niemi, 2018). Still, the worries raised by our interviewees concerning Hugo's future, in particular in relation to development, learning or even change, are worth noting. In our view, without future-orientated plans, the wider questions about targets and commitments of care and services, or even considerations about good life, are overrun by practices that merely keep the service users 'content' and fulfil their basic needs regarding housing, food and hygiene (but nothing else). The element of warehousing, the 'narrowness' of the lives of the care users, is not accidental or merely a result of insufficient resources. We would argue that it is also the result of the lack of ethical engagement with the meaning of a good life for persons with PIMD. In other words, the system in its all goodwill has focused on meeting the basic needs for food, rest and bodily health but ignored more general engagement to think and vision what kinds of ideals, norms and values should guide its policies and practices.

The current services offer very limited opportunities to our research participants to experience anything new. It is likely that Hugo's interests and preferences will stay the same, and they continue to be met in a similar manner. In other words, Hugo will stay the same because he is not given the chance to change. While Hugo appears content, it is a different matter whether he lives a good life within a service system that too often settles for warehousing and stagnation. In his care workers' view, a good life is about genuine opportunities for new experiences ('get out of the house'), to learn new skills and maintain the ones he has. These opportunities require options and resources from the service system. Similarly, attaining these rights would require the service system to approach individuals with PIMD and their needs in a new way: not as fixed objects of care but as changing subjects with dreams and aspirations. If we do not know what they might be, we can either give up and resort to warehousing or offer these persons new sources of experience in order to work out what new skills and experiences would be in line with their personalities.

Epilogue: making sense of age-appropriateness

The normalisation principle has taught us that chronological age is a significant factor in the organisation of societal services, including the intellectual disability service system. When they are perceived as children, people with intellectual disability cannot be granted the rights and status that humans in general are entitled to. Sensitivity to chronological age thus seems justified in order to guarantee the respect and recognition to which people with intellectual disability are entitled to as fellow human beings. But, when age-related concerns are expressed in very concrete terms with references to, for example, fashion (Bronston, 1976), they very soon become outdated since such phenomena change constantly. Age-related norms are inherently cultural and contextual. It is not a law of nature that it is appropriate for someone to wear high heels and make up after the age of 15 or to take afternoon naps before the age of seven or after 70. This is despite the fact that age is often seen as an objective fact defined chronologically by the number of years one has lived. But there is nothing inherent in numbers and the number of years one has lived. What matters is the way chronology is given meaning by using it 'as an organizing principle for individual and social life' (Laz, 1998, p. 92).

Age is in many ways comparable to gender. Biology sets some limits on gender and age categories, but it is the cultural expectations conveyed through socialisation that makes males and females become masculine or feminine, or that makes children become adolescents and adolescents become adults. In other words, 'age and gender become attributes of individuals as they learn, internalize, and ultimately act in accordance with norms associated with particular roles' (Laz, 1998, p. 94). Chronological age, like gender, controls and guides people's behaviour by setting standards for acceptable or desirable behaviour, appearance, clothing and other signifiers that enable us to categorise people as women, middle-aged or what have you.

But perhaps these considerations do not compromise the legitimacy of normalisation and its principle of age-appropriateness. After all, the original advocates of normalisation were well aware of the cultural and contextual nature of disability and normality (Nirje, 1985; Wolfensberger, 1972, p. 28) and they understood that concepts such as 'normal life' or 'age-appropriate' should be understood in terms of a given culture. The standard for 'normal rhythm of the day' or 'normal development experiences of the life cycle' (Nirje, 1970) is set by the cultural context, not by some universal principle. The goal of normalisation was always the attainment of the cultural norm.

When unpacking the significance of age for persons with profound intellectual disability, developmental psychology comes inevitably into play, especially in the Western world. As Priestley (2003, p. 65) argues, 'Discourses of normal child development are significant, because they impact directly on disabled children's lives.' It is developmental psychology, after all, that has set the standards for 'normal' child development where children are seen to develop through a sequence of predictable and measurable stages (Priestley, 2003, 64). Children are expected to learn to crawl, walk, talk, read, write and so on at a certain age; this is why schools, for example, are organised around assumptions regarding normal child development (Kivirauma & Kivinen, 1988). While the intention of these psychological accounts may be purely descriptive, in reality they have become normative justifications for various institutional arrangements such as removing children with special educational needs to special classes or special schools (Kivirauma, 1998). Ultimately, however, it is the norms and competencies of *independent* adulthood that define the goals and milestones of normal psychosocial development (Priestley, 2003, pp. 65, 120).

Erik Erikson's influential theory of psychosocial development is a textbook point of departure (in the Western context) to understand human development and the significance of age. Erikson argued that human beings develop in eight stages, and their psychological needs are determined in relation to social requirements. Each developmental stage involves distinct tasks that are triggered by a *crisis*, and successful completion of these tasks and resolving the related crises results in the acquisition of basic *virtues* that one needs to lead one's life successfully through its different phases. For example, at school age, children typically learn specific skills such as reading and writing and struggle to accomplish achievements and abilities valued in society (industriousness vs. inferiority). Should they fail, they develop a sense of inferiority but, if they succeed at this developmental stage, they develop the virtue of competence (e.g. Knight, 2016).

Similarly, during adolescence, the transitional phase between childhood and adulthood, young people search for a sense of self and identity (identity cohesion vs. role confusion). According to Erikson, at this stage of development young people explore ideological and occupational options and various social roles with an aim to integrate them with their talents, interests and social involvements in order to experience some kind of psychosocial unity and purpose in their lives: 'Identity, then, is an integrative configuration of self-in-the-adult-world' (McAdams, 2001, p. 102). Adolescents, thus, try to make sense of themselves and build their identity in the midst of erupting genital sexuality that 'signals the coming of full-fledged adult status in love and work' (McAdams, 2001, p. 102). Successful adaptation to one's bodily changes and examination of one's sexual and occupational identity leads to the virtue of fidelity. And, as a young adult, one is expected to resolve the conflict between intimacy and isolation, form long-term relationships and develop the virtue of love (Knight, 2016).

It is of secondary importance here what Erikson meant exactly by 'virtue of fidelity' or 'virtue of love', or how sound his theory is in the first place. Rather, the point here is that his theory reflects and possibly in part explains (because of its influence) how we in Western societies attach certain expectations and norms to certain age periods. Because of its inbuilt normativity, Erikson's theory of psychosocial development resembles, interestingly, Aristotle's virtue ethics. Despite very different starting points and ways of making sense of human lives, they both aim to illuminate what makes one's life go well, what the preconditions are for an individual's well-being and a good life. In both theories, virtues are essential for succeeding in life or living a good life (or successful and a happy life).

Erikson's aim was to describe how human beings, in fact, tend to develop and what kinds of capacities and virtues they usually need to fair well. Aristotle's ethical theory, on the other hand, is a normative theory where virtues serve the aim of being good and acting well in a moral sense (Nichomachean Ethics, 1102 b 26; NE 1144 b 18). He saw virtues as traits of character or dispositions that make a person good and enable him or her to live the good life (Nichomachean Ethics, 1106 a 15–17, 22–24). He divided virtues into intellectual and moral, which are both habits or habitual dispositions to act well under the guidance of reason; living the good life implies both good judgement as to right and wrong and character traits based upon internalised moral values that enable one to live the good life (e.g. Hursthouse & Pettigrove, 2018; Hutchinson, 1995).

Both Erikson's and Aristotle's theories assume adult human beings to possess a sufficient degree of intellectual capacities. To be virtuous, to be able to live an adult life and the good life, requires the kinds of capacities that are unattainable to many persons with intellectual disability. From this perspective, intellectual disability may be seen as something that contradicts or compromises humanity, or that high intellectual capacities are seen to give humanity and human lives special value (as many philosophers argue; see Appendix). Children with intellectual disability fail to develop in ways psychological theories and sociocultural demands assume humans develop. In particular, people with profound intellectual and multiple disabilities are unable to live up to the expectations set by societal institutions that presume people to develop in a certain way and pace. This is not only because of their cognitive capacities (or mental age, as developmental psychologists may put it) but, rather, because persons with PIMD do not go through the expected and desirable stages of psychosocial development.

Persons with PIMD are a group of people that troubles the cultural conventions and expectations regarding age. It makes sense to arrange intellectual disability services, at least to some extent, according to cultural norms with reference to age-appropriate behaviour, fashion, appearance and so on – simply to avoid infantilising persons with intellectual disability. Nevertheless, it is clear that age-appropriateness is a problematic principle for persons with PIMD. People like Hugo do not, cannot and should not be bothered about 'acting their age'. If the freedom to choose one's life according to one's own liking applies to all people, then the prior entitlement of all people, including persons with PIMD, is to have a life that is in line with their preferences, interests and well-being. If a life for Hugo that looks like him, as it were, is in conflict with the principle of age-appropriateness, that is just too bad for that principle.

People with intellectual disability continue to be conceptualised, especially in the media, in terms of their 'mental age', thus being on the level of, for example, two-year-old children. These kinds of descriptions tell very little about the people in question. Even if one accepted such descriptions, probably no one would deny that a 50-year-old person with the alleged intellectual capacities of a two-year-old would have 50 years of life experience. He or she has likely developed various emotional attachments, aesthetic tastes, preferences regarding bodily pleasure, and so on. But, since persons with PIMD need assistance to develop new likings on their own, we face the question about the limits of introducing new sources of experience and pleasure to them.

Consider stimulants: to what extent it is justified to introduce them to persons with profound intellectual disability? Some of our research participants drank coffee but none of them drank alcohol. That may be because they are, in fact, seen to be like children, and children are not supposed to drink alcohol. Or it could be due to the fact that alcohol is by default considered to be a problem for people with intellectual disability as they are assumed to end up misusing it (Simpson, 2012). What is often forgotten is that alcohol is central to many social occasions; it plays a role in cultural integration and especially a symbolic role in the transition to adulthood, as Simpson (2012) points out. Alcohol, however, continues to be a matter of worry and risk in intellectual disability services, instead of matter of cultural inclusion or exclusion, let alone a matter of autonomy and entitlement. To view exclusion from alcohol as an example of social and cultural exclusion makes sense regarding individuals with intellectual disability who are capable of expressing their will clearly and conducting their own lives, possibly with assistance, but nevertheless by themselves. But the issue is more complicated when it comes to individuals with profound intellectual disability.

Our intention here is not to provoke, let alone suggest that we should start giving persons with PIMD alcohol with the intention of getting them drunk. We merely wish to point out the problematic nature of age-related norms and the principle of age-appropriateness in relation to persons with profound intellectual disability. If we think that it is acceptable to offer them, for example, coffee, why could we not offer them a glass of white wine to go with fish? While alcohol may not be a matter of right, and one can well lead a good life without being able to enjoy, say, white wine, alcohol does perhaps constitute a complication regarding the meaning of youth and adulthood of persons with PIMD. For, if we think that abstinence is the only possibility for adults with PIMD (other than for possible medical reasons), disability scholars and policymakers promoting the principles of normalisation and age-appropriateness would need to accept that they are not fully fledged adults with a right to pursue things and activities generally valued in their culture.

Thus, the meaning and significance of youth and adulthood is far from clear with persons with profound intellectual disability. That becomes even more evident in the case of sexuality, the topic of the next chapter.

Chapter 6: Sexuality

Introduction: confronting the denial

This chapter explores the difficult issue of sexuality in people with PIMD. The need for writing this chapter arose from an embarrassing realisation of ignorance and negligence regarding the possibility of erotic life for this group of people. One of the main intellectual and ethical commitments of our research project from the very beginning was to represent the lives of the research participants in their full complexity. It was only after the field-work that Simo realised that the 'full complexity' of their lives had not included sexuality – it was not at the centre, not even on the fringes of the initial research agenda. This chapter is a part of the process of understanding and coming to terms with the sub-conscious exclusion of a crucial element of humanity from a research that had the intention of providing a thorough picture of the lived experiences of profound intellectual and multiple disabilities.

Our failure to consider the possibility of sex in the lives of persons with PIMD is by no means a rare fault in disability studies, which as a research field has focused on examining various social and structural practices and mechanisms that exclude disabled people from mainstream society. Since PIMD is a phenomenon virtually absent from disability studies, it is unsurprising that the sexual experiences of people with these conditions have not been given consideration. Still, literature on sexuality with reference to 'milder' forms of intellectual disability does exist in relation to issues such as abuse, autonomy, consent, family planning, gender expectations, identity, inappropriate behaviour, parenthood, family and staff member views, sterilisation and vulnerability (e.g.

How to cite this book chapter:
Vehmas, S. and Mietola, R. 2021. *Narrowed Lives: Meaning, Moral Value, and Profound Intellectual Disability*. Pp. 135–154. Stockholm: Stockholm University Press. DOI: https://doi.org/10.16993/bbl.f. License: CC-BY 4.0.

Abbott, 2015; Banks, 2016; Booth & Booth, 2000; Desjardins, 2012; Evans, McGuire, Healy, & Carley, 2009; Hamilton, 2010; Hollomotz, 2010; Lyden, 2007; McCarthy, 2014; Turner & Crane, 2016; Wilson, Parmenter, Stancliffe, & Shuttleworth, 2011). The absence of people with PIMD in this research literature is striking but also unsurprising due to some serious ethical and methodological concerns. These include, for example, uncertainties about the criteria of consent and abuse, as well as how to make reliable judgements about the ability to consent (Brown & Turk, 1992). Apart from independent private masturbation, the almost inevitable notion regarding sex and PIMD appears to be something of an absolute no-no. At least, this is the mentality that Simo caught himself having subconsciously.

This unreflected prejudice of sex for people with PIMD as unacceptable seemed wrong and needed to be analysed. So, what we wish to do here is to confront this prejudice in the light of our ethnographic observation and interview data. We will do this by using Simo's experiences and prejudices as a starting point,[18] and analyse them through the project's empirical data, as well as with some reflections on the ethically justified ways to enhance sexual pleasure for this group of people.[19] The personal plays a significant role in the general discussion of this chapter. Exposing the personal in this context is only appropriate as we are in the position to produce knowledge about persons who cannot do it themselves. This kind of power imbalance needs to be acknowledged as non-disabled academics have a special responsibility 'to pay particular attention to issues of their own identity, their own privilege as non-disabled people, and the relationship of these factors to their scholarship' (Linton, 1998, pp. 152–153).

In addition to the very limited cognitive and communicative capacities, our research participants also have physical impairments

---

[18] The reason why Simo's role in this chapter is so prominent is that it was motivated and directed by his personal experience and thinking. It is also a way to ascribe responsibility to him of its somewhat controversial contents.

[19] For the analysis in this chapter, episodes representing physical affection that were not part of nursing or care were separated from the ethnographic data. References to the data are based on these episodes, as well as Simo's discussions with Reetta and Sonja.

that restrict their mobility or ability to act independently. For example, Frida and Hugo are entirely dependent on other people regarding any activity; they are not capable of wheeling themselves and their hand movements are very limited, which means that they cannot feed themselves, let alone masturbate independently should they wish to do so.

During his previous encounters with people with profound intellectual disability, Simo had become aware of their expressions of sexuality but he had apparently pushed that knowledge somewhere into the subconscious. This might have been due to the inappropriateness of some of these expressions (e.g. public masturbation). Sexuality in the lives of people with PIMD apparently did not appear to Simo to be something positive, a source of pleasure and affirmation. Rather, the positive potential of sexual pleasure for them was overrun by his own anguish. The main concern was not, in fact, to protect persons with PIMD from exploitation and abuse but to protect Simo himself from the unpleasant feelings their sexual manifestations caused him.

Considering that the founding ethical conviction of this project was the recognition of the inalienable worth of persons with PIMD as fellow humans (Vehmas & Curtis, 2017), as well as an ambition to understand what makes a good life for them, it is necessary to address the issue of sexuality – better later than never. An account that dismissed a basic entitlement such as sexuality would be defective as it would fail to do justice to their personhood, and their equal value as humans with the possibility to explore and express their sexuality.

Finally, it needs to be remembered that intimacy and physical affection are continuously present in interactions with people like our research participants because they need constant care and support in all everyday routines. In other words, they are constantly touched by other people, whether it is about toileting, washing, being dressed or being moved from place to another. However, while their everyday lives are filled with intimacy in terms of nursing, only rarely did Reetta and Sonja witness other moments of physical closeness or affection. This may be related to the institutional culture of some group homes and day centres, where our research participants spent a lot of time alone, with very few opportunities to express or receive physical affection or to interact with other people.

Interpreting communication and consent

We approach the issue from a secular liberal viewpoint. In terms of sex, this position would imply that virtually anything done voluntarily between two or more people is morally permissible. The possibility to express one's sexuality and form erotic relations with other people is seen as a fundamental entitlement to all citizens and often crucial to their well-being. Concerns about the possible naturalness or perversity of any kind of sexual activity are insignificant in this view; what matters morally is whether something that took place was in line with that person's preferences, and whether it brought about pleasure or suffering (Primoratz, 1999; Soble, 2002). This kind of general live-and-let-live maxim as an ethical guideline undoubtedly leaves room for interpretation in individual situations, especially when it comes to people whose capacity for autonomous choice is questionable, things are far from simple. So, even assuming that anything done as a result of free and informed consent is permissible, various difficult questions remain. For example, how explicit and specific must consent be? That is, when can we infer in the case of non-verbal persons with limited or no mobility that they have consented to sex, and must we know in advance in exactly what kind of acts, caresses or positions they have consented to?

In our study, all our participants seemed enigmatic to other people. Anna, a non-verbal woman in her 20s with very little movement but who had recently learnt to wheel short distances by herself, was the most challenging of the research participants when it came to understanding her feelings and communication. A lot of times, she seemed to prefer to sit on her own in her wheelchair. In the noisy and often chaotic day activity centre, especially, she seemed to get distressed in the company of others, which she signalled by wailing and crying. Her frequent habit of uttering wailing sounds puzzled the care workers; they could not always tell whether she was crying, perhaps due to some pain, or whether that was actually her way of taking part in discussion. Her communication was a matter of constant and somewhat confused interpretation where the staff tried to judge whether she was reacting to the happenings around her or to her bodily state. But, even with Anna, there were situations when it was very clear what she wanted. For example, when she wanted to eat she simply opened her mouth for food, and when she wanted to drink she turned her head towards a glass. On the grounds of these kinds of gestures and signs, the care workers reported to know with certainty when she wanted, for example, to eat and drink (although a choice between two different kinds of drinks could be too demanding for her). But owing to her limited means of communication they were less certain about other things such as to what extent she wanted physical comfort and affection. Nevertheless, they were inclined to think that Anna liked strokes and hugs.

A degree of uncertainty in approximation seems acceptable when it comes to eating, drinking or even non-sexual expressions of physical affection such as hugs. But similar uncertainty would not be acceptable if we were to facilitate a person's sexual desires. In the case of men, drawing conclusions about their possible desires may appear more straightforward, but would still be far from simple. That is, an erection could well be a clear clue of sexual arousal, but there would need to be reliable means of communication in order to know that that indeed is the case and that helping that person to achieve sexual satisfaction would be based on his preferences, deliberation and free consent.

Ella was the most mobile person in our study but she was usually made to wear the kinds of trousers and underwear that made it practically impossible for her to touch her genitalia. Reetta told Simo that she had taken Ella's hands away from her private parts once or twice when Ella was sitting on her lap. When Simo asked why Reetta did that, she answered, 'because Ella's hands could've been on my face the next minute.' There was also another hygienic concern: while living in an institution years ago, Ella had the occasional habit of smearing with her faeces. One possible way to explain this problematic behaviour would be that of seeing it as a kind of substitute activity where Ella was expressing her sexuality: being cleaned afterwards probably was the only time her privates would get touched (Cambridge & Carnaby, 2000; Kulick & Rydström, 2015, p. 123). However, her behaviour had changed considerably for the better after moving to a group home and, in any case, we did not ask whether the reason for Ella's dress code was merely hygienic.

All in all, Ella's carers thought that the change in her living conditions had without doubt contributed positively to her behaviour and well-being in general. But certainty and puzzlement blended continuously in the staff's interpretations about Ella's actions. During her first days with Ella, one of her carers asked Reetta about our study and what it was all about. Reetta answered that it was about a good life and how it could be understood in the case of people with very limited means of communication, who can express their own will only very little or hardly at all. When the carer heard this, she walked to Ella, who was sitting on the floor, crouched down in front of her, and responded to Reetta with indignant tone, 'our people do express [their own will], especially Ella.' After that she told how she had worked with Ella for 20 years and how Ella had taught her what to do with her.

Other professionals working with Ella confirmed that she clearly shows, for example, whom she likes through physical gestures (like patting or sitting on a person's lap). But, while being certain about the meaning of some facial expressions, utterances and movements in some contexts, the professionals were often bewildered by Ella and what to make out of what she was trying to express, what she was feeling or thinking. It seems that their certainty over the meaning of Ella's acts and thoughts were related to two considerations. The first is the self-evident nature of some acts, such as opening one's mouth when being offered food. The second is the ethical sensitivity of the activity in question. Drawing conclusions about a person's eating and drinking appetites is a lot less precarious than judging her sexual preferences. Interestingly, one of Ella's carers compared her deliberation process about Ella's wants and wishes to the relationship between mother and child: when you feel cold yourself, you tend to put more clothes on your child – the mother thus projects her own feelings onto her child. She concluded, however, that the way to learn to read Ella is ultimately through trial and error. Fair enough, but when it comes to sexuality, there should be no room for errors. Or should there?

'Do no wrong' equals 'do nothing'?

Erotic and romantic relationships in the case of people with intellectual disability are generally considered innocent, child-like and asexual. As Kulick and Rydström (2015, p. 96) argue in relation to Sweden, the typical requirements for acceptable romantic relationships for people with congenital impairments are things such as verbal articulateness, mobility, sexual desire that is directed only at members of one's own group, innocuous public displays of affection, and little or no sex (and, in any case, no sex that would involve assistance from a staff member or helper). Meeting these kinds of standards can be difficult if not impossible for people with intellectual disability, especially those with PIMD. It is only understandable that in the case of individuals with very limited cognitive capacities, with no or very limited movement and only very limited means of communication, the safe way to deal with their possible erotic desires is to ignore them (see Kulick & Rydström, 2015, p. 86).

However, this kind of precautionary policy would conflict with a view of sex as a right. Consider the example of Denmark, analysed by Kulick and Rydström (2015). Sexuality is seen there as a positive entitlement, where individuals should have the possibility to explore their own sexuality and the professionals working with disabled people have an obligation to facilitate their access to sexual education, and, should they desire it, a sexual life. In practice this means that qualified and designated helpers (social workers with special training and competence) are obligated to 'provide or find someone who can provide help to anyone who expresses a desire for such a help ... they help individuals have sex, but they do not *have sex* with them' (Kulick & Rydström, 2015, p. 107). The helper and the individual who receives the help write a written contract about the plan of action, so that both parties are in agreement about what kind of help the person receiving help wishes to have and that the helper knows what he or she is agreeing to. These kinds of plans of action are important in order to avoid abuse or exploitation. But they are also private documents, which means that other members of the staff in, say, a group home only know that a particular resident receives assistance from a particular staff member; the details of the assistance (what, when and how) are not known by others (Kulick & Rydström, 2015, p. 107).

These kinds of policies are progressive and worthy but they do exclude people from such help if they are not capable of communicating their sexual preferences in a reliable manner. Without reliable means of communication and mutual under- standing, one cannot make an agreement. So, does this mean that it is better to do nothing? One cannot help of thinking here about the case of Anna Stubblefield. She is a philosopher who was convicted of repeated sexual assault against a non-verbal man with severe intellectual disability and cerebral palsy, and was sentenced to 12 years in prison. She claimed that their sex was consensual as the man, according to Stubblefield, was ca- pable of communication through facilitated communication.[20] Facilitated communication or supported typing is a controversial communication method where a disabled person's hand is held and guided by another person on a keyboard or alphabet board. Various experimental studies have shown the unreliability of the method. Despite its poor reputation, facilitated communication has persistent believers in disability studies. In this case, and so- mewhat unsurprisingly, only Stubblefield seemed to manage to prompt facilitated communication. And, against previous psycho- logical reports and his family's testimony, Stubblefield claimed that the man was in fact an intellectual equal to herself (Sherry, 2016).

The case of Anna Stubblefield is in many ways contentious and troubling, and, as such, it would seem to support a precautiona- ry principle of refraining from any kind of facilitation of sexual pleasure to people who lack reliable means of communication. Having said that, it would also be regrettable to submit to the kind of precautionary measures that deprive one crucial element of human well-being from persons who are unable to give infor- med consent in any conventional manner. One possible escape route from this ethical dead end could be an alternative, relational

---

[20] She was released from prison after two years when she pleaded guilty and admitted to knowing at the time of their sexual encounters that the man had been found mentally incompetent and could not legally consent (https://www.nj.com/essex/2018/05/anna_stubblefield_sentenced_for _second_time.html).

understanding of autonomy and legal capacity. The 2007 United Nations Convention on the Rights of Persons with Disabilities (CRPD) requires in article 12 that 'persons with disabilities enjoy legal capacity on an equal basis with others in all aspects of life'. This is seen to deny any substitute decision-making procedure and to require that disabled people 'are given access to the support they need to exercise their legal capacity in accordance with their will and preferences' (Series, 2015, p. 81).

Under various pieces of legislation, such as the Mental Capacity Act 2005 in England and Wales, a person is considered unable to make decisions if he or she is unable to understand, retain or use or weigh the relevant information. Legal scholars advocating the CRPD, however, argue that:

> all human persons, regardless of their decision-making capabilities, should enjoy 'legal capacity' on an equal basis – that is, the right to be recognised as a person before the law, and the subsequent right to have one's decisions legally recognized. (Flynn & Arstein-Kerslake, 2014, p. 82)

Importantly, 'the recognition of the right cannot merely extend to the areas in which we are all comfortable, because the right to legal capacity is virtually meaningless unless it is fully recognised in all areas of an individual's life' (Flynn & Arstein-Kerslake, 2014, p. 90). But how does one implement legal capacity in the case of persons with PIMD, people like Anna and Ella? It could mean various systems of support such as supported or facilitated decision-making. *Supported decision-making* takes place when one receives support from others to make a decision and communicate to others: 'This could be through helping them to obtain and understand information relevant to the decision, talking through the pros and cons of different available options, or helping a person to communicate with others' (Series, 2015, p. 85). This support model might work with some persons with PIMD as they seem to understand more than is expected from them. But, since their communication often lacks coherence, it is very difficult to judge with any kind of certainty what exactly they comprehend in various situations.

Another alternative would be *facilitated decision-making*, where a third party (facilitator) makes decisions on the person's behalf but bases their decisions on their knowledge of a person's narrative: 'The facilitator's role is to imagine what the person's will and preferences might be and to make the decisions on this basis' (Flynn & Arstein-Kerslake, 2014, p. 95). Regarding persons with PIMD and sex, this support model could perhaps imply a kind of limited and cautious facilitation of sexual pleasure. In other words, without certainty over a person's preferences and interests, active facilitation of sex (e.g. a helper facilitating an immobile person with PIMD to masturbate) would be out of the question. However, other people may well try to find out, with the best of their ability and keeping closely in mind this particular person's personality and personal history, what he or she might want in terms of sex. Gradually, this kind of process could give necessary certainty over the person's preferences so that active steps in sexual facilitation could be taken.

Along similar lines, Boni-Saenz (2015, p. 1236) argues for a decision-making support system that 'does not exist to make the sexual decision as a surrogate for the person with cognitive impairments, but instead to facilitate her wishes and desires'. However, the ability to express, in a way or another, *volition* with respect to a sexual decision is the minimal threshold for the legal capacity for sexual consent. Without the basic level of communication of volition, one is not a legal agent, which means that in such a case the liability should flow to such individual's sexual partner or to institutions that have a responsibility for safeguarding her (Boni-Saenz, 2015, p. 1235) – a consideration relevant to the Stubblefield case.

What is sex? What is fair?

There are reasons to be reasonably optimistic that the scenario outlined above would be feasible. Only *reasonable* optimism, however, seems appropriate owing to the elusiveness of the minds of people like Anna and Ella. It is important to acknowledge the many things that we do not understand about persons with PIMD and also the asymmetrical relationship between privileged and less privileged people; we cannot fully understand another person, let alone someone with very limited cognitive and verbal capacities (Young, 1997). However, we are optimistic that an ethically justifiable sexual facilitation in the case of persons with PIMD who cannot masturbate themselves is possible simply because many of them do express desire for sexual pleasure. This is most apparent with persons like Sebastian and Leo. They are both non-verbal and have very limited mobility but are capable of masturbating, and both are provided with the privacy to do so in their group homes. It should be noted that we have no data where and how the sexuality of the women in our study manifests. This mirrors in its part the gendered nature of the issue: men tend to be seen more sexual than women and are thus likely to be granted more opportunities to express their sexuality than women. This imbalance is also represented in research literature on sexuality and intellectual disability, where there is little research on how women with intellectual disability experience their sexual lives (McCarthy, 1999, 2002, 2014; O'Shea & Frawley, 2020).

Another reason to assume that many persons with PIMD do have erotic desires of some sort is their clearly expressed need for physical affection. Naturally, persons with PIMD (just like all people) are different in terms of their preferences for intimacy and affection. For people like Ella and Sebastian, physical affection is clearly important and something they actively seek. But both of them do so only in relation to *some* people: to ones they like or fancy, ones they have formed a relationship with, the kinds of people they seem to trust. But then persons like Anna, Frida and Leo are much more reserved and, while they seem to enjoy physical affection, they do so only occasionally.

Naturally, one needs to be sensitive in this context as to what counts as sexual activity and sexual pleasure, especially for someone with profound intellectual disability. People's sexual tastes vary greatly and it is difficult to define what in fact makes acts sexual, what kinds of acts count as sex (Halwani, 2010, pp. 123–151). For example, in Sanders and Reinisch's (1999) well-known study, 60% of respondents did not consider fellatio to be having sex and 20% did not even see penile–anal intercourse as sex. Some philosophers have argued that human sexuality is not merely a matter of pleasures of sensation but rather it is about activities that involve intentional pleasure and thoughts pertaining to it (Primoratz, 1999, p. 22). In particular, it is about mutual recognition of arousal between persons (Nagel, 1979, pp. 39–52). These kinds of conceptions emphasising the psychological element related to sexual pleasure may or may not be plausible, and whether they apply to people with PIMD remains an enigma. A more relevant consideration in this context is the relationship between sexual activity and sexual pleasure. In some accounts, sexual acts should be understood in terms of production of sexual pleasure. This means that virtually any act (such as holding hands or giving a foot massage) is sexual if it produces sexual pleasure. But this kind of account has unfortunate implications regarding abuse because, on such an analysis, placing the penis into the vagina would be sexual only if it produced sexual pleasure. Thus, a victim of a rape would not be able to claim that she was forced into a *sexual* activity despite the fact that intercourse was compelled on her (Soble, 2002).

One could argue, however, that, if there is no sexual pleasure involved in an act on either side, then it is not sexual abuse. In cases of abuse, the act must include pleasure to the abuser in order to be sexual. The rape victim can legitimately claim that she was used *as a means* by a person engaging in a sexual activity by virtue of deriving sexual pleasure from that activity; the victim was not participating or engaging in sexual activity because it was something that was done to her by someone who was. But this response seems inadequate. Imagine a couple who had intercourse that ended in one partner's ejaculation. However, both feel that they did not in fact enjoy the act. Even the one who ejaculated could plausibly claim that, even though he felt some physical sensations when he ejaculated, they were not pleasurable to him for psychological reasons (e.g. the way he felt about his partner). Thus, it seems false to see sexual pleasure as something purely physical because all physical sensations are arguably interpreted sensations (at least in hindsight); we feel something, but exactly what we feel or felt is influenced by our psychological, social and cultural consciousness.

Jeff McMahan and Peter Singer (2017), in their commentary on Anne Stubblefield's case, question whether the victim in this case was in fact wronged. This is because he is 'profoundly cognitively impaired' and was not necessarily wronged by Stubblefield simply because 'he cannot understand the normal significance of sexual relations between persons or the meaning and significance of sexual violation'. They also argue that, since the experience was apparently pleasurable for the man Stubblefield had sex with, 'it seems that if Stubblefield wronged or harmed him, it must have been in a way that he is incapable of understanding and that affected his experience only pleasurably' (McMahan & Singer, 2017).[21] In McMahan's and Singer's consequentialist mindset, there is no moral wrong involved in an act with individuals who cannot consent to sex unless it brings about harmful consequences to them. But conceptualising the issue merely in terms of consequences or autonomy seems terribly one-sided in cases where the ethics of exploitation is evident. The morality of actions does not depend merely on the point of view of the one towards whom the action is performed but also on the position of the one who is performing the action. In other words, wherever there is someone to whom an obligation is owed, there must also be someone who has an obligation. For example, a claim like 'we should not perform painful medical experiments on human beings' means that human beings are the kinds of beings who have the right of being protected from painful medical experiments but, also, that us humans as moral agents are the kinds of beings who have an obligation to refrain from doing certain actions (see Appendix).

Perhaps, then, it would be reasonable to conclude in this context that the relationship between sexual acts and sexual pleasure is twofold. Firstly, any act that harms no one involved but produces, or at least has the intention of producing, sexual pleasure to those involved with the act, is indeed a sexual act and in itself morally good or neutral. Secondly, if the act, however, is any way harmful in terms of a person's integrity or well-being, and involves acts typically regarded as sexual (e.g. intercourse, fellatio, sexual touching, showing pornography), then that act is indeed sexual. Pleasure cannot be the sole criterion for sexual acts

---

[21] McMahan's and Singer's view suggests that persons with PIMD are incapable of appreciating sexuality in terms of intimacy, as a sense of mutual closeness and connection. This view is empirically very problematic (as should become clear in this chapter) but it also implies that persons with PIMD are like animals who are allegedly merely capable of mating (e.g. Umberson, Thomeer, & Lodge, 2015; see also Chapter 7).

because in that case hardly any act would count as sexual abuse if it caused no particular pleasure or displeasure to the victim.

One could argue that the previous speculations about the definitions of sex complicate the issue unnecessarily. Why not make things more simple, and use a common-sense definition of sexuality as an activity that directly engages genitals, breasts and/or anuses? That may be a reasonable response and undoubtedly practical in a policy context, albeit insufficient to take into account the complexity of sexual acts and desires. But, at the end of the day, what is crucial is to set some coherent criteria for sexual acts that would aid us to judge when an act is indeed sexual, and also when abuse is sexual.

In this context, it is crucial to return to the significance of gender. When it comes to intellectual disability and sexuality, at least in any affirmative sense, the default position seems to be male: men with intellectual disability are seen as agents who legitimately may seek intimacy and sexual pleasure. But for women with intellectual disability, the reality is somewhat different: they are seen as sexually naïve, more vulnerable to sexual abuse than men and consequently in need of more protection (O'Shea & Frawley, 2020; Young, Gore, & McCarthy, 2012). This seems like a reasonable reaction to the fact that women with intellectual disability are indeed more likely to experience sexual abuse than men (e.g. Cambridge, Beadle-Brown, Milne, Mansell, & Whelton, 2006; Gil-Llario, Morell-Mengual, Ballester-Arnal, & Díaz-Rodríguez, 2018). And, especially in the case of individuals with profound intellectual disability, sensitivity to the significance of gender is undoubtedly appropriate considering the long history of sexual abuse of women with intellectual disability (McCarthy, 2002). Perhaps men with intellectual disability in general are indeed more transparent than women regarding their sexuality (possibly because they masturbate more often than women (Kijak, 2013)) and therefore perhaps enabling or facilitating their sexual desires is less precarious. Remembering that the perpetrators of sexual abuse of women with intellectual disability are often care workers (e.g. Mansell, Beadle-Brown, Cambridge, Milne, & Whelton, 2009), there is every reason for transparency in any possible policy with the aim of enriching their sexual lives.

Bearing this in mind, there should be verifiable, cogent reasons to assume that facilitating sexual pleasure for persons with PIMD would be justifiable in terms of their preferences, their well-being, and making their lives better. If a person shows no interest in expressing his or her sexuality, 'then there is no justification for trying to make him or her interested just because most other people find sexuality one of life's blessings' (Carson, 1992, p. 86). In other words, there is every reason to exhibit epistemic modesty (Kittay, 2010) but, despite that, other people do need to make judgements about the preferences of people with very limited cognitive and communicative capacities.

What does seem clearly important to many persons with PIMD is an entitlement to physical and emotional affection (Wilson et al., 2011). Just as they have the right to proper nutrition, living conditions and health care, they should have an equal right to flourish emotionally and sexually. In fact, all the aforementioned things are crucial elements of well-being and a good life and thus matters of social justice, and would remain so regardless of one's particular metric of justice. Whether one defines justice in terms of primary goods (Rawls, 1971) or capabilities (Nussbaum, 2006), it would be reasonable to argue in either case that sexual and emotional well-being are matters of entitlement and, accordingly, people with PIMD have the right to receive responses for their needs for physical affection and emotional attachment. That is clearly what people like Ella want and need, and that is what they are entitled to. There is of course divergence to the extent that persons in this group are capable or interested of forming emotional ties to others, or experience and value sexual satisfaction. But, since many of them have such interests, the minimal threshold for a life with dignity for them is one in which this capability is acknowledged and facilitated rather than denied and prevented (Boni-Saenz, 2015; Kulick & Rydström, 2015, pp. 286–287).

Conclusion: how to move forward?

It would be hazardous to come up with *precise* instructions on exactly how intimacy and sexuality should be enhanced for persons with PIMD. This is simply because of the great variety of characteristics and capacities among this group of people. But what does seem safe to suggest is a general ethical claim to include sexuality as a concern in their care as valid as any other matter usually seen important for human flourishing. The caring staff working with persons with PIMD should not approach the issue by asking 'is there a reason to assume that this person *has* a desire for sexual pleasure?' but, rather, by asking 'is there a reason to assume that this person has *no* desire for sexual pleasure or fulfilment?' If not, the next question would be 'how can we know what his or her sexual preferences might be?' 'Does the person express any kind of behaviour that suggests a search for sexual stimulation (e.g. the person rubbing themselves or touching their privates directly)?' (Boni-Saenz, 2015; Cambridge, Carnaby, & McCarthy, 2003; McCarthy & Cambridge, 2006).

For most people with PIMD the only ethically feasible way to achieve sexual pleasure and satisfaction would probably be masturbation. Gill (2015, pp. 98–99) points out correctly, we think, that masturbation among people with intellectual disability is generally seen as beneficial 'insomuch that it allows for a reduction in potential disruptions in the institution or group home, but is not seen as an asset for sexual experience'. There is an uncomfortable difference between enabling and enhancing an act in terms of behavioural issues as opposed to sexual satisfaction. When masturbation is conceptualised as a physiological necessity that removes one's physical discomfort or as a way that prevents disturbing behaviour occurring publicly, it is probably considered less problematic to help that person to masturbate than it would be based on sole motivation to make erotic pleasure and satisfaction possible for him or her.

We are inclined to think that persons with PIMD have the right to facilitated masturbation when it is clear that it would be in their interest. However, for women a more cautious policy would probably be in order considering their higher risk for abuse. What is important, however, is to acknowledge that even doing nothing is a way of doing something. It may be reasonable to conclude that the risks outweigh the possible benefits in a given case, with the implication that a particular person will not be granted the possibility to explore his or her sexuality. Whatever the decision or policy would be, it needs to be intentional, done in an open and honest way.[22]

Admittedly, reducing sexuality merely to masturbation represents a very limited view; touch, closeness and intimacy are vital elements of our sexual lives as well. Intimacy, in the sense of physical and emotional closeness, typically arises over time, from a series of encounters because intimacy exposes us to a vulnerable position in relation to the other person and also to the possibility of exploitation (LaFollette, 1996, pp. 108–114; Popovic, 2005). Trust is therefore a necessary condition of intimacy: 'trust and sensitivity heighten intimacy; their absence diminishes it' (LaFollette, 1996, p. 111). Intimacy can be seen as an essential element of one's security, subjectivity and sense of self (Jamieson, 2011). It is thus clear that intimacy can both diminish and improve one's well-being. This is especially clear in the case of persons with PIMD, who in their relationships are particularly dependent on other people's willingness to care rather than harm them; they have no choice but to trust people close to them.

Among the persons we followed, Sebastian was the one who most clearly expressed his sexuality as well his need for physical affection. The head of his housing unit remarked casually in an interview that they provide him the privacy to express his sexuality and that 'yeah, he does masturbate. Yeah. There is no question about that.' Her expression in Finnish ('*Joo kyllä hän masturboi. Joo. Ei siis mitään*') indicated clearly that Sebastian's masturbation was in no way a problem but rather seen as a natural part of his life. But it seems that Sebastian might want more than just autoerotic pleasure. It became clear in the early stages of Sonja's fieldwork that Sebastian was very fond of her. Sometimes he approached Sonja, pantomimed kisses to her, smiled at her and finally engaged in a long hug with her. Sebastian has become very selective over the past few years regarding who he wants to engage in

---

[22] In the human rights discourse, this would mean the implementation of three central obligations: *respect* (refrain from interfering with the enjoyment of the right), *protect* (prevent others from interfering with the enjoyment of the right) and *fulfil* (adopt appropriate measures towards the full realisation of the right) (UN, 2008, p. 11).

physical affection with – Sonja was among those few and he no longer accepts physical comfort, for example, from his mother. It would not be unusual to view Sebastian's changed preferences as part of a maturation process and his acts and ways to approach some people (like Sonja) as indications of a desire for reciprocal affectionate, or even sexual relations. But, even assuming that he desires such relationships, the problem how they should be made possible in an ethically justified way would remain.

While working on this issue, with the aim of understanding better the erotic lives of persons with profound intellectual disability, we have been wondering why there is such a lack of engagement with these issues in research. There is an increasing number of works on sexuality in disability studies nowadays but, in particular, the work based on the cultural studies approach (e.g. McRuer & Mollow, 2012), which utilises conceptual frameworks such as crip theory, provides hardly any practical insight to enhance the sexual satisfaction of disabled people (Kulick & Rydström, 2015, pp. 13–16; Shakespeare, 2012). The focus in these studies is the formation of cultural norms and sociocultural imagery around sexuality and disability. Too often the result is the kind of account where the carnal elements of sexuality evaporate into the 'erudite theoretical ether' (Kulick & Rydström, 2015, p. 172).

This raises the question of exactly what kind of research would enhance in practice the sexual fulfilment of persons with PIMD? Would, for example, the case report presented by Shelton (1992) provide a model for research that would engage appropriately with the carnal experiences of sexuality of persons with PIMD? He presents a case of a 32-year-old man, 'Mr C', with profound intellectual disability who tried to masturbate by lying face down on a cold, hard floor of the bathroom area used by other residents, 'with his penis tucked between his legs, presumably to encourage an erection, and then rocking from side to side in an attempt to achieve ejaculation' (Shelton, 1992, 82). The whole process would last one to five hours, caused him injuries, provided him minimal success rate regarding ejaculation, and often resulted in aggressive outbursts towards other residents. An intervention was proposed where he was taken to privacy in his own room when he began to demonstrate his inappropriate masturbation technique.

Once lying on his bed, 'his pants and trousers were removed from around the genital area, and the author would then take hold of Mr C.'s wrist and place Mr C.'s fingers on his genitals, coupled with the verbal prompt, "Rub"' (Shelton, 1992, p. 82). After five weeks and 10 sessions, Mr C.'s injuries cleared up and no new injuries were acquired through his new masturbation technique. His previous mean of 122 minutes spent masturbating reduced to 14 minutes and the overall rate of successful ejaculation was increased by 15%.

Shelton's report raises various questions: why were Mr C's pants and trousers just pulled down, and not taken off? Was all that happened that Mr C's fingers were placed on his penis, he actually understood what the verbal prompt 'rub' meant, and started moving his hand up and down? Or did Shelton, in fact, manually help Mr C to move his hand and thus helped him to understand what 'rub' meant in practice? The article does not tell. If we assume, however, that Shelton indeed manually assisted Mr C to masturbate, was it morally the right thing to do? Many individuals with profound intellectual and multiple disabilities would likely need, literally, hands-on guidance to learn to masturbate. In order to find consensus about the ethically justified limits of sexual facilitation, we would need more research-based practical examples of such assistance. There are books like *The Ultimate Guide to Sex and Disability* (Kaufman, Silverberg, & Odette, 2004) and *Loneliness and Its Opposite* (Kulick & Rydström, 2015) where various examples are presented about sexual facilitation in practice, but not specifically in relation to persons with PIMD.

Whatever one may think about Shelton's article and the intervention it describes, he is correct to emphasise that at the heart of the matter is the element of risk:

> the question of how willing staff are to take risks – not in a reckless and cavalier way, but in a calculated and reasoned fashion – and thus allowing each client the opportunity to experience those things which the great majority of people experience during their sexual development. (Shelton, 1992, p. 84)

Finding a balance between overprotection in the name of care and abandonment in the name of self-determination is far from easy with this group of people. The idea of *dignity of risk* underlines that people with intellectual disability under care need to learn and achieve things the hard way, that they also need to learn to take prudent risks in order to grow, learn and develop (McDonald & Kidney, 2012; Perse, 1972; Tøssebro, 2005). Dignity of risk would ideally allow individuals to pursue sexual experiences and relationships while recognising potential risks (Wade, 2002). It is a policy worth pursuing in the case of individuals with intellectual disability who are capable of expressing their will clearly and conduct their own lives. However, policy based on dignity of risk is far from simple regarding persons with PIMD; who should be in charge for evaluating the risk *with* them or *for* them? Who exactly should be granted epistemic authority to the mental states (Carlson, 2010, p. 122), including sexual preferences, of a person with profound intellectual disability? Parents? Professionals? Where does the limit go between acceptable and unacceptable level of confusion, emotional inconvenience or even heartbreak that often go with sexual development?

These are very practical, tangible issues that the research community, especially the field of disability studies, needs to engage with. Unpacking ableist ideologies, narratives and images related to disabled sexualities is not enough in order to improve the sexual lives of disabled people. There is clearly a need for reassessment in disability studies so as to research the sexuality of persons with profound intellectual and multiple disabilities in the first place, as something other than as an expression of the cultural imagery.

Chapter 7: Animalised Lives

Animality and disability: is there a common ground?

The history of intellectual disability is, to a large extent, a history of segregation, subjection, cruelty and downright brutality (e.g. Hughes, 2020; Scheerenberger, 1983; Stiker, 1999). People with limited cognitive capacities have been seen as animal-like, subhuman and of lesser value than other humans. And, as already mentioned in the introduction to this book, notions of people with PIMD being psychologically and morally on a par with non-human animals are prevalent in contemporary moral philosophy (e.g. McMahan, 2002; Singer, 2009). Understandably, the mere comparison between non-human animals and humans with intellectual disability, made very casually in the philosophical literature, is seen in disability studies empirically and morally inappropriate; to say that a human is psychologically like a pig is seen to suggest that he or she should be in the same moral category as pigs as well (e.g. Vehmas & Watson, 2016). And indeed, from disabled people's perspective, the relationship between disability and animality has not been particularly affirmative or in any way positive.

Only relatively recently have there been calls for a positive engagement with the animality of people with various impairments. Some scholars have argued that posthumanism provides a platform for a positive change in the valuation of disabled people and disabled lives. Posthumanism argues, among other things, that human beings should not have a priori ethical primacy over non-human animals, and that any moral hierarchy as well as the division between humans and animals is false and

How to cite this book chapter:
Vehmas, S. and Mietola, R. 2021. *Narrowed Lives: Meaning, Moral Value, and Profound Intellectual Disability*. Pp. 155–175. Stockholm: Stockholm University Press. DOI: https://doi.org/10.16993/bbl.g. License: CC-BY 4.0.

based on 'ethical parochialism' (Wolfe, 2010, p. 61). Accordingly, anthropocentrism and its conviction of the superior moral value of humans compared to other species should be replaced with 'the recognition of trans species solidarity' (Braidotti, 2013, p. 67). Following the posthumanist philosophy of Rosi Braidotti, disability scholars Goodley, Lawthom and Runswick-Cole (2014) suggest that it is not problematic to make a comparison between non-human animals and disabled people, because all humans are ultimately animals too:

> The problem is not that some categories of human are treated like animals; the problem resides in the unconscious desire of the human condition to treat animals in inhumane ways; and treat some humans as if they were animals. We think that reinvigorating discussion around human/animal relations around disability might provide the necessary conditions and impetus for revaluing animals and humans as sharing a posthuman space of becoming. (Goodley et al., 2014, p. 355; see also Nayar, 2014, pp. 130–131)

While we remain reserved regarding the emancipatory potential of posthumanism, we do recognise the use of animal and monster studies in relation to disability, in particular in unpacking the structures and cultural mechanisms that have marginalised and demonised some humans as monstrous, beastly or animal-like (Nayar, 2014, pp. 111–120). It could also be argued that analysing the similarities between certain disabled human lives and animal lives would help us to understand better the causes of their exclusion from equal moral consideration compared to so-called normal humans.

Admittedly, some analogies between these two groups do seem to exist. They are both categories that have been defined by (normal) humans, and naturalised through centuries of representations that in turn have naturalised exploitative interactions between humans and animals (Nayar, 2014, 133), between normal humans and disabled humans. Neither 'animal' or 'disabled' is a category constructed *purely* on empirical, descriptive grounds based on inherent, biological features. Animality and disability are not merely matters of neutral difference but, also, deviances; they represent deviations from a life with full moral value. The anthropomorphic gaze defines certain categories as animals and of lesser value, whereas the ableist viewpoint represents disabled lives as animal-like and as forms of subhuman existence. In particular, those individuals that fail to exhibit, in a culturally accepted manner, things like autonomy, rationality, self-consciousness and communication are humans only in the biological sense but not in the moral sense (e.g. Cavalieri, 2001, p. 76; Sapontzis, 1987, pp. 28–29).

One main motivation for our study was that PIMD seems to represent an antithesis to the ways Western philosophy has depicted the ways humans ought to be, and what kinds of lives they should live. Because of their impairments, people with PIMD cannot live a good life or achieve high levels of well-being, at least in the way as these concepts have traditionally been understood in philosophical ethics (e.g. McMahan, 2002, p. 153); from a philosophical perspective, persons with PIMD are mentally and spiritually like non-human animals who just happen to have human bodies. It is far from clear to what extent philosophers' conceptions about well-being and good human lives have affected policies and practices concerning individuals with PIMD.

A quick glance at Western disability history, however, shows that various groups of people, ranging from clergy to the common people, have been more than eager to question the humanity and equal moral worth of persons with various impairments. Those with limited intellectual, communicative and physical capacities were especially likely, for example, to be among those 'ugly and deformed' in ancient Greek society that were selected as scapegoats and who carried the blame for current evils by undergoing ritual expulsion or execution (Garland, 1995, pp. 23–26). Or in the Middle Ages, by being in the wrong place at the wrong time, their impairments were seen as signs of witchcraft and they ended being tortured by the Inquisition (Neugebauer, 1996, pp. 22–23). And, certainly, they were among those who in the 19th and 20th centuries were non- and involuntarily institutionalised, sterilised, or even systematically exterminated (e.g. Grunewald, 2008, pp. 107–120; Harjula, 1996, pp. 148–169; Proctor, 1988, pp. 95–117, 191–193; Trent, 1994, pp. 142–144, 192–202). The following discussion is our attempt to make sense of the comparison or metaphor of disability as a form of animality: how such a metaphorical account can be applied to the lives of persons with PIMD, and whether it helps to understand and engage with their lives better.

Is it wrong to compare disabled humans to animals?

Before going any further, we need to think whether there is any point of analysing the lives of persons with PIMD in terms of animality – beside it offering a venue for middle-class academics to exercise intellectual gymnastics. Does this way of conceptualising actually help us to understand the lives and minds of persons with PIMD better, and could it offer us ways to make things better for them? The answer probably depends on how the function of the comparison is understood in the first place. In other words, is the point to compare individual humans and animals, their individual characteristics, and thus argue in lines similar to Temple Grandin (Grandin & Johnson, 2005, pp. 6–8), who claims that, due to her autism, she thinks like a cow simply because the brains of autistic people and some animals work in the same ways? This approach would be similar to the one philosophers like McMahan (2002) and Singer (2010) represent, although the normative arguments and conclusions they make on the basis of these comparisons are somewhat different to those of Grandin. Another possibility would be to concentrate on the cultural and social mechanisms that result in the morally marginalised status, even oppression of these two groups; what are the similarities and differences in their marginalisation?

Probably the more contentious possibility is the first one, to compare the characteristics of some humans and animals. And that is because to compare a group of people, especially a group that is already marginalised, who are unable to defend themselves and thus are exceptionally vulnerable to abuse (like those with PIMD), can be seen as a way to degrade them, to put them in subhuman status. Eva Feder Kittay is among those who strongly oppose the comparison between humans with PIMD and non-human animals. In her view,

to respond to the challenge to articulate the differences between a human animal with significantly curtailed cognitive capacities and a relatively intelligent non-human animal means that one first has to see the former as the latter. That is the moment of revulsion. Relating with that stance to my daughter as my daughter is an impossibility. (Kittay, 2010, p. 399)

Kittay argues that, to make the comparison between persons with PIMD and non-human animals, one must first see them as animals, and to do this is to ignore morally relevant features that they possess. Making the comparison itself forces one to take up a perspective that misrepresents the nature of those with PIMD. Hence, the very act of making such comparisons is morally inappropriate. But this claim does not seem credible. Why cannot we view those with PIMD and non-human animals as they are, and compare their respective features in the light of some 'objective' criteria regarding, for example, cognitive functioning? Why should the very act of making such a comparison force us to view those with PIMD as animals? After all, we often make casual, metaphorical comparisons between humans and animals: someone is restless, thus is running around like a headless chicken; someone has the patience of a cow; someone is sly as a fox and so on. These kinds of comparisons usually do not bother us in any way. Perhaps the difference between them and the philosophical comparisons (by McMahan and others where the equal moral worth of those with PIMD compared to other humans is questioned) Kittay refers to is the fact that the latter have highly controversial ethical motivation and purpose.

It is far from arbitrary to shy away from such comparisons because not so long ago they were used in making people with intellectual disability subhuman and dispensable. Singer himself has noted to Kittay that his intention is not to insult people with PIMD by comparing them to pigs, because 'I think pigs are wonderful lovable creatures' (Kittay, 2019, p. 128). But, as Crary (2018) argues, Singer appeals here to the same paradoxical logic as the Nazis; in both accounts, cognitively disabled human beings are denigrated 'by association with traits that are precisely valued in the animals who possess them' (Crary, 2018, p. 337). In other words, it is a different matter to playfully compare our single qualities to the similar qualities of animals with the intention of making us look comical, endearing or detestable than to compare an already-marginalised human being to a non-human animal with the intention of questioning his or her full moral status. Thus, while there is no reason to think that comparing humans with PIMD to non-human animals *as such* is morally inappropriate, such comparisons are morally problematic due to their associations and possible implications.

Another question is the empirical accuracy of comparisons across species, whether they make sense or portray accurately beings in different species. That is, the empirical accuracy or inaccuracy of comparisons across species goes both ways; they either do or do not do justice (in a descriptive sense) both to humans *and* animals. For example, consider people who identify as autistic (like Temple Grandin) and who claim that they think like cows or compare themselves in some other affirmative way to non-human animals. Such descriptions may be helpful for them but whether they portray an accurate picture of non-human animals, like cows, is a different matter. Also, what is affirmative and positive for highly intelligent autistic people like Grandin may not work similarly for those who have very limited cognitive capacity to invent themselves or communicative capacity to represent themselves to others. One alternative is to put aside empirical disputes about the similarities between humans and animals and concentrate instead on the ethical issues around human–animal relations. Researchers working on human–animal communication have done just this kind of shift of focus. A couple of decades ago the purpose and goal of communicating with animals was to try to teach animals language in order to discover something about cognition, the evolution of human language and questions about how different humans are from animals. Now the focus, especially in humanities and social sciences, has moved to ethics and how to engage respectfully with non-human others (Kulick, 2017). Perhaps, then, one should not waste too much time with empirical comparisons but move on to ethical discussions on how to combat ableism without trampling on animals (Crary, 2018).

Animal liberation as a way to disability liberation?

However, the question whether there is something morally *wrong* with asymmetric similarity judgements remains. And that is because of the associations of this particular comparison. It was not

so long ago that disabled people were systematically exterminated, when they were made to live in inhumane conditions with no
autonomy or dignity, and when they made their living as human
oddities in freak shows where people could gape at them like animals in zoos.[23]

Sunaura Taylor (2017) has argued that animals and disabled
people are oppressed by similar forces. While she herself as a
disabled person does not mind being compared to an animal
(because we are all animals), she acknowledges that the comparison to animals in terms of their moral worth provides mainly
risks for persons with *intellectual* disability: 'For a group of people who have won basic rights and protections only within the
past few decades, this is a truly offensive and frightening gam-
ble' (Taylor, 2017, p. 47). Hence, we should instead compare the
shared oppressions of animals and disabled people (Taylor, 2017,
p. 95). She argues that the reasons for this shared oppression
lie within a failed conception of animality and humanity that is
ultimately based on ableism: on the anthropocentric view that
has set typical human traits and abilities such as language, rationality and complex emotions as the benchmark for the moral
worth of beings.

It is ableist values that are at the core of the animal industries
and the ways they perpetuate animal suffering and exploitation.
While animals and disabled humans experience marginalisation
and domination in different ways (e.g. humans are not processed
into meat), it is ableism that renders both non-human animals
and disabled humans less valuable and discardable (Taylor, 2017,
pp. 41–43). For example, the mercy killing of animals is affected

---

[23] It could be argued that we have to take into account the evolutionary
plateau we live on at the moment (see Williams, 2006, p. 148), and the
range of abilities it provides us with; we live in a disablist world that
continues to question the moral worth of persons with PIMD. When we
pursue theoretical explanations that would reduce or hopefully remove
the devaluing and marginalisation of this group of people, we have to
take into account the reality where it is implemented. And the reality is
perhaps still too ignorant and dismissing about disability rights in order to suggest comparisons between disabled humans and nonhuman
animals (Vehmas & Watson, 2016).

by human ableism and exemplifies the two prominent responses to disability: destruction and pity. We kill disabled animals
because we equate disability with suffering; they are better off
dead than being inflicted by disability. This is a natural response
considering the fact that the 'assumptions and prejudices we hold
about disabled bodies run deep – so deep that we project this human ableism onto nonhuman animals' (Taylor, 2017, p. 23).

We are not convinced, however, that ableism is an appropriate
concept to be used in this context. After all, ableism is a belief system that impairment or disability is inherently negative and makes people less than fully human; disability 'is cast as a diminished
state of being human' (Campbell, 2009, p. 5). Considering the
meaning of the concept: is it, in fact, true that ableism is the reason
for the mistreatment, and in general for the lower moral worth of
both animals and humans with disabilities? We think not, because
ableism and disablism[24] are first and foremost *human* prejudices
about disabled *human* lives.[25] This is not to deny that there may
be some common roots to the lower status of these two groups.
After all, it can plausibly be argued that both animals and disabled people are commodities in a capitalist machinery where their
bodies and lives are controlled in order to maximise the profit of
their input. Animals, for example, are sometimes made immobile
and bred so huge that they can hardly walk, just to maximise their
profit to the food industry (Taylor, 2017, p. 32).

Disabled people, for their part, are judged to be disabled in terms
of their economic contributions and value to society. According
to the British social model of disability, the political economy of

---

[24] 'Ableism' and 'disablism' are sometimes used interchangeably as synonyms for 'discrimination against people with disabilities'. However, in
Campbell (2009), for example, ableism refers to the cultural dominance
of non-disabled norms. It seems that Taylor is using the term this way,
as a form of cultural dominance that results in the oppression of both
disabled people and nonhuman animals.
[25] Interestingly, ableism also permeates animal rights discourse; vegans are
represented as healthy and attractive, whereas 'eating animals leads people to be fat, diseased, lazy, unhealthy, and unattractive' (Taylor, 2017,
p. 43). Thus, even ableism in animal rights communities seems to be directed against humans, not against animals, which in its part goes to
show that ableism as such cannot be equated with speciesism.

society ultimately dictates which conditions are considered to be impairments (and thus disabling), and it dictates the institutional responses to disability, which in the capitalist mode of production become commodities (Oliver, 1990). Especially in a private social service and health care system (e.g. in the USA and nowadays to some extent also in the Nordic countries), aids and equipment, medication and rehabilitation have become objects of commerce, and a huge market (Albrecht, 1992, pp. 14, 21, 68). But to conceptualise disability and disability services only in terms of economic exploitation would be one-sided. This is because disability is, importantly, also a crucial feature of the welfare state; it is an administrative category and device for social policy that entitles the members of this category to privileges in the form of social aid, and exemptions from certain obligations of citizenship such as work and military service (Stone, 1984, pp. 3–13).

It is thus clear that both animals and disabled people continue to be victims of exploitation, which is a crucial element of oppression (Young, 1990). But, as Taylor admits, the exploitation of these two groups manifests in different ways; disabled people have been used to medical experiments in concentration camps and institutions hidden from the public eye, but they have never been processed into meat and it is safe to claim that their unveiled use in medical experiments would not be tolerated even if it did result in cures for various illnesses. Considering the history of eugenics, institutionalisation and so on, it is clear that humans with intellectual disability have been treated and exploited like animals, but in secrecy, or under some moral justification; for example, institutionalisation was believed to serve the good of disabled people as well as being a mark of progress and civilisation (e.g. Kivirauma, 1987, pp. 200–201), whereas the sterilisation laws served the common good (e.g. Burleigh, 1994, pp. 40–46). As regards animals, such moral reasons were not needed. So, animal and disabled human lives seem to be evaluated, treated and also exploited differently. Why is this?

For an exploitative mindset, things, including living beings, have only instrumental value. In the case of animals, their instrumental value is evaluated either in terms of practical utility (e.g. draught animals and guide dogs) or economic profitability (e.g. livestock and racehorses).[26] For an exploitative mindset, animals with no instrumental value are simply irrelevant; there is no reason to be bothered about their well-being or ill-being. But, in the case of disabled people, the instrumental and exploitative logic works perhaps a bit differently. People with disabilities, especially those with PIMD, are conceptualised in negative sense when they are seen as useless; they eat from the common table without bringing anything to it. This instrumental logic when evaluating the worth of individual humans was taken to its extreme conclusion in Nazi Germany, where people with intellectual disability where conceptualised as 'empty shells of human beings' and 'human ballasts' (Lifton, 1988, p. 47). It was a child with PIMD who marked the beginning of euthanasia for disabled children. Notoriously, there was a petition to allow the mercy killing of an infant called Knauer, who, according to Hitler's personal doctor, Karl Brandt, was 'born blind, an idiot — at least it seemed to be an idiot — and it lacked one leg and part of an arm' (Burleigh, 1994, pp. 94–95). Consequently, approximately some 300,000 disabled people were murdered between 1939 and 1945. However, the euthanasia programme of disabled people was carried out in secrecy and the real cause of their deaths were forged because the public opinion would not have tolerated the killings (e.g. Burleigh, 1994, pp. 156–174, 227–248; Proctor, 1988 pp. 191–193).

Perhaps due to the Nazi Germany atrocities, it is nowadays ethically and politically inappropriate to evaluate the moral value of human beings purely and openly in terms of their productivity. It is safe to say that there exists a large consensus among political theorists and the general public that economically unproductive people should be taken care of, and it is thought that they share the same moral value as the rest of humankind, and that they should be treated accordingly. Naturally, the reality is a lot more complex

---

[26] Livestock and racehorses are undoubtedly good examples of animals that are exploited, but does this apply to guide dogs similarly? Perhaps there is a difference in that the reason for the use of guide dogs can be seen as ethically more justified than the use of livestock or racehorses. Even if this were the case, guide dogs are, in any case, trained and used non-voluntarily for the advantage of humans. In other words, they are exploited. Whether it is a morally justified form of exploitation is a separate issue.

and a lot less politically correct; it can plausibly be argued that these days neoliberalism contributes to the devaluing of disabled bodies and minds, thus resurging practices from the Industrial Revolution that dictate who are fully human (Hughes, 2012). But these kinds of cultural conceptions that place lower value on disabled people are not expressed explicitly in economic-instrumental terms, the way they indeed are expressed in relation to animals. It is generally accepted (although increasingly problematic) to view non-human animals as morally less valuable than humans, to treat them as means for profit, and nothing else (as is the case with livestock). It would not, however, be appropriate to think about disabled people in similar lines even if they were, in fact, treated instrumentally and animalised in various ways.[27]

So, although it is completely reasonable to argue that there are similarities in the ways animals and disabled people are being mistreated, exploited and even oppressed, the species does make a difference. Consider again the example of animal mercy killings: conceptions of human disability being tragic are projected onto animals with the result that we kill them out of mercy (Taylor, 2017, p. 23). It is true that human beings in general think that disability is something undesirable but what undesirability means in practice, and exactly how undesirable it actually is, is related to one's species. That is, it is not insignificant in the case of mobility impairment to consider its bearer's species; a broken leg (let alone a missing leg) for a deer is great disadvantage as it will not be able escape predators, whereas for humans a missing limb is a disadvantage mostly for environmental reasons, and not a deadly one, anyway. So, beings across species have different criteria for well-being and a good life. There are undoubtedly some sources of well-being or ill-being that are universally bad (e.g. excruciating pain), irrespective the subject's species. That is, causing

---

[27] Pets are a special group of animals whose moral status is not directly related to their species but, rather, to their relationship with their owners. In in some philosophical accounts their moral status is seen somewhat similar to that of people with PIMD (see Vehmas & Curtis, 2017). But from that view there is long way to the conclusion that persons with PIMD could be put down for their own good when they suffer from incurable sickness, as is the case with pets.

excruciating pain by torture to a human being (whether he or she is disabled or not) is always wrong, as is torturing a pig, because torturing is in and of itself morally wrong. However, torturing a human would be even *more* wrong than torturing a pig (Curtis & Vehmas, 2016a; 2016b; see Appendix).

Animality in practice: architecture

As the previous discussion probably made clear, it remains somewhat unclear to us whether conceptualising the lives of persons with PIMD in terms of animality would, all things considered, be useful. So, what we will do next is to unpack some elements of their lives in our data in terms of animality, and see whether such analysis is productive. We have chosen the following three factors: architecture, the warehousing mentality in care work, and the view of persons with PIMD as menace.

Considering that adults with PIMD typically do not go to work and do not study, their living conditions are perhaps the most important factor when evaluating their everyday lives. Until very recently, persons with PIMD have been placed in Western countries in dire conditions in institutions that often have been a mixture of prison and piggery. Places like Willowbrook in Staten Island, NYC, were in the 1960s and 1970s overcrowded and filthy, where children were even used as guinea pigs in medical experiments (Rothman & Rothman, 2004). Some inhumane living conditions in the past could have been partly due to the contemporary beliefs about the lack of sensory acuity of individuals with intellectual disability; that is, that they are insensitive to heat and cold. This belief was popular into the mid-1800s and often resulted in the institutions' residents being denied heat during the winter (Wolfensberger, 1972, p. 18). But often the animalisation of disabled people has manifested in more subtle ways. For example, architectural solutions in institutions speak powerful language of the animality of their residents:

> putting a drain in the middle of a living room floor ... interprets the person who lives in such a room as an animal who must be 'kept' and cleaned as in a zoo. A non-enclosed toilet says that its user has no human feeling of modesty. Bars on the windows, or

even an isolated location of a building, suggests that the building's inhabitants are a menace to society. (Wolfensberger, 1972, p. 40)

In his analysis of the living conditions of people with intellectual disability in institutions in the 1970s and before, Wolfensberger (1972) described various other ways where architecture and design of a building creates an atmosphere where the residents are expected to act in primitive, uncontrolled ways – in subhuman ways. Examples of such design solutions are walls, floors and furniture made of indestructible materials, as well as locked areas and living units in remote locations. These kinds of solutions have the intention of minimising the risk of self-harm or harm to others. In reality, they first and foremost exclude living conditions that could in any way be depicted as cosy, and minimise the possibility of residents having any natural encounters with ordinary people. Also, since individuals with PIMD have been perceived as subhuman, they have not been believed to be capable of meaningful choices. The possibility to express control in traditional institutions over one's environment has been very limited even regarding such basic things as lighting, as well as water and room temperature, which were often controlled mechanically, or by the members of the staff. And, since the residents have been seen as lacking judgement and capacities for rational decision-making, they have had no genuine rights to things such as privacy (e.g. toilets and bedrooms had no doors), property (e.g. great limitations to space and access to one's own possessions, no entitlement for payment for one's work), communication and individuality (e.g. being managed in groups when, for example, showered and toileted) (Wolfensberger, 1972, pp. 64–66).

Currently, individuals with PIMD live mostly in group homes that are in no way comparable to institutions like Willowbrook when it comes to spaciousness, hygiene and medical care. But, when considering the living conditions of our research participants, some similarities prevail. One of them is the institution-like aesthetics in many group homes; in those places one does not feel like entering someone's home but a reasonably pleasant hospital ward. Unlike in the UK or Australia, for example, in Finland group homes are commonly still located in purpose-built separate housing units that usually more closely resemble nursing homes than private homes. The premises are built and owned either by the local council, a private company or a third-sector care provider organisation. These units are often designed by architects who have specialised in designing care spaces rather than homes for people. This tradition is very much present in the building projects that take place as part of the ongoing deinstitutionalisation process. While these problems have been recognised in the public discussions concerning deinstitutionalisation in Finland, the tradition of building care units primarily according to the requirements set by functionality prevails (Mietola, Teittinen & Vesala, 2013). One key question is whether the new homes should be designed and built on the terms of the staff (building functional working spaces for them) or the residents (providing them with ordinary homes). The interests of the staff and residents may be seen to conflict with one another, especially in the case of houses for persons with extensive needs, who require special equipment and aids.

It was obvious in the case of some group homes in our study that they had been designed to be sites for care work rather than ordinary homes. The first appearance of these spaces was that they were functional but dull, and that looked and felt like small-scale hospitals rather than someone's home (see Clement & Bigby, 2010, pp. 73–76, 82–85, 90–92). They were often dominated by corridors and wide-open spaces, with very little furniture in the common areas. In two of the four group homes in our research, the kitchen area (the residents had no kitchen in their own apartments)[28] was either closed from the residents (considered a staff-only space) or designed to be inaccessible for wheelchair users and thus made impossible for them to participate in preparation of the meals. In two of the units, there were observation cubicles (called offices) near the entrance, with windows opening to corridors that enabled the staff members to observe in- and outgoing residents.

---

[28] Typically, group home apartments in Finland have a provision for a kitchen but they are often not built, especially in the case of persons with PIMD. Their apartments are typically 20–30 square metres (sometimes smaller), consisting of a room and a bathroom.

Alongside these obvious markers of institutional design, in some of the group homes the institutional atmosphere was amplified by the decoration (or the lack of it) in the common spaces of the group home. In one of the group homes, for example, the large living room that was connected to the dining area had a TV, a small sofa, and a beanbag placed along the walls of the wide space. The residents were usually sitting in their wheelchairs, placed in-between the TV and the furniture. The sofa was rarely used by either the residents or the care workers. All in all, the living room was not inviting or homely in any conventional meaning of the word – it was more of a lobby or entrance hall, looking and functioning better as a through-passage than as a living room. In another group home, the living room was not really a room but more of a narrow space in-between a corridor and a dining area, with a big electric box (with a sticker saying '*sähkökaappi*' ('electric box')) placed on the wall, behind the sofa. Moreover, the sofa was facing the TV, which had Plexiglas covering it.

Considering the institutional architecture and decoration devoid of beauty in many group homes, an analogy to a modern, clean cowhouse is not far-fetched; cows cannot appreciate beauty, can they? If persons with PIMD are assumed to lack aesthetic sensibilities, it would seem pointless to spend resources on attractive furniture, colours or art. If they are like cows, why bother? It needs to be pointed, however, that many group homes are different and base their living conditions on the premise that the aesthetic environment makes a difference in the lives of those with PIMD. So, alongside dull, institution-like group homes, we have witnessed group homes that are architecturally ambitious both in terms of functionality and aesthetics, and where attention has been paid to interior architecture and design, as well as seasonal decoration (e.g. Halloween, Christmas) that has been planned and implemented together with the residents.

Warehousing versus caring

The second, and perhaps the most important, similarity between notorious institutions like Willowbrook and some current institutional arrangements is the lack of programme, method and purpose. Consider the following example of a visit to a day activity centre. Reetta and Simo arrive at the centre around noon and find a group of persons with PIMD (including one of our research participants) sitting by themselves in a room with music playing while the staff were having a coffee break in the room next door.[29] The staff continued their break for another 30 minutes or so, and, after that, they wheeled their 'clients' to another room and announced that now was the time for a music session.

What followed was some 45 minutes of music videos shown from YouTube. The music videos (which were mostly Finnish 'teenage pop') were picked by the care workers according to each participant's taste in music (based on the evaluations by the care workers together with the music therapist that visited the day centre once a week). The videos were projected onto a screen while the participants were held by the care workers, or sitting by themselves in their wheelchairs. Irrespective of the interaction between the care workers and the participants, the session's atmosphere felt mechanical, almost apathetical. Reetta witnessed similar music sessions where the persons with PIMD were left on their own to listen and watch videos while the care workers did paperwork. The problem with these kinds of session was that they were executed for groups without consideration of individual differences (for example, some of the participants had significant visual impairments, which made us wonder whether showing videos was the best way to engage them with music).

What was typical of this day activity centre was that, while they did have written plans and 'timetables', too often the activities were carried out mechanically and indifferently, with little consideration of the differences of the service users' capacities and preferences. Too often, it seemed that these 'activities' were completely random, just a way of killing time. Exceptions to these dull routines were the sessions provided by some external professionals like music or physical therapists, who once a week came to the centre to meet some of the clients individually. However, it needs to be remembered, once again, that the staff members

---

[29] They were usually the same couple of records playing that could be best described as muzak or elevator music (e.g. panpipe versions of easy listening hits).

in day centres can do only as much they realistically can. They repeatedly complained about sudden changes in staff due to, for example, sick leave. Some day centres were not even allowed to hire replacement workers. Thus, even in cases where there were planned activities, they had to be cancelled or modified due to the lack of staff resources. These kinds of problems were typical of both day activity centres and group homes.

We would argue that the kind of service culture that has no clear programme or method does not provide proper care for persons with PIMD. What it does provide is what could be depicted as warehousing services. Just like some reasonably well maintained dwelling places for livestock (e.g. piggeries and cowhouses), these kinds of group home and day centre are merely expensive warehouses that provide very little activity or dignity to persons with PIMD. Also, the music sessions we witnessed reminded us of the way music is sometimes used with animals; music can be played, for example, to make cows voluntarily approach an automatic milking system (Uetake, Hurnik, & Johnson, 1997), improve the welfare of laboratory animals (Alworth & Buerkle, 2013), or mitigate stress for kennelled dogs (Kogan, Schoenfeld-Tacher, & Simon, 2012). In other words, the function of music in all the aforementioned cases was not to make people with PIMD, milking cows, laboratory rats or kennelled dogs learn something, to provide them with means of development and change. The function of music in all these cases was to keep the human and non-human animals content and docile.

When it comes to living arrangements, however, it needs to be remembered that the group homes are, as the name suggest, our research participants' homes, and, when you are at home, it is important to have the opportunity to do absolutely nothing. People usually do not want their homes to be like activity centres, with timetables and directed activities. However, the problem with many of our research participants is that they need assistance even in 'chilling out', because they need help with virtually anything that includes choices of some sort. The crucial point is to judge whether certain kinds of living or activity arrangements enable a good life, or whether their actual function is to maintain the system's conviction in its own legitimacy; are their practices merely 'good enough', like patches on a sore that would need more thorough care?

PIMD as a menace

One dimension of the animality of persons with intellectual disability is the view of them as menaces, as threats to the safety of other humans (Wolfensberger, 1972, p. 67). In the early 20th century especially, intellectual disability was not only linked with various social vices but seen as a prominent and persistent cause of those vices (Trent, 1994, p. 141). People with intellectual disability were seen sexually promiscuous, breeders of feeble-minded offspring, and victims and spreaders of poverty, degeneracy, crime and disease. In other words, they were responsible not only for the corruption of the genetic stock but also for the degeneration of common morality and, ultimately, the ruin of the whole of civilisation (Metzel, 2004, p. 425; Rothman & Rothman, 2004, p. 449). In order to prevent them from spreading 'misery, pauperism, degeneracy and crime' (Trent, 1994, p. 142), it was morally and politically pivotal to confine individuals with intellectual disability to segregated institutions, where their alleged immoral tendencies could be controlled more efficiently.

Now, the eugenic and moral hysteria of the early decades of the 20th century has calmed down, and people with PIMD live increasingly in ordinary residential areas due to deinstitutionalisation. But, still, they are often anything but welcomed by their neighbours. The view of people with intellectual disability as a menace to social order and morality is still one element of the not-in-my-backyard mentality (e.g. Dear, 1992); they are seen to lack control of their impulses, which makes them unpredictable and potentially violent (Wilkinson & McGill, 2009) – a view well presented in John Steinbeck's *Of Mice and Men*, where Lenny, a benign man with an intellectual or learning disability of some kind, unintentionally kills a young girl because he could not control his physical strength when trying in panic to prevent her from screaming. Persons with PIMD, however, have multiple impairments and often very limited mobility, which means that they do not pose a physical threat to others. Rather, they are seen and experienced as a nuisance in that they cause inconvenience to other people, like to the young care worker in a group home in our study, who once snapped loudly with frustration, 'Oh no! He's pissed himself again!' when one of the residents wet his trousers (luckily, these kinds of incidents were not common). Also, some practices were clearly based more on the interests of the care workers than those of our research participants. For example, Ella was fed at her day centre, whereas at home she was allowed to eat by herself, and make a mess and be covered in food afterwards. Because of this, she took a shower at least once a day. In some other group homes, things were different; the residents were allowed to take a shower according to a set timetable (e.g. once every three days), which undoubtedly was more convenient for the staff.

But often the menace caused by a person with PIMD to others can be a matter of emotional inconvenience, as in the case of sexuality. Wolfensberger (1972, p. 167), for example, concluded that one reason that the sexuality of those with intellectual disability makes us feel uncomfortable is that 'such individuals are not fully human, and though perhaps capable of mating like animals, they cannot "marry"'. In other words, the sexual acts and desires of people with PIMD can be perceived as animal acts and desires because allegedly they are not capable for deep emotional connection or respect towards their possible sexual partners. If human sexuality is not merely a matter of pleasures of sensation but about activities that involve intentional pleasure and thoughts pertaining to it (Primoratz, 1999, p. 22), or if it is about the mutual recognition of arousal between persons (Nagel, 1979, pp. 39–52), individuals with PIMD are not capable of experiencing *human* sexuality, let alone having *human* sex. They are exhibiting bare animal lust. Such conception would be only logical if those with PIMD are not seen as fully human, and incapable of experiencing romantic and erotic relationships in a spiritual sense of the word (whatever that may mean), or at least not suitable sexual subjects. When confronting sexual manifestations in the case of PIMD, doubt or even aversion may seem natural reactions. Just like in the case of children or animals, to regard persons with PIMD as sexual beings is socially inappropriate and prohibited. Considering this, it is hardly surprising that it feels perverted to see anything sexual in people who are widely portrayed as asexual and consequently have been desexualised (Hunt, 2018, p. 63).

Conclusion

In this chapter, we have analysed profound intellectual and multiple disabilities in terms of animality. The motivation for this endeavour has been normative: to see whether such an engagement would provide helpful ways to represent the everyday lives and lived experiences of people with PIMD. Therefore, the first part of the chapter was dedicated to normative discussion on whether conceptualising PIMD in terms of animality is accurate, fruitful and ethically justified. In other words, would it be intellectually, ethically and politically useful to conceptualise disability (and especially PIMD) as an animal-like condition in terms of individuals and their characteristics, or, alternatively, in terms of cultural and societal beliefs and practices? In the latter part of the chapter, we aimed to do just this: analyse the quotidian lives of persons with PIMD as animalised lives. Was that helpful? Does such conceptualisation have any other than mere shock value? After all, to say that people with PIMD live like cows is more likely to get a reaction rather than a mere 'their living conditions are dull and institution-like'. These kinds of concerns are anything but trivial. They are examples of the research ethics discussed in Chapter 2; what kind of knowledge research produces about persons with PIMD, and what impact it potentially has on their lives.

We continue to have mixed feelings about the metaphorical use of animality when analysing the lives of persons with PIMD. Analysing the lived experiences of a group of disabled people by comparison to some other group of people is not uncommon ('people with a given impairment are like...') but when such comparison is extended to non-human animals one cannot help but ponder whether we need to compare disabled people and their lives to anything at all. Are such comparisons necessary to enlighten their lives and to help other people engage with them? We are, however, inclined to think that such comparisons, even to animals, may be helpful intellectually and, to some extent, ethically as well, as they may help us to engage with the dullness and brutality of the institutionalised everyday lives of persons with

PIMD. This notion relies on the assumption that metaphors may be helpful in terms of ethical engagement despite the fact that they have force for better and for worse (e.g. Fraser, 2018). It would not be far-fetched to argue that making comparisons between disabled people and non-human animals would support the kind of understanding where disabled people are, in fact, seen to be like animals. And, if they are seen to be like animals, it would seem justified to treat them like animals, that is, as creatures that can be used as mere instruments to gain profit or as dispensable objects that can be eliminated should they have no instrumental value. Such a horror scenario may or may not be exaggerated.

But, despite these reservations, Grue and Lundblad (2020) are right to point out some common interest for animals and those people who cannot 'speak for themselves' in a culture where the ability to express one's voice is seen as a precondition for citizenship and moral standing. Even disability activism has worked on the terms of those who are articulate and has excluded individuals with PIMD and other conditions who have very limited capacities to express their own voice. If the principle 'nothing about us without us' is strictly applied, and if nobody else has the legitimacy to speak for persons with PIMD than themselves, they will have no voice, no social standing whatsoever. It would not be implausible to assume that, if one engages with the lived, personal experiences of those who cannot speak for themselves in any conventional sense of the phrase, one would become more receptive to those experiences irrespective of that being's species. Or, as Grue and Lundblad (2020, p. 125) argue, 'in seeking acceptance for one's humanity, there is little to be gained in looking beyond one's species. But if the goal is, rather, to seek acceptance of one's vulnerability, it may be inevitable.'

Chapter 8: Conclusion

When we began this study, our aim was to make sense of persons with PIMD – not just to understand their everyday lives but also to understand something about their inner lives. We soon realised, however, that we needed to be methodologically humble and acknowledge that we could not provide any kind of 'objective' account of our research participants, let alone their mental states. What we could do was to take part in their lives, observe empathetically, and try to understand and report the best we can what goes on in their lives. Through such an engagement we hoped to gain some understanding of what makes a life go well for persons with PIMD, or what a good life could mean for them.

What did we see happen in the lives of persons with PIMD and in the practices of the care system? We discovered that, in the everyday lives of our research participants, a good life materialises only in a very limited sense. Key factors that have contributed to this state of affairs are the following: (1) the institutionalisation of lives of people with PIMD; (2) the social isolation experienced by some service users; (3) that the lives of our research participants are encompassed by the disability service system; and (4) that the people we came to know often lived non-individualised and non-personalised lives.

Institutionalised lives. The lives of the people with PIMD who participated in our study, and, we believe, the lives of people with profound intellectual and multiple disabilities more generally, were embedded in institutional practices and routines that determined what and when happened in their lives. A consequence of this is that very little, in fact, happened in their lives: the rhythm and content of their everyday living was structured by basic care tasks

How to cite this book chapter:
Vehmas, S. and Mietola, R. 2021. *Narrowed Lives: Meaning, Moral Value, and Profound Intellectual Disability.* Pp. 177–184. Stockholm: Stockholm University Press. DOI: https://doi.org/10.16993/bbl.h. License: CC-BY 4.0.

like dressing, feeding and toileting. Care workers characterised the people they cared for as having narrow lives (*kapee elämä*).

Socially isolated lives. While all the research participants were constantly surrounded by other people (in that they lived in group homes and participate in day activity centres), they had little genuine opportunities for social interaction. Social isolation is particularly pronounced in those group homes and day centres that serve only people with severe or profound intellectual disability. In these contexts, usually all service users are in need of support in interaction. But, with very limited staff resources (each care worker is in charge for several people simultaneously), chances for assisted communication and interaction are slim.

Lives encompassed within the disability service system. Despite the fact that all the research participants lived in ordinary neighbourhoods (their group homes were located in suburban areas), they were not included in the community in any way. They spent the overwhelming majority of their time in the group home where they lived and the day activity centre they participated in. They usually moved between their home and day centre with accessible taxis. Only seldom did they use public transportation. Their presence in the public space was very circumscribed. The research participants interacted socially almost exclusively with the staff members, other service users and sometimes their family members.

Non-personalised, non-individualised lives. Owing to the way services in Finland are currently structured, the research participants had virtually no say concerning their everyday lives – not even about something as basic as what and when to eat. The principle of self-determination thus played barely any role in their lives. The services, furthermore, also neglect different aspects of service users' personalities and individual needs. For example, chronological age is not taken into account when services are planned or delivered. This means that our research participants who are of different ages lived fairly similar lives. Their lives were determined by their impairments and the institutional responses to their 'impaired existence', not by their personalities.

The reality that this summary portrays is undoubtedly grim. While, as we noted in the introduction, major advancements have taken place since the early stages of Finnish intellectual disability care, the personalities of people with profound intellectual disability continue to disappear under the PIMD label. We began this book with an anecdote related to the definition of PIMD and the significance of it. Conceptualisations of profound intellectual disability are important because, as our discussion (especially in Chapter 3) shows, conceptions of competence make a significant difference in how care work is organised and implemented. The fact that persons with PIMD are as diverse as any other group of people is acknowledged and highlighted by care workers. But this awareness among the staff had no recognised status in the care system, which was directed by a diagnostic ethos where the individuality of our research participants was often ignored. As a result, the practices and activities in group homes and day activity centres reproduced a homogenous group of people with a capacity to appreciate, generally speaking, only sensory stimuli. Care workers emphasised that many of those people who have profound intellectual disability have a capacity and desire for so-cial interaction. However, in most group homes this desire was ignored – a circumstance that, in our view, was not only due to insufficient staff resources. Rather, it was the result of a ware-housing mentality in which the threshold for an acceptable stan-dard of care meant keeping the residents fed and clean. Everything beyond that was optional.

One challenge for us during the writing process of this book was to provide a balanced account that would analyse and repre-sent the lives of our research participants with respect without falling into sentimentality: how do we address various ethical and practical issues that are intellectually difficult to resolve and emo-tionally uncomfortable to deal with, such as the grounds of moral status and issues to do with sexuality? And how do we repre-sent the lives of persons with PIMD in a way that simultaneously acknowledges their limitations and illuminates their capabilities: the things they *can* do, and possibly *could* do, if they only were given the chance? This difficulty was expressed in care workers' accounts as well. Staff members emphasised the individuality of persons with PIMD, but at the same time they hesitated to say what they thought our research participants were in fact capa-ble of understanding. Caution in making detailed descriptions of the individuality of persons with PIMD seems reasonable consi-dering that one is talking on behalf of people who cannot speak for themselves. In our view, such caution implies a commitment to epistemic modesty in order to avoid romanticised, stereotypical or prejudiced portraits of people with PIMD.

This book has offered critical accounts of the Finnish disability services and the care work provided for people with PIMD. However, our analyses and descriptions are unlikely to surprise care workers, because they are in line with the views they themselves expressed to us. In this sense our study presents the critique that already exists within the contexts we have researched. It elaborates and extends that critique, and presents it to a wider audience.

Our findings show that the current practices and circumstances are not completely in line with the current Finnish policy commitments regarding equal moral worth, rights and opportunities. Despite criticising the service system, professionals in all our research contexts were, interestingly, confident that their practices were good, and that they provided appropriate living conditions for their service users. Had they not believed in their ethical and professional standards, they most likely would not have let us access their workplaces in the first place.

We did not witness any mistreatment or abuse of the service users during the fieldwork. Our general impression was that the people with PIMD we worked with were treated with respect and that they were provided with appropriate basic care. Despite the lack of social engagement in our participants' lives, which we discussed in Chapter 4, we also witnessed some care workers' affectionate attachment and responsiveness to our research participants. While the shortcomings of the care culture in many group homes and day centres were evident, some of the care workers' skill in interpreting our participants' communication, as well as their commitment to their work, was impressive. Group homes and day centres are different, and so are the people working within them.

We pointed out in the introductory chapter that humanities and social science-based disability studies has largely ignored people with PIMD. While some advancement has taken place in terms of including persons with PIMD in disability studies research (Nind & Strnadová, 2020), people with profound intellectual disability are still by and large left 'out in the cold' (Chappell, 1998). Such negligence is difficult to reconcile with the political and epistemic premises of the field. It is, after all, one of the crucial aims of disability studies to make sense of how disability materialises as an antithesis for ideological concepts such as ability, norm and normalcy and how those concepts are constructed in ways that 'create the "problem" of disabled person' (Davis, 2013b, p. 1). By unpacking the social construction of such concepts and their manifestations, we are better equipped to contemplate what it means to be disabled and what it means to be human (Goodley, 2014, p. x), and how people with impairments are 'disabled by society's failure to accommodate their needs' (Barnes, Oliver, & Barton, 2002, p. 5). Thus, disability studies has redefined physical and intellectual impairments as a political issue instead of being just a personal, medical problem, and it has insisted that disability is an issue of social justice (e.g. Abberley, 1987; Linton, 1998; Shakespeare, 2006; Watson & Vehmas, 2020).

In order to understand what it means to be a person with PIMD, one needs to engage critically with the individual and the social dimension of disablement. In other words, we need to 're-cognise the profundity and complexity of what is going on within the individual, which interacts with disabling environmental and attitudinal factors' (Nind & Strnadová, 2020, p. 2). Persons with PIMD are among those people who force disability studies to reflect upon the meaning and significance of impairment, and the diversity of the disability experience (e.g. Vehmas & Watson, 2014). Such engagement combined with the theoretical tools provided by disability studies can help us to understand PIMD as an issue of ethics and social justice.

For the past few decades, disability studies scholars have argued that non-disabled people's views on disabled lives are often based on the idea that disability equals tragedy (Oliver, 1990). Anyone who has no personal relations of any kind to people like Anna or Sebastian seems likely see them only in terms of their impairments. Such a narrow – indeed, bigoted – view is evident in many philosophical accounts that present persons with PIMD only as examples, as stereotypes, who are defined entirely by what they allegedly lack: self-consciousness, the ability to experience aesthetic pleasure, the ability to perceive and enjoy deep personal relationships, and so on (e.g. McMahan, 1996 – see the discussion in the following appendix). As we saw in Chapter 3, care workers told us that it takes time and effort to learn to know people with PIMD as persons – people who have their own unique 'mixture of odd talents and personal quirks', as Ferguson & Ferguson (2001, p. 71) put it. It is through such time-consuming commitment that an individual with profound intellectual and multiple disabilities begins slowly to emerge as a person: Hugo as an inquisitive, easy-going guy or Ella as a charming middle-aged woman with the ability to make other people warm to her.[30]

The philosopher David Hume and later many care ethicists have argued that sympathy or benevolence to particular persons is a fundamental moral capacity that prompts moral action (e.g. Baier, 1987). A faceless figure with no recognised personality does not necessarily require emotional or moral consideration, the kind of response that would acknowledge his or her equal moral worth.[31] When an individual with a character 'behind the impairment' (as the care workers we worked with liked to put it) begins to emerge, it becomes difficult to dismiss that person in a moral sense. He or she needs to be treated like a person – someone who is valued for his or her own sake, whose happiness and well-being are taken as intrinsically important (Ikäheimo, 2009). In the case of persons with PIMD, such recognition requires a conception of personhood and well-being that transcends individual capacities. It is clear that, for persons with PIMD, well-being and the possibilities of a good life are, to a great degree, enabled or neglected by other people. Even their individuality, with its related wants and wishes, requires other people's recognition in order to materialise.

---

[30] Interestingly, Eva Kittay describes her daughter Sesha in a way that is somewhat similar to how the care workers depict Ella, as being charming (e.g. Kittay, 1999, p. 151). Eva also told Simo in personal communication how her friend, the well-known psychologist Walter Mischel, once told her that Sesha has great survival skills 'because she knows how to make people love her, and that is the most important survival skill of all'.

[31] People's moral consideration in this respect varies. Consider, for example, responses to the 2004 Abu Ghraib torture pictures, which mostly caused outrage but were minimized by many conservative commentators (Tétreault, 2006).

People with profound intellectual and multiple disabilities are no longer referred to as 'blockheads' or 'creatures at the lowest level' (Harjula, 1996, p. 64), nor is their dignity violated as grossly and openly as it was as recently as 50 years ago, when they were forced to live in inhuman conditions. But, despite all the practical and moral advances, some ethically problematic features remain in the lives of people with PIMD.

The first is the concern over their moral value: what kind of value is accorded to them, in both theory and in practice. Estimation of the value of people with limited cognitive capacities has changed only little in mainstream Western philosophy over the past 300 years. Since John Locke, human value has been based upon a psychological conception of personhood that posits capacities such as rationality and language as *the* property that make human beings distinctively human. The second, related concern is that people with profound intellectual and multiple disabilities are still seen as animal-like and, as we discussed in Chapter 7, perhaps even treated like animals. This materialises in a care culture that settles for warehousing. When people with PIMD are not considered to be human beings proper, they are not given the opportunity to experience and explore activities and experiences that commonly are usually valued by humans (such as aesthetic pleasures, or sex). This kind of care culture is a continuation of the long tradition of institutionalisation where disability services are run on the conditions set by the service providers rather than service users.

The general picture that we drew from our data is that persons with PIMD are not provided with possibilities to live a good life in the sense that they might flourish as individuals. Instead, the service system settles for a 'good enough' life, which means that the function of the services is to keep these individuals fed and cleaned properly. Too often, that is all. This is a kind of warehousing mentality that sees persons with PIMD as static individuals with predefined, age-independent, deindividualised needs, interests and skills.

This book has shown that this mentality has resulted in narrowed lives. But we have also argued that this is not an inevitable state of affairs, predetermined by the impairments of people like

Anna, Ella, Frida, Hugo, Leo and Sebastian. Instead, their lives are to a large extent determined by disability policy, care culture and ethical engagement, or the lack of it. Thus, in order to properly understand the lives of persons with PIMD, we also need to critically engage with *our* moral values and social arrangements.

In other words, it is not just about them. It is about us, too.

Appendix: On Moral Status

By Benjamin L. Curtis and Simo Vehmas

Introduction

As was explained in the first chapter, our research project and this book were initially motivated by philosophical debates regarding the moral status of people with profound intellectual disability. Someone unfamiliar with philosophical discourse may find these debates bizarre at best, for at least two reasons. The first is that a mere speculation about the moral status of persons with PIMD in any other way than affirmative may seem offensive. The other reason is the fact that philosophers often do not bother to communicate their ideas in an accessible manner, which may make their philosophising seem abstruse and insular. While we have tried to do our best to write on these issues as clearly as we could in earlier publications (e.g. Curtis & Vehmas, 2016a; Vehmas & Curtis, 2017), we have probably succumbed to an unnecessarily technical style of writing as well. Having said that, the issue of moral status is notoriously complicated and it is very difficult to do justice to the whole complexity of it without a degree of technicality. In this appendix, we aim to discuss the issue as clearly as we can and explain what the philosophical issues involved are. Where the material is technical, we try to spell out the concepts involved in detail. We also try to articulate where we think they go wrong, and why it is important that we do.

The philosophical analysis of this appendix has been a parallel project to ethnography. It differs from the rest of the book in that it concentrates on unpacking the strengths and weaknesses of different philosophical arguments without discussing the issue in the light of our data. This is simply because we evaluate *normative arguments* and our data cannot either verify or falsify those arguments. What data can do is to provide empirical material for philosophical arguments and show whether philosophers have used empirical knowledge appropriately. But, as such, data cannot prove whether, for example, psychological or relational properties are the normative foundation of one's moral status. In other words, there is no empirical evidence that would tell us, for example, why it would be wrong to kill people for fun. Solving that kind of question requires conceptual evidence.

The fundamental ethical principle that underpins the project that led to this book is that human beings with profound intellectual disability are beings with moral status equal to, and deserving of the same respect as, human beings without them. This principle entails that the interests and well-being of people with PIMD matter as much as anybody else's, and that those of us who do not have such impairments have a duty to understand them better, in order to discover what those interests truly are and how their well-being might be facilitated. Let us record this principle as follows:

> Equality: Human beings with profound intellectual disability have the same moral status as statistically typical non-disabled adult human beings.

We expect the equality principle will strike many readers of this book as blindingly obvious, or as being in some sense self-evident, or undeniable. We expect this because the equality of *all* humans, no matter what their ability, is often taken to be a foundational moral truth. Its spirit is captured in our fundamental legal documents, and is taken by many to encapsulate the very core of what it is to have civilised values at all. To give just one example, it is captured in the very first line of the Universal Declaration of Human Rights, which reads:

> Whereas recognition of the inherent dignity and of the equal and inalienable rights of all members of the human family is the foundation of freedom, justice and peace in the world. (UN General Assembly, 1948)

It may therefore come as a surprise to some to learn that, according to the standard view of moral status in the philosophical literature (known as moral individualism), the equality principle is false. In fact, according to moral individualists, because people with profound intellectual disability lack certain 'status-conferring' intrinsic properties, such as the capacity for high-level thought, they therefore have a *lower* moral status than non-disabled adult humans, and the *same* moral status as certain non-human animals (e.g. cattle or rats). As a being's moral status determines how a being may be treated, one consequence of this is that to farm and eat humans with profound intellectual disability is, in and of itself, no worse (morally speaking) than farming and eating cattle. And another is that experimenting on humans with PIMD is, in and of itself, as permissible (morally speaking) as experimenting on lab rats. Moral individualists recognise that there might be *instrumental* reasons not to do these things (e.g. because it will upset non-disabled people who care about disabled individuals), but there is no non-instrumental reason not to. These consequences are endorsed by those who defend moral individualism. Here, for example, is Jeff McMahan, probably the most prominent defender of the view:

> [S]uppose that a certain animal lacks any status-conferring intrinsic property that would make it impermissible to kill that animal as a means of saving several people's lives. Suppose further that there are no [instrumental] reasons that oppose killing it – for example, it is no one's pet. ... According to moral individualism, if it is permissible to kill the animal, it should also be permissible – again assuming no [instrumental] reasons apply – to kill, for the same purpose, a human being who also lacks any relevant status conferring intrinsic properties. (McMahan, 2005, p. 355)

We expect many readers will find these consequences morally shocking, and may even think that anyone who endorses them thereby betrays some gross moral failing. But it is important to realise that, within the philosophical literature, it is not only a mainstream view; it is the most widely endorsed view and considered standard by many. And this matters, because philosophical views do trickle out from the academy into society, through popular books, or because philosophers sit on ethical advisory panels and are consulted on governmental policy documents with ethical implications. Indeed, McMahan himself sits on such panels, as do other moral individualists. And so it is important that we engage with their arguments in their own terms and attempt to show where they go wrong.

We expect that many readers of this book will be tempted by a very quick response to moral individualism. This is to simply stamp one's foot and declare 'We *know* all humans have an equal moral status, and that's the end of it!' But we want to urge against giving *only* this kind of response. It is not that it is a *bad* response. In fact, as we will see, it is a fundamentally sound response and one that is important to make. But the point is that we should also be interested in taking moral individualism and the arguments in favour of it seriously. We should not be content with saying *that* moral individualism goes wrong, but also attempt to say *where* it goes wrong. If we are to deepen our moral understanding of human equality itself, and our understanding of the moral value that humans with PIMD have, a close examination of these arguments is essential.

Before we begin the main discussion, we wish to include a few words of autobiography, for reasons related to what we have just said, and for other reasons that will become clear. We (Benjamin and Simo) have been working on the issue of moral status and profound intellectual disability since 2010. We began working together precisely because each of us recognised the influence of the arguments put forward by moral individualists against the equality principle, but we also shared the feeling that their conclusions are morally shocking, and that therefore those arguments *must* be wrong. But, in the spirit of intellectual modesty, we admit that since then we have struggled to say *precisely* where the arguments of the moral individualists do in fact go wrong. In a pair of early papers we developed an account according to which moral status can be grounded in relational terms (Curtis & Vehmas, 2014; Vehmas & Curtis, 2017). It is a position that we now, at least partially, reject. However, as we will explain, we do think that that position contained a kernel of truth, and we now think that we have at least the beginnings of a correct response to moral individualism. And so in this appendix we outline the point that we have arrived at. We also admit that we have no *fully* worked out answers and that there is much work still to be done in this regard. The outlines of an alternative position are now becoming clear, but our work here is ongoing, and we still need to work out its details. At any rate, we hope that this appendix gives the reader a good sense of the philosophical debate we are engaged in, its importance, and where we now stand in that debate. We also hope it makes clear that the overall empirical project from which this book issued has serious philosophical underpinnings.

The structure of what follows, then, is this: in Section 1 we first explain and defend the idea that we can continue to accept the truth of equality without giving a detailed positive account of its truth, and reject moral individualism without being able to say where it goes wrong. Given what we have said above, we nonetheless recognise the importance of saying where moral individualism does go wrong. In Section 2 we explain the basic principle that underlies the moral individualist position: the principle that an individual's moral status must be grounded in the possession of intrinsic properties alone. In Section 3 we explain why moral individualists think that the only intrinsic properties that can do the job are psychological properties, and show why this leads to the rejection of equality. Then in Section 4 we consider what seem to be the only two possible responses to moral individualism – to maintain that all humans are psychologically equal in some important respect, or to adopt a relational account of moral status. We reject both of these responses, but then in Section 5 argue that there is in fact a further (third) response available that has been overlooked. This is to accept that intrinsic properties are important, but that their *significance* can be relational. We think that this response holds great promise. Finally, in Section 6 we finish by saying a little about how we think it might be developed.

1. Equality as a Moorean moral belief

We have already noted that we suspect many readers will be tempted by a quick response to moral individualism, i.e. to reject the view *without* saying where it goes wrong. Although we have also said we urge against giving *only* this response, we have also said that this response is fundamentally sound and one that it is important to give. Why is it important? Because moral individualists have a very well worked out, unified theoretical position, one that has been developed in a great amount of detail and that is agreed upon by many working in the field. Jeff McMahan, mentioned above, has provided what is, in effect, a book-length defence of the view in *The Ethics of Killing* (McMahan, 2002), supplemented by numerous journal articles (e.g. McMahan, 1996, 2005, 2008, 2009, 2016). And many other philosophers, including James Rachels and Peter Singer, have book-length defences of the same basic view, supplemented by numerous further journal articles of their own (e.g. Rachels, 1987, 1990, 2002, 2004; Singer, 1979, 1989, 2010, 2016). Not everything within their books and articles pertain *precisely* to the issue of moral status and profound intellectual disability. And nor is it the case that the proponents of moral individualism agree on *every* detail of the view. But everything that they have written forms a more or less coherent network of mutually supporting views that also supports moral individualism. And, even if they disagree on some of the details, they agree on the fundamentals.

In short, then, to oppose moral individualism is to oppose a large body of well-supported unified theory. By contrast, the opposition to moral individualism in the literature is largely unsystematic and often theoretically unsatisfying, for reasons we will come to. While many have written rejecting the view, the positive opposing views have been developed in a multitude of ways, in much less detail, and with little agreement on even the broad outlines of what the correct alternative view should look like (for an overview of the multitude of opposing views, see Wasserman, Asch, Blustein, & Putnam, 2017). As such, it is important to give the short answer to moral individualism to thwart the following line of argument from the moral individualists (here we summarise the general moral individualist view of the opposition):

> Generally speaking, in every domain of enquiry, we should believe the best current theory. With regard to moral status, that theory is moral individualism. It is true that some have developed other views, but there is much disagreement, and they have not been developed in anything like the same detail that moral individualism has been. As such, the alternative views should be considered promissory notes at best. Until they have been worked out in the same

level of detail as moral individualism, and shown to withstand criticism in the way that moral individualism does, moral individualism remains our best moral theory and we should continue to believe it. It is true that moral individualism contradicts the equality principle, and so contradicts pre-theoretical moral beliefs, but sometimes we do have to give up our pre-theoretical beliefs when our best theory entails their falsity.

The above line of argument is plausible, but it fails. It fails because, although it is *better* to have a fully worked out response, we are nonetheless entitled to reject moral individualism, at least on a personal level, without having a fully worked out alternative account available. We now turn to why this is so.

While it is true that we may sometimes have to revise our pre-existing moral beliefs in light of theory, there are limits on what revisions are acceptable. Our moral beliefs, like all beliefs, are held with varying degrees of confidence, and so some are more readily abandoned than others. Those moral beliefs that are very hard to give up are our strongly held core moral beliefs, and that a moral theory is consistent with these is more important than its consistency with our more weakly held peripheral moral beliefs. An example here might be the belief that travelling by aeroplane to go on holiday is morally blameless. Moreover, certain moral beliefs are so strongly held that they act as fixed points in our moral theorising. An example here is the belief that kicking another human to death for fun is morally wrong. This is a moral belief such that our degree of confidence in its truth is invariably stronger than the degree of confidence we might have in any proposed moral theory that contradicts it. We call beliefs of this kind our 'Moorean moral beliefs', after G.E. Moore, who argued that certain kinds of belief are immune from revision due to philosophical argument (Moore, 1939). He illustrated this by considering the belief that each of us can express in the first person using the sentence 'I know that I have hands'. There are various radical sceptical arguments that purport to show that this belief is false (the most famous being Descartes's argument that, for all we know, the external world does not exist at all, and we are being deceived into thinking that it does by a demon). But Moore's point was that none of these arguments can ever be successful, for our degree of confidence in their premises can never outweigh the degree of confidence we have in the existence of our hands. In just the same way, we think that the belief about kicking human beings to death for fun is not merely a widely held pre-existing moral belief but a Moorean moral belief – it is a belief that is so central to our moral outlook that it simply not open to revision in the light of theory. More to the point, we think that equality *also* captures a Moorean moral belief. Thus, one can be confident that moral individualism is wrong, and reject it, even if one does not have a fully worked out alternative theory to offer in its place.

Of course, moral individualists might respond to the above by pointing out that they themselves deny equality, and that, as such, it cannot be a Moorean moral belief (otherwise, they might say, they would *not be able* to deny it). Our response to this is to note that moral individualist views are formed in something of an empirical vacuum. It is easy enough to deny the Moorean nature of equality and to maintain the lower moral status of humans with profound intellectual disability only so long as such humans are thought of in the abstract, and only so long as one has little physical contact with, and little first-hand knowledge of, what such humans are really like. But we do not think that anyone who has actually spent time getting to know humans with profound intellectual disability could deny that they have the same moral status as non-disabled humans, and so deny the Moorean nature of equality.

To summarise, our basic position is this: our belief in the principle of equality is a fundamental moral belief of such importance that we are entitled to hold it to be true even without having available a theoretical justification for it. In addition, we are personally entitled to reject any moral theory that contradicts it without saying where that theory goes wrong. And so, because moral individualism does contradict equality, we are personally entitled to reject it without saying where it goes wrong. However, for the reasons given above (i.e. because moral individualism is such an influential view), it is also important that we *do* examine where moral individualism goes wrong. And so it is to this task that we now turn.

2. Grounding moral status

It is worth noting to begin with that moral individualists agree, at least to some extent, with what we have said above. Although they do not think equality captures a Moorean moral belief, they do recognise that it is a highly intuitive principle, and that rejecting it leads to accepting highly counterintuitive consequences like those we signalled in the introduction (e.g. that to farm and eat humans with PIMD is, in and of itself, no worse than farming and eating cattle). They also agree that our moral theories should cohere, in large part at least, with our intuitive moral judgements. However, they think that (in the absence of any other plausible moral theory) moral individualism is strong enough to warrant believing it true, and so strong enough to give up belief in the principle of equality, and to accept the highly counterintuitive results. The basic principle that they invoke, they think, is itself highly intuitively plausible, and allows us to explain a huge number of our pre-theoretical moral beliefs. And for this reason, they think, we should accept that it is true. What, then, is this basic principle? It is this:

> Status intrinsicality: An individual's moral status must be grounded in its possession of morally relevant intrinsic properties.

Moral individualists then argue that it is only an individual's intrinsic psychological properties that are morally relevant, and that individuals with profound intellectual disability do not possess such properties sufficient to ground a high moral status. So, they think that the principle of equality cannot be maintained. Let us spell out this view in more detail.

We start off with the idea of 'grounding'. Status intrinsicality contains the notion that moral status must be 'grounded' in further properties. What does this mean? The general idea is that a property needs to be grounded when that property is not a simple unanalysable one, that is, one that cannot be defined or explained in terms of any more basic or simple property. Plausible examples of properties that are simple and unanalysable, and so do *not* need to be grounded, are the fundamental physical properties like mass and charge. For example, electrons are taken by physicists to be fundamental particles – they are not 'built up' from any more fundamental particles. They are basic carriers of charge, specifically negative charge. So, physicists say that electrons are objects that possess the property of *having a charge of -1*. The 'having of this property' is not explainable in any more basic terms. It is simply a brute fact of nature: electrons have such a charge, and that is all there is to say about the matter.

To return now to status intrinsicality, the principle states that an individual's moral status cannot be fundamental in the same way that an electron's negative charge is fundamental to it. The idea is that there must be something more we can say, some further property or properties in terms of which its possession by an object (in this case a person) can be explained. It is useful to consider some simple examples to illustrate. Consider shape properties, for example the properties of *being square* and of *being round*. These are properties of macroscopic objects – TV sets are square, and beach balls are round, for example (very roughly speaking). But, we can ask, are these simple, unanalysable properties of these things, or are they *grounded* in some more fundamental properties? And here the answer is quite clear. They are *not* simple unanalysable properties. TV sets are square *because* they are made up of fundamental particles arranged in a certain way (i.e. squarewise) and beach balls are round *because* they are made up of fundamental particles arranged in a *different* way (i.e. roundwise). That is to say, being made of particles arranged squarewise *explains* why TV sets are square, and being made of particles arranged roundwise *explains* why beach balls are round. Thus, shape properties are *grounded* in the further property of being made up of particles arranged in a certain way.

However, there is more we can say about this simple example. *Being square* and *being round* are both *intrinsic* properties of objects. That is, whether an individual possesses the property of *being square* or *being round* depends *only* on the way that thing is in itself, and does not depend on the way that any *other* thing is. Roughly speaking, you can tell that something is square, for example, just by looking at *it*. You do not need to consider any *other* thing. Contrast shape properties like this with familial properties of persons like *being a sibling*. These latter properties, unlike the former, are *extrinsic* or *relational* properties. That is, whether a person possesses the property of *being a sibling* depends on that person standing in relations to *some other thing*. Roughly speaking, again, you cannot tell that someone is a sibling just by looking at *her or him alone*. Barack Obama is a sibling, for example, and this is not a simple unanalysable property of him. But in this case what grounds the fact that he is a sibling is not that he is himself a certain way, but rather that he stands in certain familial *relations* to some other things, i.e. his brothers and sisters. Thus, the property of *being a sibling* is *grounded* in the fact that things possessing them bear certain relations to other things.

The above examples, then, enable us to spell out the moral individualist position more clearly. Moral individualists hold that a person's moral status is, like a ball's roundness, not a simple unanalysable property, and so must be grounded in some further property or properties of the person. And, they maintain, a person's moral status is an *intrinsic* property, and so again akin to a ball's roundness (rather than, for example, a person's being a sibling). So, they maintain, an individual's particular moral status cannot be grounded relationally, that is, in terms of what relations that individual stands in to other things, but must instead be grounded in the possession of some further intrinsic property or properties of the individual *themselves*.

Let us take stock. So far all we have done is explain the content of the basic principle held by moral individualists, i.e. status intrinsicality. According to that principle, moral status must be *grounded*, and it must be grounded by the possession of intrinsic properties. We have not, as of yet, explained *why* they think status intrinsicality is true. We will come to that in due course. But, for now, let us suppose that it is true, and consider what follows from it.

3. Intrinsic properties as the grounds of moral status

If we assume that an individual's moral status must be grounded in its possession of further intrinsic properties alone, and we wish to maintain equality, meaning that *all* human beings have an equal moral status higher than that of any non-human animal, it follows that that there must be some intrinsic difference between *all* human beings on the one hand and *all* non-human animals on the other that explains this. But what can this difference be? It seems that there is no plausible candidate.

One obvious candidate of an intrinsic property that is shared by *all* humans and *no* non-human animal is the purely biological property of *being human* (i.e. of having the genetic constitution of a human being). But moral individualists reject this property on the grounds that a purely biological property is not a morally relevant property. On this score, they have a point. It is indeed hard to see how being made up of cells comprised of certain kinds of nucleic acid sequences could, in and of itself, explain why an individual has any kind of moral status at all. Consider asking: 'Why should I not torture this human being? Why would it be wrong to do so?' And consider the reply: 'Oh, because the adenine, guanine, cytosine and thymine in the cells that make up that person's body are ordered in a special way.' This, it is clear enough, offers no explanation whatsoever (i.e. it is entirely unilluminating).

If intrinsic biological properties cannot do the job, what other intrinsic properties can? Simply put, moral individualists maintain that none can. They think, in short, that there are no morally relevant intrinsic properties that are shared by *all* humans and *no* non-human animals. This is because they think the only kinds of intrinsic property that *can* do the job of grounding moral status are psychological properties. It is only psychological properties, they maintain, that can do any *explanatory* work. And because certain human beings, and in particular people with profound intellectual disability, lack psychologies sufficient to ground a high moral status, they possess a lower moral status than non-disabled human beings.

Consider that the intrinsic psychological properties stressed by moral individualists are those such as the capacity to feel pain and emotion, to reason and reflect, to think, to plan for the future, and to regret the past. To see that they can do the explanatory work moral individualists are so impressed by, consider that human beings have the capacity to feel pain. And now consider asking the question we considered above once more: 'Why should I not torture this human being? Why would it be wrong to do so?' Unlike the previous answer we considered (i.e. the one framed in terms of genetic properties), the following answer *does* offer an explanation and *is* illuminating: 'Because it would cause her to feel extreme levels of pain.' If one recognises the badness of pain, one can appreciate that torturing a human being is wrong *because* it would give rise to pain. In other words, that it would give rise to such pain is what *explains* why it is wrong.

Both humans and non-human animals can feel pain, of course, and so the above explanation for why it is wrong to torture a human being also applies to non-human animals. In this regard, then, there is no difference between humans and non-human animals. However, moral individualists do allow that there is a difference between *some* human beings and at least some (and perhaps all) non-human animals – a difference that is grounded, it should now be clear, in a difference in intrinsic psychological properties. Specifically, they argue that the possession of high-level psychological properties (e.g. the ability to entertain propositions in thought, to reason, to form a conception of oneself and one's life as a coherent whole) give rise to reasons to treat those who possess them in a certain way, and that those reasons simply do not hold in the case of those, like some non-human animals such as sheep and cattle, who lack high-level psychological properties. For example, moral individualists argue that their view can explain why it is morally worse to farm and eat human beings possessing high-level psychological properties than it is to farm and eat cattle. What explains this, they can say, is that the former possess high-level psychological properties and the latter do not. Thus, the possession of high-level psychological properties is thought by moral individualists to be 'status-conferring': humans with high-level psychological properties have a higher moral status than non-human animals that lack them.

So, moral individualists want to explain the *general* difference in moral status between humans and non-human animals in terms of the possession of high-level intrinsic psychological properties. *Generally* speaking, they think, humans have a higher moral status than non-human animals *because* humans possess high-level psychological properties that non-human animals lack. Here there is some disagreement about the details among moral individualists. They disagree about the precise way to spell out *how* the possession of high-level psychological properties confer status in this way. But all are agreed that they *do* confer such a status. To give one example of how this is spelled out, though, we can consider Jeff McMahan's account. He argues that individuals who possess high-level psychological properties have available to them higher levels of well-being. Although non-human animals may lead lives containing simple exuberant joy, for example, humans who possess high-level psychological properties lead lives containing more complex psychological goods, which, he maintains, are therefore *better* lives (i.e. are lives that contain more well-being). Hence, he argues, it is morally worse to kill a human who possesses high-level psychological properties than it is to kill a dog, because the lives that humans lead are better (contain more well-being) that those that dogs lead, and so such humans lose more than dogs do by being killed:

> [I]t seems that even adult human life tends to contain its share of exuberant joys that rival in intensity those experienced by dogs. They are simply not so conspicuous as they are within the lives of dogs, where they dramatically punctuate days otherwise given over to torpor and sleep. Human well-being, by contrast, is more continuous, dense, and varied, so that the ecstatic moments, which may be more diffusely spread over longer periods, are less salient. And what fills the intervals between these moments is normally altogether better than the dull vacancy of a dog at rest. ... Hence, assuming that a typical person's future would be of a significantly higher quality than that of a typical animal (of whatever species), the conclusion [is]: persons typically lose considerably more good by dying than animals do. (McMahan, 2002, p. 196)

Along similar lines, Rachels (1986) presents the life of Bertrand Russell as an example of 'an extraordinarily full life' (p. 50) and says that 'in most cases the life of a "normal" human is to be preferred to the life of a mentally retarded human' (p. 58) because the mentally retarded human would not be able to live a complex life like a 'normal' human who has got more to lose than the 'retarded' human:

> A young woman dies: it is bad because she will not get to raise her children, finish her novel, learn French, improve her backhand, or do what she wanted for Oxfam; her talents will remain

undeveloped, her aspirations unfulfilled. Not nearly so much of this kind could be said about a less sophisticated being. Her death is worse because there are *more reasons* [emphasis in original] for regretting it. (Rachels, 1986, p. 57)

We are now in a position to see more clearly why moral individualists hold that humans with profound intellectual disability have a lower moral status than non-disabled humans, and equal to that of some non-human animals. The reason is that, according to moral individualists, although humans with profound intellectual disability possess the capacity to feel pain (just as both humans and non-human animals do), they lack high-level psychological properties (just as non-human animals such as cattle do, but unlike non-disabled humans). And so, although humans with profound intellectual disability possess *some* status-conferring intrinsic psychological properties, they do not possess those required to confer the high moral status had by non-disabled humans. They are, in this sense, psychologically comparable to non-human animals like cattle. And so, because it is *only* intrinsic psychological properties that can ground moral status, humans with profound intellectual disability possess the same moral status as non-human animals, and a lower moral status than non-disabled human beings.

4. Relational accounts of moral status

If we agree, as we think one should, that moral status properties are not simple unanalysable properties, then there is an onus upon us to explain its grounds. We do think that moral individualists have a point that purely biological intrinsic properties (like having a certain genetic constitution) cannot by themselves do this job. And we can think of no intrinsic properties other than psychological ones that can plausibly do the job by themselves either. So, how are we to respond to moral individualism? It *seems* that there are only two responses available. The first is to argue that, despite what moral individualists think, human beings with profound intellectual disability *do* possess psychological properties that set them apart from non-human animals and that explain why they have a higher moral status than them. The second is to reject the idea that *only* intrinsic properties can ground moral status, and instead adopt a relational account. We consider and reject the first response, before turning to the second, which will occupy us for the rest of this section. It comes, in fact, in two guises, both of which we will argue also fail. However, considering the second response will enable us to see that there is in fact *another* (i.e. a third) response available, and it is one that is much more promising. We then consider that response in Section 5.

With regard to the first response to moral individualism, then, the salient question to ask is this: is it really true that humans with profound intellectual disability are psychologically comparable to non-human animals? Some scholars have argued that this is not the case, and that, despite suffering from reduced psychological abilities, those with profound intellectual disability still possess a distinctive kind of *human* psychology, which explains their high moral status. Eva Feder Kittay, for example, has written in such a vein about her daughter, Sesha. She writes:

> I am not going to rehearse the things that Sesha can or cannot do and what a dog can or cannot do. Such comparisons are otiose and odious as well as senseless. What Sesha can do she does as a human would do them, though frequently imperfectly, but it is humanly imperfect, not canine perfect. However, even with all that Sesha cannot do and seems not to be able to comprehend, her response to music and her sensitivity to people is remarkably intact. Perhaps her responsiveness to music is more than remarkably intact; it is quite simply remarkable. What a discordant set of abilities and disabilities she exhibits! This unevenness is a feature of many severely and profoundly retarded persons. (I will now stop calling them 'individuals' and begin to speak of those with severe cognitive impairments as the persons I believe they are.) Such unevenness is not a feature of the animals with whom McMahan equates them. (Kittay, 2005, pp. 27–28)

We agree entirely with what Kittay says here. But there is another sense in which we disagree, and it is the latter sense that is relevant to a proper assessment of moral individualism.

The sense in which we agree is this: it is entirely clear from what Kittay writes that her daughter, Sesha, does indeed possess psychological capacities of a sufficiently high level to ground a high moral status (i.e. one equal to that possessed by non-disabled humans). However, this itself is not a relevant fact in criticising moral individualism. Moral individualists are quite clear that they are not using the term 'profound intellectual disability' in any kind of diagnostic sense. That is, they are not claiming that all individuals diagnosed with profound intellectual disability have a lower moral status than non-disabled humans. Instead they explicitly use the term 'profound intellectual disability' (or some other equivalent term) by *definition* to mean 'those human beings who do, as a matter of fact, lack the relevant high-level psychological properties sufficient to ground a high moral status' (see, for example, McMahan, 2005, p. 358 for an explicit statement to this effect).[32]

We think that moral individualists could have chosen a different way to express themselves in order to avoid confusion on this matter (and to avoid causing undue offence), but this is not a substantive criticism of their position itself. If they are to be shown to be wrong, what needs to be shown is not that some of those diagnosed with profound intellectual disability in fact possess psychological properties of a sufficiently high level to ground a high moral status. Instead, what needs to be shown is that there do not exist *any* humans who lack such properties. And this, we submit, is not credible. Given that profound intellectual disability falls on a spectrum, it seems highly likely that there *do* exist human beings for whom it is not plausible that they possess any high-level psychological properties. Perhaps it can be maintained that such humans do still possess a distinctly human psychology, but this does not mean they are not psychologically comparable to non-human animals in a morally relevant sense. To say that such humans are psychologically *comparable* to non-human animals is not to say they have the psychology *of* a non-human animal, but only that their psychology is at an *equivalently developed* level to that of non-human animals such as cattle. It does not matter whether they have psychologies that are *different* from

---

[32] It seems that moral individualists (at least McMahan) are not talking about people like Sesha when they use expressions such as 'severely mentally retarded'. This raises the question about the empirical relevance of their arguments, which, in our view, moral individualists overlook; in order to have any relevance, the conceptual claims in this context require empirical substantiation (Vehmas & Curtis, 2017).

the psychologies of non-human animals, only that they are comparable in this sense. And so, because it seems likely that there are humans with psychologies that are comparable in this sense, we conclude that the first response to moral individualism fails.

We turn now to the second response to moral individualism. This is the rejection of the idea that it is only *intrinsic* properties can ground moral status. To give this response is to maintain that moral status properties can be like a person's property of *being a sibling* rather than a ball's property of *being round*, and in particular that the high moral status possessed by humans with profound intellectual disability is like this. It is thus to maintain that what *explains* why humans with profound intellectual disability have a high moral status is that they stand in certain relations to other things – that is, to give a *relational account* of moral status itself.

This has been a popular response to moral individualism, and in fact it is one that we have previously defended. Before we come to this, though, first note that anyone who defends a relational account of moral status faces two challenges: (1) to give an account of *which* relations are constitutive of the high moral status possessed by humans with profound intellectual disability, and (2) to give an account of how standing in those relations *explains* why such individuals have a high moral status. The first challenge has been met in a number of different ways by different writers. Some have argued that the relevant relation is simply the biological relation of *co-membership in the human species* (e.g. Scanlon, 1998). Others, recognising that citing purely biological relations face the same kinds of difficulties that citing purely biological intrinsic properties face, have emphasised the idea that it is in fact broadly *social* relations that matter, although the kinds of social relation appealed to differs.[33] In an earlier publication, we, for example, called the relevant relation 'the human community relation' and described it as follows:

> It is the relation that each of us stands in to each other by being a member of the human community. It is the relation that holds

---

[33] This is the view taken by Kittay (2005) and our previous selves (Curtis & Vehmas, 2014; Vehmas & Curtis, 2017), among others (other examples include Mullin, 2011 and Jaworska & Tannenbaum, 2015).

between a human and the rest of the human community when he or she is born of human parents, brought up and cared for by humans, and in general, treated as a human within the human community. We don't intend the brief list in the previous sentence to be taken as anything like a list of necessary conditions. The relation holds between different individuals and the rest of the community in different ways. It holds between you and the rest of the community because you participate fully within in it. For example, you vote, work, and pay taxes, as well as engage in emotional and social interactions with other humans. It holds between humans with [profound intellectual disability] and the rest of the human community in a different way. They cannot vote, work, and pay taxes, for example [but] it is not *required* that those who are related to the human community *participate* within the human community, in the sense of partaking in those activities that [statistically] normal human beings take part in. All that is required for the relation to hold is that an individual is *taken into* the human community: that he or she is treated by the community as human. (Vehmas & Curtis, 2017, p. 510)

However, we now think a relational view of this kind, no matter which relation is cited as being relevant, cannot be defended. We think this because we now do not think the second challenge can be met. It is not possible to give an adequate account of how standing in a relation of any sort can *explain* why an individual possesses a high moral status (or, indeed, any moral status at all).

To see why this is so, we want to first consider an objection from McMahan to the kind of view we previously defended. We think that the objection fails – but considering it will lead us to a more powerful objection that we think succeeds (as we will see, there is a sense in which it is in fact a *simpler* objection). McMahan's objection, then, is this:

[I]f the only factor that relevantly differentiated [those with profound intellectual disability] from animals with comparable capacities was that [those with profound intellectual disability] are specially related to us, it would follow that it would be permissible, other things being equal, for those who are *not* specially related to them to treat them in the ways in which we treat animals. ... This means that, if intelligent and morally sensitive Martians were to arrive on Earth, they would be justified, other things being equal, in treating [humans with profound intellectual disability] in the ways in which we treat animals with comparable capacities. They would, of course, be required to exercise forbearance out of respect for us, for we are (or at least some of us are) specially related to [those with profound intellectual disability]; thus any harms the Martians might inflict on [those with profound intellectual disability] would constitute indirect offenses against us. But this would, it seems, be the *only* reason Martians might have not to subject [those with profound intellectual disability] to forms of treatment that we reserve for animals: for example, eating them, hunting them, experimenting on them, and so on. It is doubtful that this conclusion would be congenial to commonsense intuition. If that is right, an appeal to the special relation we bear to [those with profound intellectual disability] cannot provide a full justification for our treating animals considerably less well than we believe we are required to treat [those with profound intellectual disability]. (McMahan, 2002, pp. 222–223)

In other words, McMahan claims here that, although we might save the view that *we* (i.e. humans) ought not to farm and eat humans with profound intellectual disability by endorsing a relational account of moral status (i.e. such an account would give *us* a moral reason not to do this), such an account is still open to the objection that this would not apply to those (such as intelligent Martians) who do *not* stand in the appropriate relation to such humans (i.e. it would not provide *them* with a moral reason not to do this). If this objection were correct, we think it would show that a relational account cannot work. Our pre-theoretical view regarding the fact that humans possess the moral status that they do, we think, is the view that this is a *categorical* or *objective* fact about them – it is the view that *every possible rational agent in every possible circumstance* ought to treat them with due respect (and so, for example, must refrain from farming and eating them). It is thus not only that *we* ought not to do certain things to individuals with moral status properties that needs to be explained by an account of moral status, but that these things *ought not be done to them by any rational agent under any circumstances.* So, if an account of the moral status of humans with profound intellectual disability (or any other human, for that matter) turned out to allow that some possible moral agent could permissibly farm and eat them, or that there was some possible circumstance in which this was so, then the account must fail. Then it would not deserve to be called an account of moral status at all.[34]

Now, as it happens, we think that McMahan's objection does not in fact show that relational accounts cannot explain the categoricality and objectivity of moral status, for it is possible to maintain that an individual *can* gain a categorical and objective moral status by standing in a relation to other things. As we put it in our 2017 paper:

> The bestowment view, then, is the view that objective [status] can be bestowed upon an individual by its standing in a relation to something else. Once bestowed, that value then functions to bind *all* evaluators, not merely those who stand in the bestowing relation to it. In a case where these values are *moral* values, their being possessed can then give rise to obligations that hold objectively. (Vehmas & Curtis, 2017, p. 508)

However, we also now think that there is an objection that *does* show that a relational account cannot explain the categoricality and objectivity of moral status. In fact, the objection is a perfectly simple one. To see what it is, first note that if any individual's moral status is entirely constituted by the holding of certain relations, then if those relations were to have failed to hold, then that individual would not have had that moral status. Next, note that the kinds of relations cited as constituting the moral status of humans with profound intellectual disability are purely *contingent* relations; they do not hold as a matter of necessity (in any sense of 'necessity'). And so there could be possible circumstances in which those relations do not hold, and humans with profound intellectual disability would fail to possess a moral status. In such circumstances, it would *then* be permissible for

---

[34] We are, in this sense, moral realists. We think that moral reasons are objective and apply to all rational agents. We are aware that many outside of the philosophical literature hold 'constructivist' positions according to which morals are constructed by us, and thus are not binding on all rational agents. We do not have the space to evaluate this view here, but we think that adopting such a view is a grave error, for ultimately it leaves its proponents with no grounds whatsoever to rationally criticise divergent moral views, even those they themselves find most pernicious.

intelligent Martians to treat humans with profound intellectual disability as it is permissible to treat non-human animals. They would do nothing wrong by farming and eating them (or at least nothing worse than we do to non-human animals like cattle). And so, relational accounts must fail.

5. A further response to moral individualism is possible

Let us briefly summarise the position we have arrived at. We have outlined the moral individualist's account of moral status, according to which the moral status of humans with profound intellectual disability must be grounded in the intrinsic psychological properties of those humans. However, such humans may not possess any intrinsic psychological properties sufficient to ground a high moral status. Accordingly, we have considered how we might respond to moral individualism. However, as we have outlined, it seems that the only alternative account available is a relational account of moral status, which fails for the reasons just given. So, we think that *both* moral individualism *and* relational accounts of moral status fail to account for the moral status of those with profound intellectual disability. Where do we go from here?

In fact, we think that we can learn from the failure of both accounts. Moral individualism fails because it fails to identify an intrinsic property possessed by humans with profound intellectual disability that explains why they have a moral status equal to non-disabled human beings. And relational accounts fail because they fail to identify relations that can do this job. But what if we combine the two accounts? What if we could find an *intrinsic* property possessed by *all* humans (with or without profound intellectual disability) that has a *relational* significance? In fact, we now think that we can do just that.

In order to explain this idea further, it is useful to reconsider the simple examples of grounding that we began with. We contrasted shape properties of objects like *being square* with familial properties of persons like *being a sibling*. The former, we said, gives an example of a property that is grounded by intrinsic properties, and the latter an example of a property that is grounded by relational properties. We then went on to say that moral individualists view moral status properties as being like *being square* and that those who defend relational accounts view moral status properties as being like *being a sibling*. However, there are properties that, in a sense, fall into a half-way house between *being square* and *being a sibling*. For these properties, it is unclear whether they should be thought of as being grounded by intrinsic properties or relations. One plausible example, in this regard, is the colour properties of objects, such as *being red*. Colour properties are certainly not simple unanalysable properties, and so must be grounded. However, there is a sense in which the possession of *being red* by an object is grounded by intrinsic properties of the object, *and* a sense in which its possession is grounded by relations. The sense in which it is grounded by intrinsic properties is the sense according to which something is red just if it has a certain intrinsic physical structure that means it reflects light only of a certain wavelength, that is, according to something like the following schema:

X is red = X possesses an intrinsic structure Y that reflects light of a certain wavelength.

And the sense in which it is grounded relationally is the sense in which something is red only if it looks red to normal observers under normal conditions, that is, according to something like the following schema (which mentions other things other than the individual itself, i.e. observers):

X is red = X would give rise to red experiences in normal observers under normal conditions.[35]

The salient point here can be put in the following way: if we want to explain what colour properties are, what we should do is explain their intrinsic structure, and explain how that intrinsic structure interacts with the environment to give rise to certain experiences in observers. In other words, *being red* is a matter of having a certain *intrinsic* structure that has a *relational* significance.

Our leading idea, then, is that moral status properties are just like colour properties in the above sense. What we need to do is to

---

[35] NB The notion of a 'normal observer' and 'normal conditions' needs to be spelled out carefully. There is a large literature on how to do this, but we pass over this complication here. The intuitive notions are clear enough for our purposes.

identify certain intrinsic properties possessed by *all* humans (including those with PIMD), as moral individualists think we must. But, unlike moral individualists, we do not think that we must confine ourselves to thinking that those properties only have an *intrinsic significance*, meaning that we can explain why those properties give rise to the possession of a high moral status by considering *only* humans with profound intellectual disability. Instead, we think we must look to explain their significance *relationally*, that we must make reference to things *other* than those with profound intellectual disability to explain why they are morally relevant properties.

We need not stop there. We can draw further on the failure of moral individualism and relational accounts of moral status to learn more about what an explanation of moral status of people with profound intellectual disability must look like. We noted that any explanation of their moral status must account for its categoricality and objectivity; it must explain why any possible rational agent in any possible circumstance must treat those with profound intellectual disability with the respect we maintain they deserve. And the account we are now considering gives us a way to do this. What we must do is identify an intrinsic property possessed by those with profound intellectual disability that any rational moral agent, by virtue of being a rational moral agent, *must* respond to. It is the *relational* fact that any rational moral agent must so respond that will explain the significance of the *intrinsic* property itself. It is this that is missed by moral individualists, who think that the moral status of people with profound intellectual disability is to be explained by mention of their intrinsic properties *alone*. But there is also something here that is missed by those who defend relational accounts of moral status. If such an account is to work, there must be some *intrinsic* property possessed by all humans with profound intellectual disability for rational moral agents to respond to in the first place. If there is no such property, there is simply nothing that rational moral agents *must* respond to, and so no way to establish the necessity of the relation in question, which is precisely what is needed to establish the categoricality and objectivity of the moral status of people with profound intellectual disability.

So, to summarise the above: what we need to identify is some *intrinsic* property possessed by all humans with profound intellectual disability and lacked by non-human animals like cattle, and explain its moral significance *relationally* by explaining why any rational moral agent, by virtue of being a rational moral agent, must respond to it by treating people with profound intellectual disability with the same respect with which they treat non-disabled humans. To put things another way, what we learn from the above is that the most important questions to ask in moral theory are not *merely* questions about single individuals but those questions along with questions about pairs or groups of individuals and the relations between them.

To apply the above idea to the debate surrounding humans with profound intellectual disability, we should build our theories about what we owe such humans on an explanation of what moral value our relations with them have. In so doing, we should focus on the intrinsic properties possessed by those with profound intellectual disability, but not solely on *their* intrinsic properties. We should also consider how *our* intrinsic properties and how *we*, as rational moral agents, should respond to *their* intrinsic properties by virtue of being rational moral agents. That is to say, we should not forget to leave out the role *we* play in the story, as *responders* to the properties *they* possess.

6. Possible personhood and the virtue of empathy

We take our cue in this final section from a recent paper by the philosopher Shelly Kagan, who has tentatively argued that the intrinsic property of *possibly being a person* is a property with moral significance (Kagan, 2016). We think that this view has great promise, so long as it is worked out in line with the basic idea we have expressed above (Kagan himself frames it in moral individualist terms). Here we offer some tentative suggestions about how this might be done.

Firstly, what is the property of *possibly being a person*? To explain this, we must first explain what the property of *being a person* is, which is used in a semi-technical sense in the philosophical literature. It is used to pick out the property that is possessed by all statistically typical adult human beings by virtue of their possessing the high-level intrinsic psychological properties mentioned above in Section 3. In short, a person in the philosophical sense is an individual with reason and reflection, who is capable of entertaining propositional thoughts, planning for the future, and so on. And so *possibly being a person* is the property that is possessed by any individual who is *not* in fact a person (i.e. who does *not* in fact possess those high-level intrinsic psychological properties) but who *could have been* (i.e. who *could have possessed* those high-level intrinsic psychological properties). The idea, then, is that it is an intrinsic property of humans with profound intellectual disability that they *could have been persons* (in case they are not). This in turn is justified in terms of the metaphysical nature or essence of what it is to be a human being. Human beings, in their very nature, could have been persons, while non-human animals could not. Cows, for example, by virtue of being intrinsically cows, could not have possessed the high level of intrinsic psychological properties that statistically normal non-disabled humans possess. Thus, *no* cow could have been a person.

If the above is right, this identifies an intrinsic property, that of *possibly being a person*, that is possessed by all humans with profound intellectual disability, and lacked by non-human animals. How, then, are we to explain its relational moral significance? Our answer is to appeal to something like a virtue ethical account, according to which it is constitutive of being a good moral agent to respond to this property appropriately, by conferring greater care and concern upon those who could have been persons than those who could not. One initial line of thought is to appeal to something like the virtue ethical notion of *empathy*. We may suppose that empathy comes in different forms, and that it takes a special form with regard to humans with profound intellectual disability. Thus, we can say, one should empathise in this special way with those who could have been persons but are not. These humans have sustained something like an existential loss in that they do not possess all the attendant goods that go along with being a person. And, because of this, they are owed a great deal of empathy, in the special sense we have indicated. Any moral agent should respond to their existential loss appropriately, by treating such individuals with utmost respect, as having a moral status equal to the rest of human beings. We suggest that properly spelled out this special notion of empathy entails acting towards such individuals with a special concern with their well-being. It involves making an attempt to understand what that well-being consists in, and in attempting to make their lives go as well as possible.[36]

Thus, the idea here is that any rational moral agent, *by virtue of being a moral agent*, should respond to this intrinsic property of people with profound intellectual disability by treating the individuals in question with the utmost respect, i.e. as having a moral status equal to that of non-disabled human beings. To be somewhat more specific, we suggest that acting empathetically in this special sense towards such individuals involves being concerned with their well-being to a higher degree than we are concerned with the well-being of non-human animals like cattle. Note, however, that this is an initial tentative account. We do not mean to hang our account here on precisely the notion of 'empathy'. Although this term seems appropriate in some respects, it seems inappropriate in other respects, and perhaps another term is better. In particular, 'empathy' may seem to suggest something like 'pity', which we do not intend. A good analogy here is perhaps with the elderly, who are no longer able to do the things youth allows because of the bodily changes that naturally occur

---

[36] This line of thought has a resemblance to the Rawlsian idea that the undeserved inequalities resulting from natural and social lottery should be compensated for somehow (Rawls, 1971). So, persons with PIMD in this scheme have suffered from bad luck in the natural lottery by being born with less favorable biological potential than the rest of us. Often, they have been unlucky in the social lottery as well by living in a social environment that caters poorly to their various needs. To admit that PIMD as an inherent state of an individual is more or less undesirable does not necessarily imply ableism, derogatory pity or any other harmful prejudice where disabled people's subjectivity is taken away from them and where they are nothing but objects on whom non-disabled people project fears about their own vulnerability. Rather, the acknowledgement of the undesirable dimension related to PIMD is an opportunity for moral agents to pay extra attention to the well-being of those fellow human beings who possess only rudimentary capacities of their own to flourish.

as humans age, and have thereby sustained a loss. Those who are younger should empathise with them for this, and treat them in an appropriate manner because of this, but this does not amount to pity. At any rate, a proper treatment of the issue will need a thorough exploration of what the virtues consist in, and how responding to those individuals with profound intellectual disability because they could have been persons, is partly constitutive of being a virtuous agent. We are not yet sure how to spell this account out in detail. But it does have an intuitive appeal, and we are convinced that some account of this kind can be made to work.

Conclusion

The above, then, is where we currently stand on these issues. Clearly, details need to be filled in, and further development is needed. But, if we are right, all the pieces of the puzzle will finally fall into place. We can allow that humans with profound intellectual disability possess an intrinsic property, that of *possibly being a person*, and maintain that it is the relational significance of this property that grounds their high moral status. Some of them could have been persons, but are not, and this is something any good moral agent should be appropriately responsive to, by displaying some virtue, perhaps one related to that of empathy. And so any good moral agent should be concerned to ensure that the well-being of humans with profound intellectual disability is fully understood, so that their lives can go well.

We finish, then, where we began, by restating the fundamental ethical principle that underpins the project that led to this book: human beings with profound intellectual disability are beings with moral status equal to, and deserving of the same respect as, any other human being. As we also stated at the beginning, this principle entails that their interests and well-being matter as much as anybody's, and that we therefore have a duty to understand them better, in order to discover what those interests truly are, and what their well-being truly consists in. As we hope to have demonstrated in this appendix, we now think that we have, at least in outline, an understanding of how this is to be justified philosophically.

Analysed Policy Documents

Government resolution on program to arrange housing and services for people with intellectual disabilities. http://stm.fi/documents /1271139/1357028/Kehitysvammaisten+asumisen+ja+siihen +liittyvien+palveluiden+j%C3%A4rjest%C3%A4minen.pdf /004d06c5-a9f4-4bad-bec0-0907edd142a6

Government resolution on securing individual housing and services for people with intellectual disabilities. Publications of the Ministry of Social Affairs and Health, 2012:15.

Implementation of the government resolution: program to arrange housing and services for people with intellectual disabilities. Letter addressed to municipalities, Ministry of Social and Health, Ministry of Environment and Association of Finnish Local and Regional Authorities, 16.19.2010. http://www.kvank.fi/wp-content /uploads/Kuntakirje.pdf

Intellectual Disability Services' Advisory Committee for Housing (IDSACH) 2010. Quality recommendations for building of housing for people with intellectual disabilities 2010–2017. 8.3.2010 http://www.kvank.fi/wp-content/uploads/laatusuositukset _asuntojen_rakentamiseen_2010_2017.pdf

Intellectual Disability Services' Committee for Housing (IDSACH) 2011. Quality criteria for individualized support. http://www .kvank.fi/wp-content/uploads/Yksilollisen-tuen-laatukriteerit _kesakuu-2011.pdf

Ministry of Social Affairs and Health 2003. Yksilölliset palvelut, toimivat asunnot ja esteetön ympäristö. Vammaisten ihmisten asumispalveluiden laatusuositus. [Individualised services, working services and accessible environment. Quality recommendation for housing services for disabled people] Sosiaali- ja terveysministeriön oppaita 2003:4.

Ministry of Social Affairs and Health 2016. Laitoksesta yksilölliseen asumiseen. Kehitysvammaisten asumisen ohjelman toimeen panon arviointia ja tehostettavat toimet vuosille 2016–2020. Seurantaryhmän loppuraportti. [From intellectual disability hospitals to individualised housing. Evaluation of the housing programme for people with intellectual disabilities and the actions for years 2016–2020] Sosiaali- ja terveysministeriön raportteja ja muistioita 2016:17.

References

Abberley, P. (1987). The concept of oppression and the development of a social theory of disability. *Disability, Handicap & Society, 2,* 5–19. https://doi.org/10.1080/02674648766780021

Abbott, D. (2015). Love in a cold climate: Changes in the fortunes of LGBT men and women with learning Disabilities? *British Journal of Learning Disabilities, 43,* 100–105. https://doi.org/10.1111/bld.12131

Albrecht, G. L. (1992). *The disability business: Rehabilitation in America.* London: Sage.

Alworth, L. C., & Buerkle, S. C. (2013). The effects of music on animal physiology, behavior and welfare. *Lab Animal, 42,* 54–61. https://doi.org/10.1038/laban.162

American Psychiatric Association. (2013). *Diagnostic and statistical manual of mental disorders* (5th ed.). Arlington, VA: American Psychiatric Association.

Aromaa, J., & Tiili, M.-L. (2018). Empatia ja ruumiillinen tieto etnografisessa tutkimuksessa. In P. Hämeenaho & E. Koskinen-Koivisto (Eds.), *Moniulotteinen etnografia* (pp. 258–280). Helsinki: Ethnos ry.

Atkinson, P. (2015). For ethnography. London: Sage.

Bacchi, C., & Bonham, J. (2014). Reclaiming discursive practices as an analytic focus: Political implications. *Foucault Studies, 11,* 173–192. https://doi.org/10.22439/fs.v0i17.4298

Baier, A. C. (1987). Hume, the women's moral theorist? In E. F. Kittay & D. T. Meyers (Eds.), *Women and moral theory* (pp. 37–55). Savage, MD: Rowman & Littlefield.

Banks, S. (2016). 'Knowing me knowing you': Disability support worker as emotional mediator? *Sexualities, 19,* 659–676. https://doi.org/10.1177/1363460715620565

Barnes, C. (1990). *Cabbage syndrome: Social construction of dependence*. London: The Falmer Press.

Barnes, C. (2003). What a difference a decade makes: Reflections on doing 'emancipatory' disability research. *Disability & Society, 18*, 3–17. https://doi.org/10.1080/713662197

Barnes, C., Oliver, M., & Barton, L. (2002). Introduction. In C. Barnes, M. Oliver, & L. Barton (Eds.), *Disability studies today* (pp. 1–17). Cambridge: Polity.

Baron, S., Riddell, S., & Wilson, A. (1999). The secret of eternal youth: Identity, risk and learning difficulties. *British Journal of Sociology of Education, 20*, 483–499. https://doi.org/10.1080/01425699995227

Barton, L. (2005). Emancipatory research and disabled people: Some observations and questions. *Educational Review, 57*, 317–327. https://doi.org/10.1080/00131910500149325

Beach, D. (2010). Identifying and comparing Scandinavian ethnography: Comparisons and influences. *Ethnography and Education, 5*, 49–63. https://doi.org/10.1080/17457821003768455

Bergmann, J. R. (1998). Introduction: Morality in discourse. *Research on Language and Social Interaction, 31*, 279–294. https://doi.org/10.1080/08351813.1998.9683594

Berkson, G. (2004). Intellectual and physical disabilities in prehistory and early civilization. *Mental Retardation, 42*, 195–208. https://doi.org/10.1352/0047-6765(2004)42%3C195:IAPDIP%3E2.0.CO;2

Berrios, G. E. (1995). Mental retardation: Clinical section – Part II. In G. E. Berrios & R. Porter (Eds.), *A History of clinical psychiatry: The origin and history of psychiatric disorders* (pp. 223–238). London: Athlone.

Bigby, C., Clement, T., Mansell, J., & Beadle-Brown, J. (2009). 'It's pretty hard with our ones, they can't talk, the more able bodied can participate': Staff attitudes about the applicability of disability policies to people with severe and profound intellectual disabilities. *Journal of Intellectual Disability Research, 23*, 363–376. https://doi.org/10.1111/j.1365-2788.2009.01154.x

Bjarnason, D. (2002). Young adults with disabilities in Iceland: The importance of relationships and natural supports. *Scandinavian Journal of Disability Research, 4*, 156–189. https://doi.org/10.1080/15017410209510790

Björnsdottir, K., Stefansdottir, G. V., & Stefansdottir, A. (2015). 'It's my life': Autonomy and people with intellectual disabilities. *Journal of Intellectual Disabilities, 19*, 5–21. https://doi.org/10.1177/1744629514564691

Björnsdottir, K., Stefansdottir, A., & Stefansdottir, G. V. (2017). People with intellectual disabilities negotiate autonomy, gender and sexuality. *Sexuality and Disability, 35*, 295–311. https://doi.org/10.1007/S11195-017-9492-X

Boni-Saenz, A. A. (2015). Sexuality and incapacity. *Ohio State Law Journal, 76*, 1201–1253. https://heinonline.org/HOL/P?h=hein.journals/ohslj76&i=1225

Booth, T., & Booth, W. (2000). Against the odds: Growing up with parents who have learning difficulties. *Mental Retardation, 38*, 1–14. https://doi.org/10.1352/0047-6765(2000)0382.0.CO;2

Boxall, K., & Ralph, S. (2010). Research ethics committees and the benefits of involving people with profound and multiple intellectual disabilities in research. *British Journal of Intellectual Disabilities, 39*, 173–180. https://doi.org/10.1111/j.1468-3156.2010.00645.x

Braidotti, R. (2013). *The posthuman.* Cambridge: Polity.

Brigg, G., Schuitema, K., & Vorhaus, J. (2016). Children with profound and multiple intellectual difficulties: Laughter, capability and relating to others. *Disability & Society, 31*(9), 1175–1189. https://doi.org/10.1080/09687599.2016.1239571

Bronston, W. G. (1976). Concepts and theory of Normalization. In R. Koch & J. C. Dobson (Eds.), *The mentally retarded child and his family: A multidisciplinary handbook* (pp. 490–516). New York, NY: Brunner/Mazel.

Brown, H., & Turk, V. (1992). Defining sexual abuse as it affects adults with learning disabilities. *Mental Handicap, 20*, 44–55. https://doi.org/10.1111/j.1468-3156.1992.tb00658.x

Burleigh, M. (1994). *Death and deliverance: Euthanasia in Germany 1900–1945*. Cambridge: Cambridge University Press.

Cambridge, P., Beadle-Brown, J., Milne, A., Mansell, J., & Whelton, R. (2006). *Exploring the incidence, risk factors, nature and monitoring of adult protection alerts*. Canterbury: Tizard Centre.

Cambridge, P., & Carnaby, S. (2000). A personal touch: Managing the risks of abuse during intimate and personal care for people with learning disabilities. *Journal of Adult Protection*, 2, 4–16. https://doi.org/10.1108/14668203200000026

Cambridge, P., Carnaby, S., & McCarthy, M. (2003). Responding to masturbation in supporting sexuality and challenging behaviour in services for people with learning disabilities. *Journal of Learning Disabilities*, 7, 251–266. https://doi.org/10.1177/14690047030073005

Cameron, L., & Murphy, J. (2007). Obtaining consent to participate in research: The issues involved in including people with a range of learning and communication disabilities. *British Journal of Learning Disabilities*, 35, 113–120. https://doi.org/10.1111/j.1468-3156.2006.00404.x

Campbell, F. K. (2009). *Contours of ableism: The production of disability and abledness*. Basingstoke: Palgrave Macmillan.

Carlson, L. (2010). *The faces of intellectual disability: Philosophical Reflections*. Bloomington, IN: Indiana University Press.

Carson, D. (1992). Legality of responding to the sexuality of a client with profound learning disabilities: Commentary on David Shelton's paper. *Mental Handicap*, 20, 85–87. https://doi.org/10.1111/j.1468-3156.1992.tb00665.x

Cavalieri, P. (2001). *The animal question: Why nonhuman animals deserve human rights*. New York, NY: Oxford University Press.

Chappell, A. L. (1998). Still out in the cold: People with learning difficulties and the social model of disability. In T. Shakespeare (Ed.), *The Disability Reader: Social Science Perspectives* (pp. 211–220). London: Continuum.

Christensen, P., & Prout, A. (2002). Working with ethical symmetry in social research with children. *Childhood*, 9, 477–497. https://doi.org/10.1177/0907568202009004007

Clegg, J., Murphy, E., Almack, K., & Harvey, A. (2008). Tensions around inclusion: Reframing the moral horizon. *Journal of Applied Research in Intellectual Disabilities, 21,* 81–94. https://doi.org/10.1111/j.1468-3148.2007.00371.x

Clement, T., & Bigby, C. (2009). Breaking out of a distinct social space: Reflections of supporting community participation for people with severe and profound intellectual disability. *Journal of Applied Research in Intellectual Disabilities, 22,* 264–275. https://doi.org/10.1111/j.1468-3148.2008.00458.x

Clement, T., & Bigby, C. (2010). *Group homes for people with intellectual disabilities: Encouraging inclusion and participation.* London: Jessica Kingsley.

Clifford Simplican, S., Leader, G., Kosciulek, J., & Leahy, M. (2015). Defining social inclusion of people with intellectual and developmental disabilities: An ecological model of social networks and community participation. *Research in Developmental Disabilities, 38,* 18–29. https://doi.org/10.1016/j.ridd.2014.10.008

Cocks, A. J. (2006). The ethical maze: Finding an inclusive path towards gaining children's agreement to research participation. *Childhood, 13,* 247–266. https://doi.org/10.1177/0907568 206062942

Crary, A. (2018). The horrific history of comparisons between cognitive disability and animality (and how to move past it). In L. Gruen & F. Probyn-Rapsey (Eds.), *Animaladies: Gender, animals, madness* (pp. 324–380). New York, NY: Bloomsbury.

Culham, A., & Nind, M. (2003). Deconstructing normalisation: Clearing the way for inclusion. *Journal of Intellectual & Developmental Disabilities, 28,* 65–78. https://doi.org/10.1080 /136682503 1000086902

Curtis, B., & Vehmas, S. (2014). Moral worth and severe intellectual disability – A hybrid view. In J. E. Bickenbach, F. Felder, & B. Schmitz (Eds.), *Disability and the good human life* (pp. 19–49). New York, NY: Cambridge University Press.

Curtis, B., & Vehmas, S. (2016a). A Moorean argument for the full moral status of those with profound intellectual disability. *Journal of Medical Ethics, 42,* 41–45. https://doi.org/10.1136 /medethics-2015-102938

Curtis, B., & Vehmas, S. (2016b). The Moorean argument for the full moral status of those with profound intellectual disability: A rejoinder to Roberts. *Journal of Medical Ethics, 42,* 266–267. https://doi.org/10.1136/medethics-2016-103437

Davis, L. J. (Ed.). (2013a). *The disability studies reader* (4th ed.). New York: Routledge.

Davis, L. J. (2013b). Introduction: Disability, normality, and power. In L. J. Davis (Ed.), *The disability studies reader* (4th ed., pp. 1–14). New York, NY: Routledge.

Davis, J., Watson, N., & Cunningham-Burley, S. (2008). Disabled children, ethnography and unspoken understandings: The collaborative construction of diverse identities. In P. Christensen & A. James (Eds.), *Research with children: Perspectives and practices* (2nd ed., pp. 220–218). New York, NY: Routledge.

Dear, M. (1992). Understanding and overcoming the NIMBY syndrome. *Journal of the American Planning Association, 58,* 288–300. https://doi.org/10.1080/01944369208975808

Desjardins, M. (2012). The sexualized body of the child: Parents and the politics of 'voluntary' sterilization of people labeled intellectually disabled. In R. McRuer & A. Mollow (Eds.), *Sex and Disability* (pp. 69–85). Durham, NC, London: Duke University Press.

Emerson, E., & Hatton, C. (2008). *People with intellectual disabilities in England.* CeDR Research Report 2008:1. Lancaster: Lancaster University.

Evans, D. S., McGuire, B. E., Healy, E., & Carley, S. N. (2009). Sexuality and personal relationships for people with intellectual disability. Part II: Staff and family carer perspectives. *Journal of Intellectual Disability Research, 53,* 913–921. https://doi.org/10.1111/j.1365-2788.2009.01202.x

Fava, L., & Strauss, K. (2010). Multi-sensory rooms: Comparing effects of the Snoezelen and the Stimulus Preference environment on the behavior of adults with profound mental retardation. *Research in Developmental Disabilities, 31,* 160–171. https://doi.org/10.1016/j.ridd.2009.08.006

Ferguson, P., & Ferguson, D. L. (2001). Winks, blinks, squints and twitches: Looking for disability, culture and self-determination through our son's left eye. *Scandinavian Journal of Disability Research, 3*, 71–90. https://doi.org/10.1080/15017410109510777

Finlex 3.4. 1987/380. Laki vammaisuuden perusteella järjestettävistä palveluista ja tukitoimista. [The Act about Service and Support Due to Disability] https://www.finlex.fi/fi/laki/ajantasa/1987/19870380

Flynn, E., & Arstein-Kerslake, A. (2014). Legislating personhood: Realising the right to support in exercising legal capacity. *International Journal of Law in Context, 10*, 81–104. https://doi.org/10.1017/S1744552313000384

Forster, S. (2010). Age-appropriateness: Enabler or barrier to a good life for people with profound intellectual and multiple disabilities. *Journal of Intellectual & Developmental Disability, 35*, 129–131. https://doi.org/10.3109/13668251003694606

Forster, S., & Iacono, T. (2008). Disability support workers' experience of interaction with a person with profound intellectual disability. *Journal of Intellectual & Developmental Disability, 33*, 137–147. https://doi.org/10.1080/13668250802094216

Fraser, R. E. (2018). The ethics of metaphor. *Ethics, 128*(4), 728–755. https://doi.org/10.1086/697448

Garland, R. (1995). *The eye of the beholder: Deformity and disability in the Graceo-Roman world.* London: Duckworth.

Gauthier-Boudreault, C., Gallagher, F., & Couture, M. (2017). Specific needs of families of young adults with profound intellectual disability during and after transition to adulthood: What are we missing? *Research in Developmental Disabilities, 66*, 16–26. https://doi.org/10.1016/j.ridd.2017.05.001

Gill, M. (2015). *Already doing it: Intellectual disability and sexual agency.* Minneapolis, MN: University of Minnesota Press.

Gil-Llario, M. D., Morell-Mengual, V., Ballester-Arnal, R., & Díaz-Rodríguez, I. (2018). The experience of sexuality in adults with intellectual disability. *Journal of Intellectual Disability Research, 62*, 72–80. https://doi.org/10.1111/jir.12455

Goode, D. (1994). *A world without words: The social construction of children born deaf and blind.* Philadelphia, PA: Temple University Press.

Goodey, C. F. (1992). Mental disabilities and human values in Plato's late dialogues. *Archiv für Geschichte der Philosophie, 74,* 26–42. https://doi.org/10.1515/agph.1992.74.1.26

Goodey, C. F. (1995). Mental retardation: Social section – part I. In G. E. Berrios & R. Porter (Eds.), *A History of clinical psychiatry: The origin and history of psychiatric disorders* (pp. 239–250). London: Athlone.

Goodey, C. F. (2001). What is developmental disability? The origin and nature of our conceptual models. *Journal of Developmental Disabilities, 8,* 1–18.

Goodey, C. F. (2011). *History of intelligence and intellectual disability: The shaping of psychology in early modern Europe.* Farnham: Ashgate.

Goodey, C. F., & Stainton, T. (2001). Intellectual disability and the myth of the changeling myth. *Journal of the History of the Behavioral Sciences, 37,* 223–240. https://doi.org/10.1002/jhbs.1032

Goodley, D. (2014). *Dis/ability studies: Theorising disablism and ableism.* London: Routledge.

Goodley, D., Lawthom, R., & Runswick-Cole, K. (2014). Posthuman disability studies. *Subjectivity, 7,* 342–361. https://doi.org/10.1057/sub.2014.15

Goodwin, J. (2020). On 'being' together as belonging: Inside golden tent. In M. Nind & I. Strnadová (Eds.), *Belonging for people with profound intellectual and multiple disabilities: Pushing the boundaries of inclusion* (pp. 59–74). London: Routledge.

Gordon, T., Holland, J., Lahelma, E., & Tolonen, T. (2005). Gazing with intent: Ethnographic practice in classrooms. *Qualitative Research, 5,* 113–131. https://doi.org/10.1177/1468794105048659

Grandin, T., & Johnson, C. (2005). *Animals in translation: Using the mysteries of autism to decode animal behavior.* New York: Scribner.

Granlund, M., Wilder, J., & Almqvist, L. (2013). Severe multiple disabilities. In M. L. Wehmeyer (Ed.), *The Oxford handbook of positive psychology and disability* (pp. 452–474). New York: Oxford University Press.

Grue, J., & Lundblad, M. (2020). The biopolitics of disability and animality in Harriet McBryde Johnson. In N. Watson & S. Vehmas (Eds.), *Routledge handbook of disability studies.* 2nd ed. (pp. 117–126). London: Routledge.

Grunewald, K. (2008). *Från idiot till medborgare.* Stockholm: Gothia Förlag.

Hall, E. (2010). Spaces of social inclusion and belonging for people with intellectual disabilities. *Journal of Intellectual Disability Research, 54*, 48–57. https://doi.org/10.1111/j.1365-2788.2009.01237.x

Halwani, R. (2010). *Philosophy of love, sex, and marriage.* New York, London: Routledge.

Hamilton, C. (2010). 'But Rachel was enjoying it too, wasn't she?' A learning disability and sexuality case study. In R. Shuttleworth & T. Sanders (Eds.), *Sex & disability: Politics, identity and access* (pp. 121–136). Leeds: The Disability Press.

Hanzen, G., van Nispen, R., van der Putten, A., & Waninge, A. (2017). Participation of adults with visual and severe or profound intellectual disabilities: Definition and operationalization. *Research in Developmental Disabilities, 61*, 95–107. https://doi.org/10.1016/j.ridd.2016.12.017

Harjula, M. (1996). *Vaillinaisuudella vaivatut: Vammaisuuden tulkinnat suomalaisessa huoltokeskustelussa 1800-luvun lopulta 1930-luvun lopulle.* Helsinki: Suomen Historiallinen Seura.

Harris, J. C., & Greenspan, S. (2016). Definition and nature of intellectual disability. In N. N. Singh (Ed.), *Handbook of Evidence-Based Practices in Intellectual and Developmental Disabilities* (pp. 11–39). New York, NY: Springer.

Hjörne, E. (2004). *Excluding for inclusion? Negotiating school careers and identities in pupil welfare settings in the Swedish schools.* Göteborg Studies in Educational Sciences 213, Acta Universitatis Gothoburgensis. http://hdl.handle.net/2077/16271

Hollomotz, A. (2010). Vulnerable adults? The social creation of risk to sexual violence. In R. Shuttleworth & T. Sanders (Eds.), *Sex & disability: Politics, identity and access* (pp. 21–39). Leeds: The Disability Press.

Honkasalo, M.-L. (2008). Etnografia terveyden, sairauden ja terveydenhuollon tutkimuksessa. *Sosiaalilääketieteellinen aikakauslehti, 45,* 4–17. https://journal.fi/sla/article/view/587

Honkatukia, P. (2017). Nuorisotutkimuksen yhteiskunnallinen tehtävä [The societal task of youth research]. *Nuorisotutkimus, 35,* 59–64.

Hudson, B. (2006). Making and missing connections: Learning disability services and the transition from adolescence to adulthood. *Disability & Society, 21,* 47–60. https://doi.org/10.1080/09687590500375366

Hughes, B. (2012). Civilizing modernity and the ontological invalidation of disabled people. In D. Goodley, B. Hughes, & L. Davis (Eds.), *Disability and social theory: New developments and directions* (pp. 17–32). London: Palgrave Macmillan.

Hughes, B. (2020). *A historical sociology of disability: Human validity and invalidity from antiquity to early modernity.* London: Routledge.

Hunt, X. (2018). *Through a different lens: Examining commonality and divergence in constructions and depictions of the sexuality of persons with physical disabilities in South Africa.* Unpublished PhD dissertation. Stellenbosch: Stellenbosch University.

Hursthouse, R., & Pettigrove, G. (2018). Virtue ethics. In *The Stanford Encyclopedia of Philosophy* (Winter 2018 Edition). Retrieved from https://plato.stanford.edu/archives/win2018/entries/ethics-virtue/

Hutchinson, D. S. (1995). Ethics. In J. Barnes (Ed.), *The Cambridge companion to Aristotle* (pp. 195–232). Cambridge: Cambridge University Press.

Ikäheimo, H. (2009). Personhood and the social inclusion of people with disabilities: A recognition-theoretical approach. In K. Kristiansen, S. Vehmas, & T. Shakespeare (Eds.), *Arguing about disability: Philosophical perspectives* (pp. 77–92). London: Routledge.

Itard, J. G. (1972). The Wild Boy of Averyon (1799-1806). In L. Malson (Ed.), *Wolf Children and the Problem of Human Nature* (pp. 91–140). New York: Monthly Review Press. (Original work published 1801)

Jamieson, L. (2011). Intimacy as a concept: Explaining social change in the context of globalisation or another form of ethnocentricism? *Sociological Research Online, 16*, 151–163. https://doi.org/10.5153/sro.2497

Jaworska, A., & Tannenbaum, J. (2015). Who has the capacity to participate as a rearee in a person-rearing relationship? *Ethics, 125*, 1096–1113. https://doi.org/10.1086/680905

Jennings, B. (2010). Agency and moral relationship in dementia. In L. Carlson & E. F. Kittay (Eds.), *Cognitive Disability and Its Challenge to Moral Philosophy* (pp. 171–182). Malden, MA: Wiley-Blackwell.

Johnson, H., Douglas, J., Bigby, C., & Iacono, T. (2012a). A model of processes that underpin positive relationships for adults with severe intellectual disability. *Journal of Intellectual & Developmental Disability, 37*, 324–336. https://doi.org/10.3109/13668250.2012.732221

Johnson, H., Douglas, J., Bigby, C., & Iacono, T. (2012b). Social interaction with adults with severe intellectual disability: Having fun and hanging out. *Journal of Applied Research in Intellectual Disabilities, 25*, 329–341. https://doi.org/10.1111/j.1468-3148.2011.00669.x

Johnson, K., & Walmsley, J. (2010). *People with intellectual disabilities: Towards a good life*. Bristol: Policy Press.

Jones, P. (2004). 'They are not like us and neither they should be': Issues of teacher identity for teachers of pupils with profound and multiple learning difficulties. *Disability & Society, 19*, 159–169. https://doi.org/10.1080/0968759042000181785

Kagan, S. (2016). What's wrong with speciesism? (Society for Applied Philosophy annual lecture 2015). *Journal of Applied Philosophy, 33*, 1–21. https://doi.org/10.1111/japp.12164

Kamstra, A., van der Putten, A. A. J., Post, W. J., & Vlaskamp, C. (2015). Informal social networks of people with profound intellectual and multiple disabilities: Relationship with age, communicative abilities and current living arrangements. *Journal of Applied Research in Intellectual Disabilities, 28*, 159–164. https://doi .org/10.1111/jar.12115

Kaufman, M., Silverberg, C., & Odette, F. (2004). *The ultimate guide to sex and disability*. San Francisco, CA: Cleis.

Kauppila, A., Mietola, R., & Niemi, A.-M. (2018). Koulutususkon rajoilla: koulutuksen julma lupaus kehitys- ja vaikeavammaisille opiskelijoille. In H. Silvennnoinen, M. Kalalahti, & J. Varjo (Eds.), *Koulutuksen lupaukset ja koulutususko* (pp. 209–240). Jyväskylä: FERA Suomen Kasvatustieteellinen Seura.

Kijak, R. (2013). The sexuality of adults with intellectual disability in Poland. *Sexuality and Disability, 31*, 109–123. https://doi.org /10.1007/s11195-013-9294-8

Kittay, E. F. (1999). *Love's labor: Essays on women, equality and dependency*. New York, NY: Routledge.

Kittay, E. F. (2005). At the margins of personhood. *Ethics, 116*, 100–131. https://doi.org/10.1086/454366

Kittay, E. F. (2010). The personal is philosophical is political: A philosopher and mother of a cognitively disabled person sends notes from the battlefield. In E. F. Kittay & L. Carlson (Eds.), *Cognitive disability and its challenge to moral philosophy* (pp. 393–413). Malden, MA: Wiley-Blackwell.

Kittay, E. F. (2019). *Learning from my daughter: The value and care of disabled minds*. New York, NY: Oxford University Press.

Kivirauma, J. (1987). *Poikkeavuus ja kansanopetus ennen oppivelvollisuutta: Tutkimus heikkolahjaisiin ja pahantapaisiin oppilaisiin kohdistettujen toimenpiteiden muotoutumiseen vaikuttaneista tekijöistä erityisesti Turun ja Tampereen kansakouluissa*. Turku: Turun yliopiston kasvatustieteiden tiedekunta, julkaisusarja A: 120.

Kivirauma, J. (1998). Normaali erityisopetuksen piilo-opetussuunnitelmana. In T. Ladonlahti, A. Naukkarinen, & S. Vehmas (Eds.), *Poikkeava vai erityinen? Erityispedagogiikan monet ulottuvuudet* (pp. 203–215). Jyväskylä: Atena.

Kivirauma, J., & Kivinen, O. (1988). The school system and special education: Causes and effects in the twentieth century. *Disability, Handicap & Society, 3,* 153–165. https://doi.org/10.1080/02674648866780141

Klotz, J. (2004). Sociocultural study of intellectual disability: Moving beyond labelling and social constructionist perspectives. *British Journal of Learning Disabilities, 32,* 93–104. https://doi.org/10.1111/j.1468-3156.2004.00285.x

Knight, Z. G. (2016). A proposed model of psychodynamic psychotherapy linked to Erik Erikson's eight stages of psychosocial development. *Clinical Psychology & Psychotherapy, 24,* 1047–1058. https://doi.org/10.1002/cpp.2066

Kogan, L. R., Schoenfeld-Tacher, R., & Simon, A. A. (2012). Behavioral effects of auditory stimulation on kenneled dogs. *Journal of Veterinary Behavior, 7,* 268–275. https://doi.org/10.1016/j.jveb.2011.11.002

Kohli, M. (2007). The institutionalization of the life course: Looking back and look ahead. *Research in Human Development, 4,* 253–271. https://doi.org/10.1080/15427600701663122

Komulainen, S. (2007). The ambiguity of the child's 'voice' in social research. *Childhood, 14,* 11–28. https://doi.org/10.1177/0907568207068561

Kulick, D. (2015). The problem of speaking for others *redux:* Insistence of disclosure and the ethics of engagement. *Knowledge Cultures, 3*(6), 14–33.

Kulick, D. (2017). Human-animal communication. *Annual Review of Anthropology, 46,* 357–378. Retrieved from https://www.annualreviews.org/doi/10.1146/annurev-anthro-102116-041723

Kulick, D., & Rydström, J. (2015). *Loneliness and its opposite: Sex, disability, and the ethics of engagement.* Durham, NC, London: Duke University Press.

LaFollette, H. (1996). *Personal relationships: Love, identity, and morality.* Cambridge, MA: Blackwell.

Lancioni, G. E., Cuvo, A. J., & O'Reilly, M. F. (2002). Snoezelen: An overview of research with people with developmental disabilities and dementia. *Disability and Rehabilitation*, 24, 175–184. https://doi.org/10.1080/09638280110074911

Laz, C. (1998). Act your age. *Sociological Forum*, 13, 85–113. https://doi.org/10.1023/A:1022160015408

Leppälä, H. (2014). *Vammaisuus hyvinvointivaltiossa: Invalideiksi, vajaamielisiksi tai kehitysvammaisiksi määriteltyjen kansalais-asema suomalaisessa vammaispolitiikassa 1940-luvun taitteesta vuoteen 1987* [Disability in the Welfare State: Status of People de-fined as Invalids, Mentally Deficient or Developmentally Disabled in the Finnish Post-War Disability Policy, early 1940s to 1987]. Turku: University of Turku, C 394.

Lifton, R. J. (1986). *The Nazi doctors: A study in the psychology of evil*. London: Macmillan.

Linton, S. (1998). *Claiming disability: Knowledge and identity*. New York, NY: New York University Press.

Locke, J. (1998). *An essay concerning human understanding*. London: Penguin. (Original work published 1690)

Lotan, M., & Gold, C. (2009). Meta-analysis of the effectiveness of individual intervention in the controlled multisensory environment (Snoezelen) for individuals with intellectual disability. *Journal of Intellectual & Developmental Disability*, 34, 207–215. https://doi.org/10.1080/13668250903080106

Lyden, M. (2007). Assessment of sexual consent capacity. *Sexuality and Disability*, 25, 3–20. https://doi.org/10.1007/s11195-006-9028-2

Lyons, G. (2011). Quality of life for persons with intellectual disabil-ities: A review of the literature. In R. Kober (Ed.), *Enhancing the quality of life of people with intellectual disabilities* (pp. 73–126). Dordrecht: Springer.

MacLure, M. (2013). Classification or wonder? Coding as an ana-lytic practice in qualitative research. In R. Coleman & J. Ringrose (Eds.), *Deleuze and research methodologies* (pp. 164–183). Edinburgh: Edinburgh University Press.

Mansell, J. (2010). Raising our sights: Services for adults with pro-found intellectual and multiple disabilities. https://www.mencap.org.uk/sites/default/files/2016-06/Raising_our_Sights_report.pdf

Mansell, J., Beadle-Brown, J., Cambridge, P., Milne, A., & Whelton, B. (2009). Adult protection: Incidence of referrals, nature and risk factors in two English local authorities. *Journal of Social Work, 9*, 23–38. https://doi.org/10.1177/1468017308098426

Marcus, G. E. (1995). Ethnography in/of the world system: The emergence of multi-sited ethnography. Annual Review of Anthropology, 24, 95–114. https://doi.org/10.1146/annurev.an.24.100195.000523

Mattila, M. (1999a). The alegal eugenic sterilisations in Finland – an international perspective. *Tartu University History Museum Annual Report, 1998*(3), 43–75.

Mattila, M. (1999b). *Kansamme parhaaksi: Rotuhygienia Suomessa vuoden 1935 sterilointilakiin asti*. Helsinki: Suomen Historiallinen Seura.

Maulik, P. K., Mascarenhas, M. N., Mathers, C. D., Dua, T., & Saxena, S. (2011). Prevalence of intellectual disability: A meta-analysis of population-based studies. *Research in Developmental Disabilities, 32*, 419–436. https://doi.org/10.1016/j.idd.2010.12.018

McAdams, D. P. (2001). The psychology of life stories. *Review of General Psychology, 5*, 100–122. https://doi.org/10.1037/1089-2680.5.2.100

McCarthy, M. (1999). *Sexuality and women with learning disabilities*. London: Jessica Kingsley.

McCarthy, M. (2002). Sexuality. In P. Noonan Walsh & T. Heller (Eds.), *Health of women with intellectual disabilities* (pp. 90–102). Oxford: Blackwell.

McCarthy, M. (2014). Women with intellectual disability: Their sexual lives in the 21st century. *Journal of Intellectual & Developmental Disability, 39*, 124–131. https://doi.org/10.3109/13668250.2014.894963

McCarthy, M., & Cambridge, P. (2006). Sexuality and intimate and personal care. In S. Carnaby & P. Cambridge (Eds.), *Intimate and personal care with people with learning disabilities* (pp. 46–61). London: Jessica Kingsley.

McCormack, N. (2020). A trip to the caves: Making life story work inclusive and accessible. In M. Nind & I. Strnadová (Eds.),

Belonging for people with profound intellectual and multiple disabilities: Pushing the boundaries of inclusion (pp. 98–112). London: Routledge.

McDonald, K. E., & Kidney, C. A. (2012). What is right? Ethics in intellectual disabilities research. *Journal of Policy and Practice in Intellectual Disabilities, 9*, 22–39. https://doi.org /10.1111/j.1741-1130.2011.00319.x

McKearney, P. (2018a). Receiving the gift of cognitive disability: Recognizing agency in the limits of the rational subject. *The Cambridge Journal of Anthropology, 36*, 40–60. https://doi.org /10.3167/cja.2018.360104

McKearney, P. (2018b). The weight of living: Autonomy, care, and responsibility for the self. *Journal of Disability & Religion, 22*, 266–282. https://doi.org/10.1080/23312521.2018.1483219

McKearney, P. (2019). The ability to judge: Critique and surprise in theology, anthropology, and L'Arche. *Ethnos.* https://doi.org/10 .1080/00141844.2019.1640261

McMahan, J. (1996). Cognitive disability, misfortune, and justice. *Philosophy & Public Affairs, 25*, 3–35. https://doi.org/10.1111 /j.1088-4963.1996.tb00074.x

McMahan, J. (2002). *The ethics of killing: Problems at the margins of life*. Oxford: Oxford University Press.

McMahan, J. (2005). Our fellow creatures. *The Journal of Ethics, 9*, 353–380. https://doi.org/10.1007/s10892-005-3512-2

McMahan, J. (2008). Challenges to human equality. *The Journal of Ethics, 12*, 81–104. https://doi.org/10.1007/s10892-007-9020-9

McMahan, J. (2009). Cognitive disability and cognitive enhancement. *Metaphilosophy, 40*, 582–605. https://doi.org/10.1111 /j.1467-9973.2009.01612.x

McMahan, J. (2016). On modal personism. *Journal of Applied Philosophy, 33*, 26–30. https://doi.org/10.1111/japp.12167

McMahan, J., & Singer, P. (2017). Who Is the Victim in the Anna Stubblefield Case? Retrieved from https://www.nytimes .com/2017/04/03/opinion/who-is-the-victim-in-the-anna-stubble field-case.html

McRuer, R., & Mollow, A. (Eds.). (2012). *Sex and disability.* Durham, NC, London: Duke University Press.

Metzel, D. S. (2004). Historical social geography. In S. Noll & J. W. Trent, Jr., (Eds.), *Mental retardation in America: A historical reader* (pp. 420–444). New York, NY: New York University Press.

Mietola, R. (2014). *Hankala erityisyys: Etnografinen tutkimus erityisopetuksen käytännöistä ja erityisyyden muotoutumisesta yläkoulun arjessa* [*Troubling special: An ethnographic study on practices of special education and formation of special in the everyday life of lower secondary school*]. University of Helsinki, Institute of Behavioural Sciences, Studies in Educational Sciences 256. http://urn.fi/URN:ISBN:978-952-10-9375-3

Mietola, R. (2018). Koko elämä palveluissa: Vaikeasti kehitysvammaisen henkilön nuoruus ja elämänkulku kehitysvammapalveluissa [Whole life in services: Youth and life course of a person with profound intellectual disability in the intellectual disability service system]. In M. Gissler, M. Kekkonen & P. Känkänen, (Eds.), *Nuoret palveluiden pauloissa: Nuorten elinolot –vuosikirja 2018* (pp. 136–146). Helsinki: Nuorisotutkimusverkosto, Terveyden ja hyvinvoinnin laitos & Valtion nuorisoasiain neuvottelukunta.

Mietola, R., Miettinen, S., & Vehmas, S. (2017). Voiceless subjects? Research ethics and persons with profound intellectual disabilities. *International Journal of Social Research Methodology, 20,* 263–274. https://doi.org/10.1080/13645579.2017.1287872

Mietola, R., Teittinen, A., & Vesala, H. T. (2013). *Kehitysvammaisten ihmisten asumisen tulevaisuus. Kansainvälisiä esimerkkejä ja vertailu Suomeen* [*Future of housing for people with intellectual disabilities. International examples and national comparison*]. Suomen ympäristö 3/2013. Helsinki: Finnish Ministry of Environment and Housing.

Mietola, R., & Vehmas, S. (2019). 'He is, after all, a young man': Claiming ordinary lives for young adults with profound intellectual disabilities. *Scandinavian Journal of Disability Research, 21,* 120–128. https://doi.org/10.16993/sjdr.590

Moore, G. E. (1939). Proof of an external world. *Proceedings of the British Academy, 25,* 273–300.

Morris, J. (1999). *Hurtling into a void: Transition to adulthood for young disabled people with complex health and support needs*. Brighton: Pavilion Publishing.

Mullin, A. (2011). Children and the argument from 'marginal' cases. *Ethical Theory and Moral Practice, 14*, 291–305. https://doi .org/10.1007/s10677-010-9241-z

Nagel, T. (1979). *Mortal questions*. Cambridge, MA: Cambridge University Press.

Nayar, P. K. (2014). *Posthumanism*. Cambridge: Polity.

Neugebauer, R. (1996). Mental handicap in medieval and early modern England: Criteria, measurement and care. In D. Wright & A. Digby (Eds.), *Mental deficiency: Historical perspectives on people with learning disabilities* (pp. 22–44). London: Routledge.

Nieuwenhuijse, A. M., Willems, D. L., van Goudoever, J. B., Echteld, M. A., & Olsman, E. (2019). Quality of life of persons with profound intellectual and multiple disabilities: A narrative literature review of concepts, assessment methods and assessors. *Journal of Intellectual & Developmental Disability, 44*, 261–271. https://doi .org/10.3109/13668250.2017.1388913

Nikander, P. (2000). 'Old' versus 'little girl': A discursive approach to age categorisation and morality. *Journal of Aging Studies, 14*, 335–358. https://doi.org/10.1016/S0890-4065(00)80001-8

Nind, M. (2007). Supporting lifelong learning for people with profound and multiple learning difficulties. *Support for Learning, 22*, 111–115. https://doi.org/10.1111/j.1467-9604.2007.00457.x

Nind, N., & Strnadová, I. (2020). Changes in the lives of people with profound intellectual and multiple disabilities. In M. Nind & I. Strnadová (Eds.), *Belonging for people with profound intellectual and multiple disabilities: Pushing the boundaries of inclusion* (pp. 1–21). London: Routledge.

Nirje, B. (1969). The normalization principle and its human management implications. In R. Kugel & W. Wolfensberger (Eds.), *Changing patterns in residential services for the mentally retarded* (pp. 179–195). Washington, D.C.: President's Committee on Mental Retardation.

Nirje, B. (1970). I–The normalization principle–Implications and comments. *Journal of Mental Subnormality, 16*, 62–70. https://doi.org/10.1179/bjms.1970.013

Nirje, B. (1985). The basis and logic of the normalization principle. *Australia and New Zealand Journal of Developmental Disabilities, 11*, 65–68. https://doi.org/10.3109/13668258509008747

Nussbaum, M. (2006). *Frontiers of justice: Disability, nationality, species membership.* Cambridge, MA: Harvard University Press.

Oliver, M. (1990). *The politics of disablement.* Basingstoke: Macmillan.

Oliver, M. (1992). Changing the social relations of research production? *Disability, Handicap & Society, 7*, 101–115. https://doi.org/10.1080/02674649266780141

O'Shea, A., & Frawley, P. (2020). Gender, sexuality and relationships for young Australian women with intellectual disability. *Disability & Society, 35*, 654–675. https://doi.org/10.1080/09687599.2019.1647148

Paju, E. (2013). *Lasten Arjen ainekset: Etnografinen tutkimus materiaalisuudesta, ruumiillisuudesta ja toimijuudesta päiväkodissa.* Helsinki: Tutkijaliitto.

Parry Hughes, R., Redley, M., & Ring, H. (2011). Friendship and adults with profound intellectual and multiple disabilities and English disability policy. *Journal of Policy and Practice in Intellectual Disabilities, 8*, 197–206. https://doi.org/10.1111/j.1741-1130.2011.00310.x

Pawlyn, J., & Carnaby, S. (2009). Introduction. In J. Pawlyn & S. Carnaby (Eds.), *Profound intellectual and multiple disabilities: Nursing complex needs* (pp. 3–14). Oxford: Wiley-Blackwell.

Perse, R. (1972). The dignity of risk and the mentally retarded. *Mental Retardation, 10*, 24–27.

Pink, S. (2009). *Doing sensory ethnography.* London: SAGE.

Pockney, R. (2006). Friendship of facilitation: People with learning disabilities and their paid carers. Sociological Research Online, 11, http://www.socresonline.org.uk/11/3/pockney.html

Popovic, M. (2005). Intimacy and its relevance in human functioning. *Sexual and Relationship Therapy, 20,* 31–49. https://doi.org/10.1080/14681990412331323992

Priestley, M. (2003). *Disability: A life course approach.* Cambridge: Polity Press.

Primoratz, I. (1999). *Ethics and sex.* London: Routledge.

Proctor, R. (1988). *Racial hygiene: Medicine under the Nazis.* Cambridge: Harvard University Press.

Qian, X., Tichá, R., Larson, S. A., & Wuorio, A. (2015). The impacts of individual and organisational factors on engagement of individuals with intellectual disability living in community group homes: A multilevel model. *Journal of Intellectual Disability Research, 59,* 493–505. https://doi.org/10.1111/jir.12152

Rachels, J. (1986). *The end of life: Euthanasia and morality.* Oxford: Oxford University Press.

Rachels, J. (1987). Darwin, species, and morality. *The Monist, 70,* 98–113.

Rachels, J. (1990). *Created from animals: The moral implications of Darwinism.* New York, NY: Oxford University Press.

Rachels, J. (2002). The value of human life. *Philosophical Inquiry, 24,* 3–16. https://doi.org/10.5840/philinquiry200224l/22

Rachels, J. (2004). Drawing lines. In C. R. Sunstein & M. C. Nussbaum (Eds.), *Animal rights: Current debates and new directions* (pp. 162–174). New York, NY: Oxford University Press.

Rawls, J. (1971). *A theory of justice.* Cambridge, MA: Harvard University Press.

Rothman, D. J., & Rothman, S. M. (2004). The litigator as reformer. In S. Noll & J. W. Trent, Jr., (Eds.), *Mental retardation in America: A historical reader* (pp. 445–465). New York, NY: New York University Press.

Saari, E. (1957). *Sielullisesti poikkeavat lapset, 3. painos* [Mentally deviant children, 3rd edition]. Jyväskylä: Gummerus.

Samuel, J., Nind, M., Volans, A., & Scriven, I. (2008). An evaluation of intensive interaction in community living settings for adults with profound intellectual disabilities. *Journal of*

Intellectual Disabilities, 12, 111–126. https://doi.org/10.1177/1744629508090983

Sanders, S. A., & Reinisch, J. M. (1999). Would you say you 'had sex' if...? *Journal of the American Medical Association*, 281, 275–277. https://doi.org/10.1001/jama.281.3.275

Sapontzis, S. F. (1987). *Morals, reason, and animals*. Philadelphia, PA: Temple University Press.

Scanlon, T. (1998). *What we owe to each other*. Cambridge, MA: Harvard University Press.

Scheerenberger, R. C. (1983). *A history of mental retardation*. Baltimore, MD: Paul H. Brookes.

Scheerenberger, R. C. (1987). *A history of mental retardation: A quarter century of promise*. Baltimore, MD: Paul H. Brookes.

Sen, A. (1992). *Inequality reexamined*. Oxford: Clarendon Press.

Seppälä, H., & Sundin, M. (2011). *TOIMI: Menetelmä psykososiaalisen toimintakyvyn kuvaamiseen*. Helsinki: Kehitysvammaliitto.

Series, L. (2015). Relationships, autonomy and legal capacity: Mental capacity and support paradigms. *International Journal of Law and Psychiatry*, 40, 80–91. https://doi.org/10.1016/j.ijlp.2015.04.010

Shakespeare, T. (2006). *Disability rights and wrongs*. London: Routledge.

Shakespeare, T. (2012). Sex and disability (book review). *Disability & Society*, 27, 894–895. https://doi.org/10.1080/09687599.2012.714255

Shelton, D. (1992). Client sexual behaviour and staff attitudes: Shaping masturbation in an individual with a profound mental and secondary sensory handicap. *Mental Handicap*, 20, 81–84. https://doi.org/10.1111/j.1468-3156.1992.tb00664.x

Sherry, M. (2016). Facilitated communication, Anna Stubblefield and disability studies. *Disability & Society*, 31, 974–982. https://doi.org/10.1080/09687599.2016.1218152

Simmons, B., & Watson, D. (2014). *The PLMD ambiguity: Articulating the life-worlds of children with profound and multiple learning disabilities*. London: Carnac Books.

Simpson, M. K. (2012). Power, ideology and structure: The legacy of normalization for intellectual disability. *Social Inclusion, 6,* 12–21. https://doi.org/10.17645/si.v6i2.1264

Singer, P. (1979). *Practical ethics.* Cambridge: Cambridge University Press.

Singer, P. (1993). Practical ethics – second edition. Cambridge: Cambridge University Press.

Singer, P. (1989). All animals are equal. In T. Regan & P. Singer (Eds.), *Animal rights and human obligations* (pp. 215–226). Englewood Cliffs, NJ: Prentice Hall.

Singer, P. (2009). Speciesism and moral status. *Metaphilosophy, 40,* 567–581. https://doi.org/10.1111/j.1467-9973.2009.01608.x

Singer, P. (2016). Why speciesism is wrong: A response to Kagan. *Journal of Applied Philosophy, 33,* 31–35. https://doi.org/10.1111/japp.12165

Soble, A. (2002). Introduction: The fundamental of the philosophy of sex. In A. Soble (Ed.), *The philosophy of sex: Contemporary readings* (4th ed., pp. xvii–xlii). Lanham, MD: Rowman & Littlefield.

Socialstyrelsen (2011). Tillsynsrapport 2011. Hälso- och sjukvård och socialtjänst. Artikelnr 2011-5-4.

Socialstyrelsen (2018a). Statistik om insatser enligt lagen om stöd och service till vissa funktionshindrade 2017. http://www.social styrelsen.se/Lists/Artikelkatalog/Attachments/20925/2018-4-9.pdf

Socialstyrelsen (2018b). Bostad med särskild service för vuxna enligt LSS. https://www.socialstyrelsen.se/Lists/Artikelkatalog /Attachments/20981/2018-6-12.pdf

Stainton, T. (2018). Sensationalism and the construction of intellectual disability. In P. McDonagh, C. F. Goodey, & T. Stainton (Eds.), *Intellectual disability: A conceptual history, 1200–1900* (pp. 128–147). Manchester: Manchester University Press.

Stewart, K. (1996). *A space on the side of the road: Cultural poetics in an 'other' America.* Princeton, NJ: Princeton University Press.

Stiker, H.-J. (1999). *A history of disability.* Ann Arbor, MI: The University of Michigan Press.

Stone, D. A. (1984). *The disabled state*. Philadelphia, PA: Temple University Press.

Stone, E., & Priestley, M. (1996). Parasites, pawns and partners: Disability research and the role of non-disabled researchers. *British Journal of Sociology, 47,* 699–716. https://doi.org /10.2307/591081

Talman, L., Wilder, J., Stier, J., & Gustafsson, C. (2019). Staff's and managers' conceptions of participation for adults with profound intellectual disabilities or profound intellectual and multiple disabilities. *Scandinavian Journal of Disability Research, 21,* 78–88. https://doi.org/10.16993/sjdr.53

Taylor, S. (2017). *Beasts of burden: Animal and disability liberation.* New York: The New Press.

Tétreault, M. A. (2006). The sexual politics of Abu Ghraib: Hegemony, spectacle, and the global war on terror. *NWSA Journal, 18,* 33–50. https://doi.org/10.1353/nwsa.2006.0064

Tilley, L., Ledger, S., & de Haas, C. (2020). Enabling people with profound and multiple learning disabilities to belong in public and community archive collections. In M. Nind & I. Strnadová (Eds.), *Belonging for people with profound intellectual and multiple disabilities: Pushing the boundaries of inclusion* (pp. 176–195). London: Routledge.

Trent, J. W., Jr. (1994). *Inventing the feeble mind: A history of mental retardation in the United States.* Berkeley, CA: University of California Press.

Turner, G. W., & Crane, B. (2016). Pleasure is paramount: Adults with intellectual disabilities discuss sensuality and intimacy. *Sexualities, 19,* 677–697. https://doi.org/10.1177/1363460 715620573

Tøssebro, J. (2005). Reflections on living outside: Continuity and change in the life of 'outsiders'. In K. Johnson & R. Traustadóttir (Eds.), *Deinstitutionalization and people with intellectual disabilities: In and out of institutions* (pp. 186–202). London: Jessica Kingsley.

Tøssebro, J., Bonfils, I. S., Teittinen, A., Tideman, M., Traustadóttir, Vesala, H. T. (2012). Normalization fifty years beyond–

Current trends in the Nordic countries. *Journal of Policy and Practice in Intellectual Disabilities, 9,* 134–146. https://doi.org/10.1111/j.1741-1130.2012.00340.x

Uetake, K., Hurnik, J. F., & Johnson, L. (1997). Effect of music on voluntary approach of dairy cows to an automatic milking system. *Applied Animal Behaviour Science, 53,* 175–182. https://doi.org/10.1016/S0168-1591(96)01159-8

Umberson, D., Thomeer, M. B., & Lodge, A. C. (2015). Intimacy and emotion work in lesbian, gay, and heterosexual relationships. *Journal of Marriage and Family, 77,* 542–556. https://doi.org/10.1111/jomf.12178

UN 2008. *Fact Sheet No. 33, Frequently Asked Questions on Economic, Social and Cultural Rights.* UN Office of the High Commissioner for Human Rights (OHCHR). Retrieved 21 November 2019 from http://www.refworld.org/docid/499176e62.html

UN General Assembly. (1948). Universal Declaration of Human Rights. Retrieved 28 October 2019 from http://www.un.org/en/universal-declaration-human-rights/

van der Putten, A. J., Bossink, L. W. M., Frans, N., Houwen, S., & Vlaskamp, C. (2017). Motor activation in people with profound intellectual and multiple disabilities in daily practice. *Journal of Intellectual & Developmental Disability, 42,* 1–11. https://doi.org/10.3109/13668250.2016.1181259

Vehmas, S. (2010). The who or what of Steve: Severe cognitive impairment and its implications. In M. Häyry, T. Takala, P. Herissone-Kelly, & G. Árnason (Eds.), *Arguments and analysis in bioethics* (pp. 263–280). Amsterdam, New York: Rodopi.

Vehmas, S. (2019). Persons with profound intellectual disability and their right to sex. *Disability & Society, 34,* 519–539. https://doi.org/10.1080/09687599.2018.1545110

Vehmas, S., & Curtis, B. (2017). Profound intellectual disability and the bestowment view of moral status. *Cambridge Quarterly of Healthcare Ethics, 26,* 505–516. https://doi.org/10.1017/S0963180116001183

Vehmas, S., & Watson, N. (2014). Moral wrongs, disadvantages, and disability: A critique of critical disability studies. *Disability & Society*, 29, 638–650. https://doi.org/10.1080/09687599.2013.831751

Vehmas, S., & Watson, N. (2016). Exploring normativity in disability studies. *Disability & Society*, 31, 1–16. https://doi.org/10.1080/09687599.2015.1120657

Verdonschot, M. M. L., de Witte, L. P., Buntinx, W. H. E., & Curfs, L. M. G. (2009). Community participation of people with an intellectual disability: A review of empirical findings. *Journal of Intellectual Disability Research*, 53, 303–318. https://doi.org/10.1111/j.1365-2788.2008.01144.x

Vesala, H. T. (2003). *Palvelujen käyttäjäurat kehitysvammaisilla henkilöillä* [The service user careers of people with intellectual disabilities]. Helsinki: Finnish Association on Mental Retardation.

Vesala, H. T. (2010). Hameennappi ja haalari: Tutkimus puhumattoman, vaikeasti kehitysvammaisen naisen itsemääräämisestä ja valinnanmahdollisuuksista. In A. Teittinen (Ed.), *Pois laitoksista! Vammaiset ja hoivan politiikka* (pp. 123–161). Helsinki: Gaudeamus.

Vorhaus, J. (2013). Capability, freedom and profound disability. *Disability & Society*, 28, 1047–1058. https://doi.org/10.1080/09687599.2012.758036

Vorhaus, J. (2014). Philosophy and profound disability: Learning from experience. *Disability & Society*, 29, 611–623. https://doi.org/10.1080/09687599.2013.831749

Vorhaus, J. (2016). *Giving voice to profound intellectual disability: Dignity, dependence and human capabilities*. London: Routledge.

Wade, H. A. (2002). Discrimination, sexuality and people with significant disabilities: Issues of access and the right to sexual expression in the United States. *Disability Studies Quarterly*, 22, 9–27. https://doi.org/10.18061/dsq.v22i4.369

Wasserman, D., & Asch, A. (2014). Understanding the relationship between disability and well-being. In J. E. Bickenbach,

F. Felder, & B. Schmitz (Eds.), *Disability and the good human life* (pp. 139–167). New York, NY: Cambridge University Press.

Wasserman, D., Asch, A., Blustein, J., & Putnam, D. (2017). Cognitive disability and moral status. *The Stanford Encyclopedia of Philosophy* (Fall 2017 Edition). Retrieved from https://plato .stanford.edu/archives/fall2017/entries/cognitive-disability

Watson, D., Jones, A., & Potter, H. (2018). Expressive eyebrows and beautiful bubbles: Playfulness and children with profound impairments. In K. Runswick-Cole, T. Curran, & K. Liddiard (Eds.), *The Palgrave handbook of disabled children's childhood studies* (pp. 130–139). London: Palgrave Macmillan.

Watson, N., & Vehmas, S. (2020). Disability studies: Into the multidisciplinary future. In N. Watson & S. Vehmas (Eds.), *Routledge handbook of disability studies* (2nd ed., pp. 3–13). London: Routledge.

Wendell, S. (1996). *The rejected body: Feminist philosophical reflections on disability*. New York, NY: Routledge.

Westerinen, H. (2018). *Prevalence of intellectual disability in Finland*. Helsinki: University of Helsinki.

WHO. (1992). *The ICD-10 classification of mental and behavioural disorders*. Geneva: WHO.

Wilkinson, P., & McGill, P. (2009). Representation of people with intellectual disabilities in a British newspaper in 1983 and 2001. *Journal of Applied Research in Intellectual Disabilities, 22*, 65–76. https://doi.org/10.1111/j.1468-3148.2008.00453.x

Williams, B. (2006). *Philosophy as a humanistic discipline*. Princeton, NJ: Princeton University Press.

Willis, P., & Trondman, M. (2000). Manifesto for ethnography. *Ethnography, 1*, 5–16. https://doi.org/10.1177/146613800222 30679

Wilson, J., Parmenter, T. R., Stancliffe, R. J., & Shuttleworth, R. P. (2011). Conditionally sexual: Men and teenage boys with moderate to profound intellectual disability. *Sexuality and Disability, 29*, 275–289. https://doi.org/10.1007/s11195-011-9203-y

Wolfe, C. (2010). *Before the law: Humans and other animals in a biopolitical frame*. Chicago, IL: The University of Chicago Press.

Wolfensberger, W. (1972). *The principle of normalization in human services*. Toronto: National Institute on Mental Retardation.

Young, H., & Garrard, B. (2015). Bereavement and loss: Developing a memory box to support a young woman with profound intellectual disabilities. *British Journal of Intellectual Disabilities, 44*, 78–84. https://doi.org/10.1111/bld.12129

Young, I. M. (1990). *Justice and the politics of difference*. Princeton, NJ: Princeton University Press.

Young, I. M. (1997). *Intersecting voices: Dilemmas of gender, political philosophy, and policy*. Princeton, NJ: Princeton University Press.

Young, R., Gore, N., & McCarthy, M. (2012). Staff attitudes towards sexuality in relation to gender of people with intellectual disability: A qualitative study. *Journal of Intellectual & Developmental Disability, 37*, 343–347. https://doi.org/10.3109/13668250.2012.704983

Index

Lightning Source UK Ltd.
Milton Keynes UK
UKHW022254080721
386862UK00006B/72

9 789176 351512